RAFIQ HARIRI

AND THE FATE OF LEBANON

Marwan Iskandar

RAFIQ HARIRI

AND THE FATE OF LEBANON

SAQI

London   San Francisco

ISBN 10: 0-86356-370-8
ISBN 13: 978-0-86356-370-6

First published in 2006 by Saqi Books
This updated and augmented second edition published in 2006 by Saqi Books

Printed in Lebanon by Chemaly & Chemaly
Binding: Fouad El-Baayno Bookbinders

SAQI
26 Westbourne Grove, London W2 5RH
825 Page Street, Suite 203, Berkeley, California 94710
www.saqibooks.com

To the young Lebanese
who lit the flame
on 14 March 2005

Contents

Acknowledgments

This book arose from my friendship with the late Rafiq Hariri. I wanted to convey the spirit and patience of the man who reshaped Lebanon and gave the Lebanese a second chance to enjoy independence.

Many friends contributed, sometimes unknowingly, to this book. Facts and incidents were reviewed with numerous people who interacted with Hariri or were actively concerned with the public good. More specific contributions were provided by my family and work colleagues.

My wife Mona corrected numerous mistakes and was patient and caring whenever thoughts escaped me and it was difficult to put pen to paper. My son Samer, a professional writer better versed in the techniques of the trade, offered guidance whilst minding parental sensibility. Adnan Iskandar, my eldest brother and former university professor and administrator, suggested the necessary flow of subject matter.

Mr Tony Saadeh, chief of research at my company, provided timely Internet research about particular people and events.

My publishers, Mai Ghoussoub and André Gaspard, exerted tremendous efforts to publish the first edition of this book by 14 February 2006, the first anniversary of Lebanon's re-awakening.

Robert Fisk, a long-time friend, allowed the first words of this manuscript to be his. He has written a moving first-hand description of the scene of the crime, which is reproduced herein.

In any such work, there are contributors who provoke thoughts and ideas without aiming to do so. To these anonymous collaborators I extend my heartfelt thanks.

Marwan Iskandar
March 2006

The Crime

by
Robert Fisk

On 14 February 2005 the former Lebanese prime minister, Rafiq Hariri, was killed by a massive bomb as he was heading home from parliament along Beirut's seafront just before one o'clock in the afternoon. Eight of Hariri's aides died in the blast, including his close associate Dr Bassel Fuleihan, along with another fourteen innocent people.

Robert Fisk, the well-known international journalist and author, witnessed the incident and recounts what happened in his book The Great War for Civilization: The Conquest of the Middle East.[1]

On 14 February 2005 I was walking along the seafront Corniche, opposite my favorite restaurant, the Spaghetteria, talking on my mobile phone to my old friend Patrick Cockburn, my replacement in Baghdad, when a white band of light approached at fearsome speed, like a giant bandage. The palm trees all dipped towards me as if hit by a tornado and I saw people – other strollers on the pavement in front of me – fall to the ground. A window of the restaurant splintered and disappeared inside. And in front of me, perhaps only 400 metres away, dark brown fingers of smoke streaked towards the sky. The blast wave was followed by an

---

1. Published by Fourth Estate, an imprint of HarperCollins Publishers, London, 2005.

explosion so thunderous that it partially deafened me. I could just hear Patrick. 'Is that here or there?' he asked. 'I'm afraid it's here, Patrick,' I said. I could have wept. Beirut was my home-from-home, my safe haven, and now all the corpses of the Lebanese civil war were climbing out of their graves.

I ran down the street towards the bombing. There were no cops, no ambulances yet, no soldiers, just a sea of flames in front of the St Georges Hotel. There were men and women round me, covered in blood, crying and shaking with fear. Twenty-two cars were burning, and in one of them, I saw three men cowled in fire. A woman's hand, a hand with painted fingernails, lay on the road. Why? Not bin Laden, I said to myself. Not here in Beirut. I was staggered by the heat, the flames that crept across the road, the petrol tanks of vehicles that would explode and spray fire around me every few seconds. On the ground was a very large man, lying on his back, his socks on fire, unrecognizable.

Then through the smoke, I found the crater. It was hot and I climbed gingerly into it. Two plain-clothes cops were already there, picking up small shards of metal. Fast work for detectives, I thought. And it was several days before I realized that – far from collecting evidence – they were hiding it, taking it from the scene of the crime. I came across an AP reporter, an old Lebanese friend. 'I think it's Hariri's convoy,' he said. I couldn't believe it. Hariri had been Lebanon's billionaire prime minister until the previous year. He had been 'Mr. Lebanon', who had rebuilt Beirut, the symbol of its future economy, the man who had turned a city in ruins into a city of light, of fine new restaurants and shops and pedestrian malls. But the Syrians believed that he was secretly leading Lebanese opposition to their military and intelligence presence in Lebanon. They suspected that his hand lay behind an American-French UN Security Council resolution, number 1559, demanding the withdrawal of Syria's remaining 40,000 troops in the country.

And now, half an hour after the bombing, his family knew he had gone; Hariri's mobile had stopped working, along with those of all his bodyguards. The convoy's anti-bomb neutralizers – a cluster of scanners on the roofs of the armoured four-by-fours – had failed to protect him. And next day, when I opened the Lebanese papers, there was a photograph of a large man lying on his back with his socks burning and he was identified as 'the martyr prime minister Rafiq Hariri'.

Foreword

by
Fuad Siniora
Prime Minister of Lebanon

This book is not about economics, nor can it be considered only on the merit of the political facts it presents. It does not, moreover, simply describe a certain phase of Lebanese history. It is rather a fusion of all these things, with one main theme: the development of Lebanon over recent years.

Marwan Iskandar parallels the story of this country with the path adopted by Rafiq Hariri on the economic, political, reconstructive and social fronts. This book is essential reading for those who would like to know more about this important period in the life of Lebanon.

Beirut, December 2005

Preface

Rafiq Hariri, for nearly three decades, from 1978 until his assassination in February 2005, played a vital role in shaping the political and economic future of Lebanon. He made important developments in education, reconstruction, political mediation, and in the restoration of near-normal conditions of living in Lebanon at the turn of the 21st century.

In 1978 Lebanon was in a state of shambles. The two years' war between Lebanese and Palestinian factions and Syrian forces had left Beirut's centre mostly burned by gunfire and ravaged, and much of Lebanon's infrastructure was destroyed. Occupation of a significant strip of southern Lebanon by Israel as of spring 1978, which continued until June 2000, further compounded the picture.

In 1978 Rafiq Hariri, a man of humble rural origins, became involved in Lebanon's political, economic and reconstruction efforts aimed at restoring the country's viability as a modern nation. As testament to his achievements, by the early 1980s over 30,000 university students from Lebanon had educational support around the globe and major efforts were under way to bring about reconciliation between Lebanese factions. In November 1989 the Taef Accord – the national reconciliation agreement – was approved, having been drafted by Hariri in consultation with leading politicians and jurists. In 1992 Hariri was elected as prime minister, serving for ten years from 1992–8 and from 2000–4.

The histories of Hariri and of Lebanon are intertwined over the past thirty years, during which Hariri was involved in practically all major efforts and decisions related to Lebanon's future. Few people would contest his role in rebuilding the infrastructure of Lebanon, and his efforts have generally been evaluated positively, although there have been criticisms relating to project costs and management.

This book provides a broad outline of Hariri's initiatives and experiences. It is not intended as an academic or even completely objective presentation. I was a friend of Rafiq Hariri and was engaged intermittently in finalizing studies for him or evaluations of public policy decrees. Completion of this book was not subject to his family's approval.

In the process of writing, it became clear to me that the background to the critical situation that prevailed in 1978 needed to be explored. The introduction to this book aims to provide a background, so that readers understand better the stage that was set for Hariri. According to my personal evaluation, Lebanon slid towards crisis in 1964, and the slide was faster and more dangerous than was anticipated because, in 1963, Lebanon lost a unique leader, Emile Bustani. It was Bustani who could have steered Lebanon clear of the Cairo Agreement with the Palestine Liberation Organization, signed in 1969, which compromised the sovereignty of Lebanon.

In the 1970s Hariri was optimistic for the future of Lebanon. Yet by the end of summer 2004 he was very sad and pessimistic. President Emile Lahoud's term in office was renewed for a further three years against Hariri's advice, and plans for modern development in the context of evolving technology and globalization could not be achieved with Syrian control of Lebanese affairs. This conviction became deep-rooted in Hariri's thinking and he gave up on forming a new government in October 2004. When he declared his resignation from the task of forming a new cabinet, he said, 'I leave my beloved Lebanon, with a heavy heart, in the hands of God'.

Following his withdrawal, Hariri rarely seemed happy. His ready smile was no longer there and his eyes were sad rather than gentle. In

November 2004 I asked him why I had only seen him happy on two occasions over the past few months, when receiving a UN distinction for rebuilding Beirut, and when having lunch with Patriarch Sfeir (Mar Nasrallah Boutros Sfeir), the head of the Maronite Church. Hariri's short response possibly summarizes his experience and expectations. He said, 'The UN prize testifies to a modern achievement on a grand scale. Look at the centre of Beirut in 1990 and at what the centre is today. As to the Patriarch, he is the only important Lebanese leader who never raises with me sectarian issues. The Patriarch only concentrates on national issues and national unity. How can I but be happy with the Patriarch's friendship and support?'

Rebuilding Lebanon, achieving national unity, regaining independence and opening up educational and professional opportunities for the young generation: these were the concerns of Hariri at the end of 2004. These were his concerns in 1978, but without the urgency of independence as Lebanon was too divided at the time.

This book is intended to show the progress towards these objectives, the costs of initiatives, mistakes committed and results achieved. It is a presentation reflecting my own, personal observation and judgment and, consequently, the book is only as good as my choice of issues to discuss and the evaluations I have made.

Marwan Iskandar
March 2006

Slide to Chaos: 1963–1975

The deaths of Emile Bustani and Rafiq Hariri served to cripple Lebanon at critical periods in its recent history. It is important to explore these two tragic events in relation to the particular political climate in which each was involved, and to the political developments that followed.

Emile Murchid Bustani was born in 1907 in the small village Dibbyeh, located on the road that runs from Sidon to Jezzine. His father taught mathematics at an American high school in Sidon, and for a while he was a church minister. In 1916, when Emile was nine years old, his father died, and his mother – a woman of strong character – left to teach in Egypt in order to support her children's education. Emile was sent to an American missionary school in Sidon as a boarding student. He was a brilliant pupil, but troublesome because of his argumentative nature and amorous inclinations (during his last year in high school he was expelled for exchanging love letters with the daughter of the principal).

Bustani spent his last year of high school at the National College of Aley, where he graduated with flying colours, and went on to the American University of Beirut (AUB), thanks to a scholarship from a Lebanese emigrant from the Maalouf family, graduating with distinction in June

1928 with a degree in sciences. After AUB, he went to Ramalla where he taught for one year before returning to complete an MSc in astronomy. After teaching astronomy for a year he then went on to the Massachusetts Institute of Technology (MIT) in the United States to study engineering. Bustani completed the two-year course in just one year, graduating in June 1933 with a Masters degree in civil engineering.

On his return home, Bustani was keen to find suitable work as he wanted to marry Laura Syriani, the daughter of a prosperous merchant family to whom he had taught English before leaving to study in the United States. He was employed by the Iraq Petroleum Company to work on the construction of a pipeline from Kirkuk to Haifa. It was during this time that he met Shukri Shammas, a hard-working engineer with whom he formed a friendship that was later to become a partnership. Before the end of 1935, Bustani's uncle, Wadih Bustani, a well-known lawyer and poet, persuaded his young nephew to establish an engineering company in Haifa. By 1937, Bustani had married and started a home in Haifa and began cultivating relations with his former employers, IPC, to secure future contracts.

The Contracting & Trading Company (CAT) was formed in Lebanon in 1937 as a partnership between Emile Bustani, Shukri Shammas, Abdalla Khoury and Raif Fawaz. The latter withdrew from the partnership after one year, and CAT proceeded to become the Arab world's largest contracting company for the oil industry in the Middle East. CAT expanded rapidly with Bustani looking for contracts, Shammas mustering engineering talent, and Khoury watching over finances and trading interests. By 1960, CAT had offices in Pakistan, Iran, Iraq, all the Gulf countries, Syria, Lebanon, Egypt, and the United Kingdom (as early as 1943 CAT had rented offices in London). With skills in civil and mechanical engineering, and a successful track record of over twenty years, also by 1960 the company employed 18,000 people, making it the biggest company in Lebanon and the Arab world.

In the 1950s Bustani became a member of parliament. Before this took place he had reverted to his original sect, a Maronite, in order that he could achieve the highest prize, the Presidency, which was only to be occupied by a member of the Maronite body. (Bustani's father had previously become a Protestant for reasons relating to clashes with the clergy and educational needs for his children.) As an active member of parliament, Bustani showed excellent debating qualities and aggressively pursued his objectives. By this time, he had become convinced that communism was bad, that pan-Arab cooperation was an essential condition for prosperity in the region, that some of the Arab oil wealth should be earmarked for development in the non-oil Arab countries of the region, and finally, that Arabs should become more versed in the techniques of the oil industry and more capable of marketing products.

Already Bustani had taken steps to fulfill these objectives in respect of his company. He had formed a 50/50 joint venture with a Scottish engineering company specializing in oil and gas, Motherwell Bridge Contracting Company. The joint venture company was named MotherCat. This was the first Arab foray into the ownership and management of a specialized Western company. Moreover, Bustani formed Sea CAT, another joint venture that would drill and search for oil whether on account of others or for itself.

This Lebanese ball of fire was moving into the playground of the Big Sisters (seven major international oil companies) that had just ceded the principle of a 50/50 split of net oil revenues with producing countries. (Up to 1955 or 1956, producing countries received a fixed fee that amounted to no more than 10–15 percent of the final price.)

During the 1960s, the oil industry was beset by arguments and legislative changes. Bustani was involved in the international debate, and as chairman of the Foreign Affairs Committee of the Lebanese Parliament, he was entrusted to organize a major Arab Oil congress scheduled for 1964. Yet in the midst of all his business and political activities, Bustani found time for leadership roles that contributed to the welfare and future of Lebanon. He became the first Arab to be elected to the Board of Trustees of the AUB, he was elected chairman of the Alumni Association of AUB graduates, and he contributed to the construction of a young ladies' dormitory at the American University campus in the name of his wife Laura Bustani.

Bustani was extrovert and charismatic. He ferreted out critics of his policies and personality, and maintained excellent relations with the national and international press. He was the first Lebanese business leader to engage on a full-time basis an editor and a journalist. Bustani always embellished his energetic drive with a knack for unearthing business opportunities. In 1956, when Israel, France and England attacked Egypt after nationalization of the Suez Canal by Gamal Abdul Nasser, who became the Arab hero par excellence, Bustani went to London where he spent a small fortune raising objections to Anthony Eden's anti-Egyptian policies. Bustani's efforts did not go unnoticed by Abdul Nasser, and a friendship developed between the two in spite of ideological differences – Nasser was pushing towards socialism whereas Bustani supported nationalism and tried to temper Nasser's socialism.

By the early 1950s, when he was 45 years of age, Bustani started working to achieve the responsibility of president of the Republic. He was an ally of Kamal Jumblatt, the well-known socialist block leader, and a fierce debater in parliament. Also, he was close to Camille Chamoun, a charismatic political leader who became president of Lebanon in 1952. Bustani considered the press and its leading figures very important for his future. For this purpose, he devoted time and resources to befriending leading figures such as Kamel Mroueh, Gibran Metni, Muhammad Samak and Yasser Hawari; he was also close to Ghassan Tueni, a rising star in the press who had taken charge of *an-Nahar* newspaper after interrupting his studies at Harvard. In 1950 Tueni had become the youngest deputy in parliament on the same ticket as Bustani. Both men were politically liberal and not truly socialists. Eventually, their alliance with Jumblatt had to give way.

During the period from the late 1950s to the early 1960s, Lebanon was a promising country with unfolding opportunities, and containable sectarian and political differences. Two developments – one natural, the other political – clouded the picture. In March 1956 a 7.6 Richter

Scale earthquake hit Lebanon, and thousands of homes were destroyed in the Chouf district and in the south of Lebanon. Bustani was nominated minister of reconstruction and, with his energy, drive and motivation, he managed to rebuild most of the damage within two years. In 1958, between May and July, a mini civil conflict erupted because the Lebanese president at the time, Camille Chamoun, and his minister of foreign affairs, Charles Malek, favoured Lebanon's joining the Baghdad Pact, an American sponsored anti-Soviet alliance extending from Iraq in the west to Turkey and Pakistan in the east. Sunni Muslims led by the late Saeb Salam and supported by a number of political blocks in Lebanon, and Gamal Abdul Nasser, opposed Chamoun's choice. By 14 July 1958 Iraq witnessed a coup d'état by the army, which favoured Nasser, and within days American forces landed in Lebanon, lest the opposition won the conflict, but, more importantly, to control developments in the region, while British forces landed in Jordan to protect the rule of King Hussein.

After these momentous developments, Lebanon settled under the presidency of General Fouad Chehab into a workable relationship with Abdul Nasser, who had accepted a Syrian-Egyptian unity that lasted for three years from 1958 until 1961. Bustani maintained excellent relations with Nasser and for this reason, and because his mind was set on attaining the presidency in 1964, President Chehab did not particularly favour him. The two men had their characters, which were poles apart. Chehab shied away from media attention, whereas Bustani did everything to have local and international reach. No matter; Bustani's style could not be cramped and his role and that of his company, CAT, were too big to ignore.

By the late1950s Bustani had pledged to become the next president of Lebanon. CAT had interests in banking, insurance, shipping, hotels, trading and real estate in Lebanon and a number of Arab countries as well as in Brazil. In modern terms, we can describe CAT as a multinational company. It built refineries, power plants, roads, schools, airports and maintenance enterprises. It had a fleet of small airplanes to carry the partners or chief executives of the company to work sites when and if needed. In fact, I myself travelled on company business in a Dove aircraft, a uni-propeller double-winged craft in which we followed the coastline from Kuwait to Muscat. In case the craft had engine trouble, it had the facility to glide and land by the shore. With such means at the company's disposal – along with the first hotel to be built in Abu Dhabi by 1962, and the first hotel to be completed in Dubai – CAT had no real competition in the region. All major oil companies sought cooperation with CAT, including Bechtel (now the largest engineering consulting company in the world) and SEDCO (South Eastern Drilling Company, based in Texas). Bustani was riding a wave of success. He was blessed with having good partners, extraordinary health, intelligence and courage. By 1963, Bustani had achieved a high-profile image. He was hugely successful in business, had an international reputation for excellence in construction, and could count a number of world leaders as his friends, including President Gamal Abdul Nasser of Egypt, Ayoub Khan of Pakistan, the sheikh of Kuwait, the sultan of Oman, the sheikhs of Abu Dhabi and Dubai, the president of Guinea, the secretary general of the United Nations, the president of the World Bank and numerous famous scientists and celebrities.

The following story, which happened just before his death, tells a lot about the man. In early March 1963, Bustani was giving a lecture in Amsterdam. While there, he read about the condemnation to death of two Lebanese in Guinea for currency smuggling. Without hesitation, Bustani arranged for immediate travel to Guinea where CAT was building a water pipeline with international finance. In Guinea, Bustani met with President Sekou Touré, a well-known socialist figure with strong ties to the Soviet Union. Bustani secured clemency for the two Lebanese, and more importantly, persuaded Sekou Touré to veer away from dependence on the Soviet bloc. By force of his personality and international reach, Bustani convinced Sekou Touré that CAT could build a network of roads to promote Guinea's development and that the World Bank would finance these works. Upon his return to Lebanon around 8 March 1963, Bustani set the legal department to work on preparing draft agreements between CAT and the government of Guinea, and agreements with the World Bank. On 18 March 1963, Sheikh Fouad El Khazen, the son-in-law of Bustani and a rising engineer at CAT, and myself were scheduled to travel to Guinea to meet with Sekou Touré and start the process of the realization of Bustani's plan. However, this was not to be as Bustani died on 15 March (Ides of March) 1963.

At the time of his death, Bustani was the leading Lebanese businessman in the Middle East. His company had a turnover of $180 million in 1961 and could compete with larger international enterprises such as Technip, Snam Projetti and Bechtel. He enjoyed political sway in Lebanon and the region, including significant influence on Gamal Abdul Nasser who he assisted in the British press in 1956 when British, French and Israeli forces occupied the Suez Canal in retaliation for Nasser's nationalization of the Suez Canal Company. Later, British, French and Israeli forces had to withdraw under American pressure, mercilessly exercised by President Eisenhower. Nasser credited Bustani with courage and admired his ability to criticize Anthony Eden in the British press.

The orientation of Emile Bustani was pan-Arab. He worked in Palestine, where he had influential relatives, after graduating from AUB. From the start of his professional contractual work, he was involved in pan-Arab projects, including the IPC pipeline network from Iraq to Haifa in Palestine and, later, Banias in Syria and Tripoli in Lebanon. He helped build schools, hotels and airports in destinations that were still relatively unknown outside the Arab world in the late 1950s and early 1960s, such as in Abu Dhabi and Dubai.

In the early 1930s, when Emile Bustani returned home from his studies in the United States, he showed intellectual signs of attachment to communist teachings. It is perhaps no wonder, given that he was coming back from a US struggling to emerge from the Depression. Much later, after thirty years of work and notable success, Emile Bustani had undergone a major change in his political and economic outlook. He believed in pan-Arab cooperation and was the first Arab statesman to call for allocating 5 percent of the oil income to finance development in non-oil Arab countries. Moreover, he was the first Arab businessman to take steps towards establishing joint venture enterprises with foreign companies with expertise in oil-related construction and services.

Bustani's idea of devoting 5 percent of Arab oil revenues to regional development of non-oil-producing Arab countries was endorsed by the Lebanese parliament and Kuwait's leadership. In the early and mid-sixties the Kuwait Fund, and later the Arab Fund for Social and Economic Development, owed their inception to Bustani's ideas, and their resources primarily to the generosity of Kuwait and, to a lesser extent, Saudi Arabia.

Bustani believed in inter-Arab enterprises and became a major investor in, and director of, the Arab Bank. In 1948, during the Arab-Zionist war, a CAT airplane carried all documents of the Arab Bank from Jerusalem to Amman and thus contributed to maintenance of the bank's records. In March 1963, Bustani was heading to Amman for a board meeting when his plane catapulted into Beirut's seaport, resulting in his death.

Bustani's business engagements, commentaries in the books he wrote and published, and lectures and pronouncements, show him to be in favour of Arab nationalism and strong ties with the West. The potential for Lebanon to become the regional base of business in the Middle East pre-occupied him and he was always willing to support regional drives by gifted people working out of Lebanon. This tendency was manifest in his admiration of business figures such as Yussef Beidas, a Palestinian who was developing an Arab capitalized and managed bank (Intra) that reached to all financial centres in the modern world; Najib Allamudine, a brilliant Lebanese mathematician and educator who was building the first modern airline in the region, Middle East Airlines; as well as Albert Abella who was developing a catering company that could meet the requirements of oil companies in the region. In 1958, when US Marines landed on the southern shores of Beirut, Abella representatives were ready to discuss supplying the American forces with provisions.

It was Bustani's vision that Lebanon could become the tourism, technical, commercial, financial, educational, media and publishing centre in the Middle East. He saw no limits to growth, and he wanted young Lebanese to achieve the highest degrees of specialization and to reach the furthest corners of the Arab world to work and demonstrate the dynamism of their country's youth.

In the early 1960s the Soviets were pushing hard to consolidate political and strategic objectives in the Middle East. Confrontations with the Americans had already forced them to back down, whether at the doorstep of the United States during the Cuban missile crisis, or earlier in Europe following the Berlin Wall crisis, resulting in the Americans building an air bridge of supply airplanes to Berlin residents in 1949. The US president at the time of the Cuban missile crisis, John F. Kennedy, stood up to the Soviets and made them back down in Cuba and withdraw installed missiles capable of reaching major cities in the United States.

As early as 1952 the Soviets had tried to test American reactions *vis-à-vis* Middle Eastern oil states. The importance of the region with regard to oil reserves and future supplies of energy was already clear to the Western world as well as to the Soviet Union, although in the early1950s oil-producing countries were still receiving only a few schillings per barrel of oil produced.

Iran is the oldest oil-producing country in the Middle East. During World War I, Winston Churchill, as minister of Britain's navy, encouraged British oil companies to secure concessions there. As far as Churchill was concerned, the need for oil was manifest in respect of naval power, first and foremost, as oil-fired ships could travel faster and further than coal-fired ships. The transformation to oil-fired ships was proceeding at a fast pace, and Churchill wanted Britain, the world's strongest maritime nation, to maintain its advantage. Oil resources were not only more efficient as an energy source for ships, but also much cheaper. The British started developing oil wells in Iran before the end of World War I, and soon realized that the region was rich with oil. They extended their interests in oil to Iraq, Kuwait and Abu Dhabi, but committed a major error by disregarding the potential of Saudi Arabia, which was left to the American companies alone.

In 1952, a French-educated, liberal oriented, elderly lawyer, Muhammad Mossadeq, was chosen by the then shah, Muhammad Reza Pahlavi, to be Iran's prime minister. Soon after his nomination, Mossadeq started to protest the terms of the oil concession and took the unprecedented step of nationalizing the oil industry. The shah objected to these measures, but was deposed and sent out of the country. Mossadeq had leftist leanings and under severe Western pressure turned to the Soviets for help.[1] Russian forces had withdrawn from northern Iran in 1946 under an American ultimatum, and showed an intention to reoccupy northern Iran if invited by Mossadeq, but he was ousted from power in 1953.

After World War II, the Americans took centre stage in international politics, and provided massive aid to Western Europe through the Marshall Plan (the European Recovery Act of 1947) and to developing countries through the World Bank (originally named the International Bank for Reconstruction and Development). The Americans had already negotiated their way to partnerships with the British in the exploitation of the oil resources of Iran and Iraq. When Mossadeq nationalized the British-American oil interests in 1952 and moved closer to the Soviet sphere, the Americans felt the strategic threat and moved swiftly.

In 1953, within months of the coup d'état of Mossadeq, the Americans had organized a brilliantly executed counter coup. The army threw out Mossadeq and declared its allegiance to the shah – Muhammad Reza Pahlavi – who returned from exile to regain the reins of power under the watchful eyes of the CIA. The leader of the American team that restored the old order in Iran was a demure, sophisticated gentleman, Kermit Roosevelt, the grandson of Theodore Roosevelt, the American president at the beginning of the 20th century.

Once the shah was restored and the Anglo-American oil company resumed its operations, Soviet military presence in the north of Iran could not be tolerated by the Americans. President Eisenhower issued

---

1.   See *The Eisenhower Diaries*, W W Norton & Co (New York/London, 1981). Concerning Mossadeq's débâcle, Eisenhower speaks of a Churchill-Truman confrontation with Mossadeq before the end of 1952.

the Soviets with an ultimatum: withdraw from all Iranian territories or American forces would be used to evict the Soviet contingents. The Soviets were not strong enough to challenge the Americans and withdrew their forces. Thus, Iran became subject to American political influence with a leader who, in the 1950s, showed reformist tendencies and adopted rational policies.

As of 1958, Egypt started showing signs of leaning towards the Eastern Camp. Gamal Abdul Nasser, who had become the leading figure among the officers who took power away from King Farouk in the summer of 1952, showed the Americans his appreciation for their stand during the Suez Canal crisis of 1956. At that time, and in reaction to Nasser's nationalization of the Suez Canal, British, French and Israeli forces occupied the canal zone and were forced to withdraw by American pressure exercised by President Eisenhower. Nasser wanted to strengthen ties with the United States, and sought to secure finance for the High Dam project, which he considered essential for the future of Egypt. John Foster Dulles, the secretary of state under Eisenhower, wanted Egypt to join the Baghdad Pact, an American sponsored alliance intended to force the Soviet Union from Turkey, Egypt, Lebanon and Iraq in the west to Pakistan in the east. Nasser could not join such a pact, particularly because he had joined Nehru and Tito in establishing the non-aligned third bloc international coalition, which aimed to reduce international differences through negotiation. The negative response of Egypt to American pressure brought about withdrawal of the offer to finance and construct the High Dam.

At this juncture, the Soviet Union took the opportunity to tie Egypt to its sphere of influence. Nasser, particularly after the Suez Canal crisis, had become the most popular Arab leader. He had charisma and could address huge crowds in colloquial Arabic for hours at a time. In 1958, Nasser nationalized farmlands and industrial and trade establishments, and turned Egypt to socialism, exercising his power as a dictator albeit with a relatively gentle touch. Encouraged by Nasser's example and the populist propaganda of his team, young officers in leading Arab countries attempted to take power into their own hands. An attempted coup d'état in Jordan was foiled by King Hussein, but a string of coups d'état in Syria and in Iraq brought the Ba'ath party to power in both countries in the early 1960s.[1]

In Lebanon, General Fouad Chehab, the chief of the Lebanese army, was elected president in September 1958. He had abstained from involving the Lebanese army in confrontations with the protesting masses in 1958: the army tried to maintain order and to prevent major conflagrations. Chehab was the natural choice for president and he was wise enough to forge an understanding with Nasser that seemed to keep Lebanon out of trouble in the late 1950s and early 1960s.

Fouad Chehab ruled Lebanon with a social conscience and iron fist exercised by his army training. Although Chehab was an elitist in his choice of key figures for senior government posts, and favoured French-trained young talent, he worked hard to introduce modern government administration with a social direction. During his presidential term from September 1958 to September 1964, Chehab saw the formation of an independent central bank, the endorsement of the national social security law, and the formation of government agencies essential for verifying good governance. Moreover, Chehab was the first president to launch a study of socio-economic conditions in deprived areas, and to start programmes of improvement for the most underdeveloped regions of Lebanon.

During the period 1958 to 1964, the Soviets were keen to strengthen links with Nasser and to foster socialist regimes in Iraq and Syria with strong ties to the USSR. They were still smarting from castigation over their encroachment in Iran and felt that they were paying back the West by attracting Nasser, and later the Ba'athist leadership, in Iraq and Syria to their side. In addition, the nebulous formation of the Palestine Liberation

---

1. Ba'athist doctrine is the brainchild of the Syrian intellectual Michel Aflack who stressed three guiding principles in his teachings: freedom, unity and socialism. Freedom was neglected by military figures practising dictatorial powers under the pretext of being Ba'athist; unity fell apart when Ba'athists in Iraq and Syria became literally enemies. Of the three guiding principles socialism survived and looked to become the guiding force in the Arab world, particularly after Egypt and Syria formed the United Arab Republic.

Organization (PLO) had seen the light of day and the Soviets were eager to help Yasser Arafat. They realized that for the PLO to become effective, it had to have bases for military action in Gaza, Jordan and Lebanon, and if possible, Syria. Formal endorsement of the PLO by Arab regimes as the sole representative of the Palestinian people was announced in Cairo in 1964. The head of the PLO chosen at that time was Ahmad Choukeiri, a Palestinian who had served as a Saudi diplomat. Arafat was chosen to develop and lead the army of the PLO.

At this time, Emile Bustani was the political figure that stood in the face of Soviet ambitions in the Middle East. He enjoyed success on a regional level, provided technical competence, and enjoyed sway over Nasser. If Bustani was to become president of Lebanon in 1964, as seemed very likely at the beginning of 1963, the Soviets feared he could turn around most of their gains in Egypt, Syria and Iraq. More importantly, he was capable of restraining Palestinian action in Lebanon because of his forceful personality, undisputed Arab nationalism, independent means, strong relations with the West and friendship with Nasser.

For the Soviet plan in the Middle East to work, Lebanon had to have a weak president after Chehab, the reformer. Accordingly, Bustani was undesirable to the Soviets. Without his influence, work towards integrating the resources of oil-rich Arab countries with the needs of less rich Arab states would recede, and instead of orderly growth there would be chaos that would serve Soviet objectives. Lebanon was rapidly becoming the tourism, technical, educational and financial centre of the Arab Middle East, and under Bustani the rich oil states would have become shareholders in the future of Lebanon. Bustani could build a bridge between so-called revolutionary Arab regimes and the oil sheikhdoms, and the whole region would have tilted towards the West if Bustani could play a leading role as Lebanon's president. His accidental death would no doubt have been welcomed by the KGB.

Around the time of Bustani's death, the Soviets took a bold step to destabilize Saudi Arabia. They supported a coup d'état in Yemen which lies to the southwest of Saudi Arabia and which had disputes with the

Saudis over the line of their border. Moreover, Yemenis and Saudis of Yemeni descent constituted a significant proportion of the total resident population in Saudi Arabia at that time. Saudi Arabia was known to have the richest oil reserves in the world. The concessions for oil production on land were in American hands, and the Saudis and Americans forged a special political relationship that was nourished by Prince Faysal bin Abdul Aziz Al Saud who later became king.

In 1963 the Soviets and Egyptians both supported the overthrow of the old dynastic and antiquated regime in Yemen. The new rulers, officers with clear affiliation to Nasser, started agitating particularly along the lines of the Saudi border and within Saudi Arabia. Prince Faysal organized strategic, military and financial aid to members of the former ruling family who had fled to the mountains that stretched close to the Saudi border. A war soon started and Egypt sent tens of thousands of soldiers to fight in Yemen, backed by hundreds of Russian tanks and tens of bombers, fighters and helicopters. It was a quagmire such as the Russians found in the 1980s in Afghanistan. The Egyptians met with military and political failure, and after the debacle of their losing the 1967 war with Israel in six days, Nasser pleaded with Prince Faysal for a peace agreement in Yemen.

The Soviets and Egyptians both wanted to destabilize the rule of Al Saud in Saudi Arabia and to hit at American oil interests. Had they succeeded in bringing about this result in the largest oil-producing state, then rulers in Kuwait, Abu Dhabi and Iran possibly would have tumbled. However, this was not to be. Men like Bustani, who sought the peaceful and speedy modernization of Arab oil-producing countries, obstructed the ambitions of the Soviets.

In September 1964 a mild-mannered lawyer, diplomat and former senior government employee, Charles Helou, was elected president of Lebanon. He had served as ambassador of Lebanon in the Vatican and as chairman of the Council for Development of Tourism, one of the semi-autonomous agencies created by Chehab's regime to overcome rigid and fossilized organizational structures, which prevented development of the Lebanese public administration from within.

Helou had no political backing except that of outgoing President Fouad Chehab, whose support was very important as Chehab had declined to accept nomination for a second term, although a sufficient majority of deputies had signed a petition requesting him to accept the nomination. At the end of his six years' term, Chehab, the military elitist, had become convinced that the Lebanese political system would not change to the better. Chehab had tried to improve social, educational and administrative conditions in the poorest regions of Hermel, the Beqaa and Akkar in the north of Lebanon. In respect of senior government appointments, he had attempted to provide young Muslim candidates with equal opportunities, without compromising standards of education and performance.

In 1964 Chehab, the outgoing president, was already disillusioned with the lack of progress in Lebanese administrative and political life, and expected no more than the efficient management of government affairs by the incoming president. Helou could write well and speak at length in French, Chehab's preferred language, and was chosen by Chehab and his intelligence team as a new president who, it appeared, they would be able to control and direct.

Helou took the responsibility that seemed destined to be in the hands of Emile Bustani had he been alive. He let Lebanon slip into financial crisis, followed by growing friction with Palestinian and Syrian-led Palestinian factions, which led to the Cairo Agreement (1969).[1] This undermined Lebanese sovereignty and planted a time bomb in the Lebanese politico-sectarian scene that exploded many times, up until the onset of a major civil war in 1975, which lasted for fifteen painful years during which Lebanon became subject to massive interference by foreign powers, mostly for the worse and only occasionally for the better.

---

1.   The terms of the agreement were ostensibly designed to regulate Palestinian activity in Lebanon, but in fact allowed the PLO freedom of action in Lebanon to recruit, arm, train and employ fighters against Israel. The Lebanese army protected their bases and supply lines.

Early in his term in office Helou sought to secure Christian approval by visiting the Vatican and President de Gaulle in France. Later he moved towards strengthening relations with Nasser. In exercising his presidential responsibilities, and as of 1966, he showed signs of mistrust against the intelligence team that had been formed by Chehab. Members of this team, who devoted considerable resources and energies to controlling Palestinian efforts at securing armaments and exercising political influence in Lebanon suddenly found themselves struggling for power against growing public criticism and insidious presidential moves. The efficiency of the intelligence apparatus was compromised without placing alternative arrangements in place. Already, political assassinations had begun and leftist leaning autocratic states were not averse to the use of murder as a political weapon. It is not only the Soviets who did this in the 1960s but also their client states such as Egypt, Iraq and Syria. One notable example was recorded in Lebanon.

On 6 May 1966 Kamel Mroueh, the publisher of *al-Hayat* newspaper and probably the most important journalist in Lebanon at the time, was shot dead in his office by Adnan Sultani, who was caught while trying to escape the newspaper premises. Sultani claimed during his trial that he was instigated, encouraged and supported to do the job by Ibrahim Koleilat, who served a prison sentence together with the assassin.

Mroueh had been anti-Nasser in his writings and pro-Western in his orientation. During the war in Yemen, he vehemently criticized Egyptian actions and motives while being a close ally and friend of Faysal bin Abdul Aziz Al Saud, who became the King of Saudi Arabia and was Nasser's political foe. Mroueh's assassin was freed during 1975–6 when the Arab Liberation Army, a rebellious faction of the Lebanese army, stormed Beirut central prison. The leadership of this rebellious faction of the Lebanese army always declared its adherence to Nasserite ideas even five years after the death of Nasser.

In the summer of 1966, a financial crisis occurred because of shortages of liquidity faced by Intra Bank, which, in the six years since its formation, had become the largest bank in Lebanon and the only Arab-owned bank with vast interests in Western banking, real estate and industry. Yussef Beidas, a Palestinian financial genius, had formed this bank in Beirut in 1960 and attracted as depositors Arab leaders from Kuwait and Saudi Arabia. Beidas financed the expansion of Middle East Airlines, the Casino du Liban, wheat imports from the US to Lebanon and Egypt, and purchase of prime real estate in Paris, New York, Frankfurt, Geneva and Sao Paolo. Moreover, Intra Bank acquired La Ciotat, the French shipbuilding yard that pioneered the building of tankers for carrying liquid natural gas (LNG), a new industry in the 1960s and which today carries the hope of combating the energy crisis worldwide.

However, in the summer of 1966, widespread rumours that Intra Bank was facing trouble did not serve to help its position. The Lebanese Central Bank was not yet two years old, and its governor, Philip Takla, was foremost a politician. At the time of Intra's crisis he was the minister of foreign affairs and during the bank's blackest days was abroad. Thus, the handling of Intra Bank's liquidity settled on Joseph Ogorlian, the brother-in-law of President Helou and the only member of the Central Bank's senior management who had experience in banking. Unfortunately, his background did not help and Intra Bank eventually transformed itself into an investment company, which still exists today.

Joseph Ogorlian was previously the general manager of the Banque du Syrie et du Liban (BSL). This foreign-owned bank – largely by French interests – had been the bank of issue and the government's bank since Lebanon and Syria were placed in French colonial hands in 1920 by the League of Nations. In the early 1960s, BSL had hoped, as did its general manager Ogorlian, to become the Central Bank of Lebanon. It was not unknown for commercial banks to assume this role, and in their drive to attain this responsibility the BSL management built vast premises in the banking district, intended to meet the requirements of a central bank and not only a commercial bank. However, BSL's aspirations were frustrated by Chehab's insistence on establishing an independent but government-controlled central bank, and frustrated further by the growth and performance of Intra Bank. Whereas BSL worked on principles of colonial privilege and presumed the superiority of French-trained bureaucrats and bankers, Intra Bank worked on the principle of extending Arab oil wealth to the Western hemisphere and enlarging the role of Anglo-Saxon-trained Arabs in handling and directing Arab money. The practices of BSL were rooted in the colonial past, whereas Intra Bank was showing the way of the future.

As senior deputy governor of the Central Bank, Ogorlian played a pivotal role in the demise of Beidas and Intra Bank. Although $22 million was granted to Intra, it had to mortgage on a vast scale and deliver property documents to the Central Bank. This operation was to be done in secret to avoid alarming depositors, but in fact became very public and served to speed up the bankruptcy of Intra. In 1970 Intra Investment Company was formed, subject to nominations of board members by the Lebanese Central Bank and the ministry of finance in Kuwait. The company's expenditures are estimated to have exceeded $1 billion in thirty-five years, and total assets exceed $300 million. Under the leadership of its chairman, Dr Muhammad Choeib, Intra Investment Company is now capable of distributing in profits per year what Intra needed in liquidity to continue functioning in 1966. Nevertheless, the forsaking of Intra in the 1960s is a prime example of what Bustani's absence meant to Lebanon. Bustani admired and supported Beidas and had he been president in 1966, Intra would have been alive and well with over $100 billion on its balance sheets. The three biggest banks of the Arab world today do not own in physical assets what Intra owned in 1966.[1]

---

1.   For further reference, see Hana Asfour, *Intra Bank, Case and Lessons*, (Beirut, 1969). The author is of Palestinian origin and was a consultant to Intra Bank. He writes: 'In Lebanon, some political leaders believed that this institution (Intra Bank) is of Lebanese identity only by name and that it is going to become the window from which rich arab subjects of petrol producing countries could sneak to invest their huge wealth in Lebanon and eventually put their hand on its sole natural resource, the Land. This would transform the Lebanese people into foreigners in their own country, similar to what happened to the Palestinian people. In order to avoid a similar fate as it was promoted by these leaders, the Lebanese government issued laws that limited the ownership of properties in cities to non-Lebanese and prohibited the transfer of agricultural land to non-Lebanese'. *Intra Bank Case and Lessons*, p. 17 (translated by the author).

Yet more dangerous waters were crossed without Bustani's strength and energy on the military and political fronts and I can only summarize the essence of what took place.

In June 1967 Egypt, under Nasser's leadership, provoked a war with Israel: the Six Day War, which also involved Syria and Jordan, was a total disaster. The Egyptian air force was destroyed on the ground, as Egyptian propaganda declared the destruction of hundreds of Israeli planes in the air. Israeli forces occupied the Golan Heights, and Jerusalem fell into the hands of Israel. All these losses came about in less than a week, and Nasser addressed the Egyptian people to admit his responsibility for the defeat and announce his resignation. Millions of Arabs took to the streets asking Nasser to retain power, which he did. However, Nasser had lost his edge. After 1967 he asked forgiveness from King Faysal for the war in Yemen, and sought aid to fortify the western bank of the Suez Canal, as Israeli forces had occupied Sinai and stretched along the eastern shores of the canal.

Egypt's failure in the 1967 war by Egypt, and Israel's occupation of vast Arab lands, drove Arab leaders to seek resistance using commando raids against Israel, whether along the eastern shores of the Suez Canal with Egyptian commandos, or by the newly formed Palestinian army of the PLO. Between 1964, the date of formation of the PLO, and 1967, a number of Palestinian factions had emerged, each with their own military formations.

The PLO worked hard to secure bases for launching attacks against Israeli targets and succeeded in establishing such bases in Jordan and Lebanon. Arafat, who soon became dominant in the PLO, assumed King Hussein would not allow free Palestinian military action, and consequently concentrated on establishing bases in Lebanon. He was helped by Syrian and Algerian resources. In the spring of 1968, Palestinian commandos attacked an Israeli plane at Athens airport, as well as conducting ineffective forays into Israel out of Lebanon. In retaliation, a few days before the end of 1968 an Israeli helicopter, protected by overflying fighters, landed in Beirut airport. Israeli commandos spilled out of the helicopter and in forty minutes blew up thirteen Lebanese civil aircraft that represented most of the fleet of Middle East Airlines (MEA). From that date onwards, Lebanese-Palestinian frictions worsened and a growing number of clashes between the Lebanese army and Palestinian and Syrian commandos increased internal tensions.

Due to severe clashes in April 1969, the then Prime Minister Rachid Karame stopped fulfilling his duties, but he did not resign.[1] He called on the Lebanese authorities to allow the Palestinians free movement and training in Lebanon, receiving support from Kamal Jumblatt, the most prominent Druze leader in Lebanon.

It became clear then that President Charles Helou and most Christian factions did not wish to abrogate Lebanon's truce agreement with Israel and to allow free rein to PLO fighters and their compatriots. The sovereignty of the country was at stake and Lebanon had only a weak president with no popular following. Helou tried to convince the Lebanese of the futility of any agreement with Palestinian factions that allowed free attacks against Israel.

Muslim Sunni leaders, Kamal Jumblatt and the Syrians, who closed their borders with Lebanon, forced an agreement on Lebanese Christians by immobilizing government and land exports for seven months, from April 1969 until 3 November 1969. At this point the Lebanese army chief, General Emile Bustani (not Emile Murchid Bustani), signed with Arafat the Cairo Agreement, which contradicted Lebanon's international

1.   In 1969 Rachid Karame refused to act as prime minister, yet he did not resign. It is interesting to note a similar attitude between him and his younger brother, Umar Karame, who was Lebanon's prime minister at the time of Hariri's assassination on 14 February 2005. Umar Karame came under severe criticism in parliament and resigned on 28 February 2005. Two days later he was nominated again for the role of prime minister. He took time to select his cabinet members, and delayed the formation of the cabinet until 5 April, when improvements to the electoral law had become impossible; even the proposed dates for holding elections between late May and mid-June were under threat. When international pressure increased in intensity, and Syria was accused of creating artificial delays, Karame was dropped, and Najib Mikatti, a man from Karame's home town with strong ties to Syria's president, Bashar al-Assad, was designated to form a cabinet. In a miraculously short period of time, Mikatti formed a fourteen-man cabinet that supervised reasonably clean elections and paved the way for improvements in other areas.

obligations and opened the country to dangerous winds of change, and the ambitions of the Palestinian leadership.

After the Cairo Agreement, Lebanon slid towards civil war. This had become inevitable. Yet had Bustani lived, Lebanon's history could have been different. The huge impact of Bustani's loss can be understood only by knowing what he could have prevented.

ONE

Hariri Comes on Stage

Following the 1975 civil war, many Lebanese with means and professional capabilities went abroad. The war of destruction and attrition had left the Lebanese questioning the future of their country, and there was a pervading feeling of pessimism. Lebanese emigrants of all creeds – and in total contrast to what was happening in Lebanon itself – met together to commiserate and exchange hope for the future.

In France, and particularly in Paris, there was a significant Lebanese community composed essentially of professionals, including lawyers, medical doctors, engineers, traders, professors, bankers and, of course, entrepreneurs. As of spring 1978, there was talk of a rising star in Saudi Arabia, Rafiq Hariri. He was going to build a huge port in Sidon, his home town in Lebanon where he had rebuilt his old school; he was offering scholarships to students; and most importantly, he was hiring capable Lebanese to work in Saudi Arabia, France and the United States.

Business opportunities in the Gulf region were expanding at a fast pace. Oil prices had risen to levels previously unheard of: $35 a barrel, as compared with $11 in 1973 and $18 in 1975. The increase in oil prices was spurred by the Iranian oil workers' strike, which caused Iranian production to drop from six million barrels a day to two million. The strike started in summer 1978 and continued until February 1979, when the shah was deposed and Ayatollah Khomeini was given the responsibility of running Iranian affairs. It was at that time that Iran became a religious state subjected to the rule of the 'wisest' – always a religious figure – and Khomeini decreed that oil production should not exceed two million barrels a day. Consequently, making up for the shortage was not expected in the short term, and oil prices increased, as did the revenues of oil-producing countries.

There was a heated atmosphere from late 1977 until mid-1982, a period during which expenditures on grandiose projects reached astronomical figures. There were bottlenecks in the availability of professionals and delivery of projects on time, and the rewards for ability to deliver were great. Hariri made a grand and unexpected entry in 1977.

In early summer 1978 Mr and Mrs Robert Debbas, members of a family who excelled in completing contracts for electrical works and who were close friends of Hariri's, invited my wife and I to lunch at the Coq Hardy, a fashionable country restaurant not far from Paris. When Hariri stepped into the restaurant the most striking features about him were his gentle eyes, his smile that flashed easily and wholeheartedly, and his youth. He was then 34 years old and had achieved all that had been reported about him, and he truly intended to develop an active port in Sidon where he was born in November 1944. Talking to Hariri was easy. I learned that he grew up in a loving family with a father who worked hard tilling the land and a mother who believed in education. He was urged to do well by his mother, just as she had urged his younger sister Bahia and younger brother Chafic.

Before the end of the 1960s, after securing a degree in accounting from the Arab University in Beirut (a university established by the Egyptians in Lebanon after the events of 1958), Hariri married an Iraqi who was his former classmate and travelled to Saudi Arabia for work, where he began his career as a teacher and later became a professional accountant.

One of Hariri's first employers was a Saudi who developed a large-scale contracting business, Redec, where Hariri had a reputation as hard-working and religious. Whenever the time came to pay part of his income as a tax and religious obligation (*zakat*), Hariri would refuse to let the company pay the tax on his behalf, and would pay out of his own small resources. Hariri was a devoted Sunni Muslim and believed strongly that God is the true benefactor and that each and everyone reaps what God wishes. This strong religious belief was fused to a political stand in support of Arab nationalism.

By 1970 Hariri had three sons from his first marriage: Bahaa, Hussam and Saad. He had to work hard to cover the needs of a growing family, and started dabbling in business for his own account. This was at the time of the first oil-price increase, when the cost of a barrel rose from $2.2 to $11–12 in 1973 – initiating a boom in Saudi Arabia that lasted well into 1982. Late in 1976 Hariri's partner, a Palestinian contractor, secured a contract for a large hotel with conference facilities in Taef, to be completed within ten months. The Saudis were preparing for an important conference to be held in November 1978 in Taef, their beautiful mountainous summer capital, where hotel and conference facilities were practically non-existent. Hariri undertook to fulfill the terms of the contract, visiting Paris to secure a loan for working capital and to involve a French company in the task – cost was no problem provided completion was realized in ten months.

While in Paris, Hariri was introduced to Joseph Abdo al-Khoury, an active Lebanese banker who had appropriated Banque Méditerranée in Lebanon and started operations in Paris. The banker was impressed by Hariri and chose to support his efforts by providing required bank guarantees, financing for working capital and an agreement with Oger, a well-known French engineering firm.

The job was completed on time. This was his first major test, which he passed with flying colours, gaining the support of Crown Prince Fahd who later became king in 1980. Hariri achieved considerable profits, and made a successful takeover bid for Oger, a company that was teetering on the brink of bankruptcy. From then on, the Saudi royal family relied on Hariri to do construction work for its most prominent members. It is estimated that the volume of work completed or contracted by Hariri between 1977 and 1982 exceeded $10 billion. The work did not involve construction only, but furnishings as well as landscaping and maintenance. The scope of work even involved the completion of a 'Palais des Congres', with highly sophisticated specifications, in Damascus. The Saudis paid for this venture, encouraged by Hariri who, in the early 1980s, had become involved with Saudi efforts to mediate between Lebanese fighting parties. He wanted to develop a strong bond with the Syrian regime, particularly as Syrian forces had controlled most of the Lebanese territory since 1976.

Between 1977 and 1982 Hariri crossed over from need to prosperity and, more importantly, from anonymity to a position of trust with the Saudi royal family, whether with regard to executing projects or assuming the role of covert or overt emissary in respect of the ongoing Lebanese crisis. Having achieved great wealth in a short period of time, Hariri revealed his true generous nature: he rebuilt his old school in Sidon, which had fallen into disrepair; he started offering scholarships to bright students through a foundation run by his sister Bahia; and he acquired agricultural land on a large scale to occupy his father in farming, his preferred activity. By this time, Hariri was enjoying substantial means, and with a background as an active member of a pan-Arab nationalist movement, had strong political ties.

In 1982 Hariri secured aid for Lebanon from King Fahd to clear the rubble from Beirut after Israel's occupation of the city in the summer. Israel had withdrawn by September of that year, after Palestinian fighters had been evicted to Tunisia. The previous commercial centre of Beirut had become an area of destruction. It was full of dirt, wild animals, displaced people, rubble, free-flowing wastewater, etc. To cross from East Beirut (the Christian district) to West Beirut (the Muslim district), passing through the centre, would normally take no more than five minutes. Few people, however, dared to zigzag through blocked streets and arteries. Those who needed to move urgently between both sections of Beirut needed to travel for hours and with expert help and protection to cover the short distance. Lebanese with urgent business on the other side of Beirut would often travel by sea to Cyprus and pick up a boat there in order to reach their destination. They would face a tiring and expensive day to travel over what, in the absence of barricades, would have been a short distance.

Hariri realized that before his engineering team completed works on cleaning the rubble, restoring water services and opening roads to traffic, restoration of Lebanese unity and the Lebanese state had to start with the declared intention of restoring the central commercial district through the implementation of a clear programme.

A research firm was engaged in 1983 to conduct a feasibility study concerning the restoration of the commercial centre of Beirut. The study was completed by June 1984, during which time 270 commercial tenants, resident in the area before 1975, were interviewed. Concurrently and on a much larger scale, Dar al-Handassah (Chaer & Partners), the largest engineering consulting operation in the Middle East working out of Lebanon, was contracted to finalize a master plan for the reconstruction of the commercial centre of Beirut.

The task of preparing and scheduling the reconstruction of the commercial centre of Beirut involved hundreds of engineers, bankers, legal experts, accountants, town planners, etc. Realization of this ambition could not proceed until an enabling law was passed in 1993 and work started by the newly established company, Solidere, to bring about fundamental change to the face of Beirut and the characteristics of Lebanon's capital. The ceremonial laying of the first building block in the commercial centre of Beirut was celebrated on 21 September 1994 in the presence of President Elias Hraoui and the Sunni leader Saeb Salam who flew from Geneva to join the ceremony.

In 1982 tragic developments in Lebanon pulled Hariri into the vortex of internal politics. During the second half of the1960s, when he went to work in Saudi Arabia, Hariri was an avid and active Arab nationalist. As a very young married man with familial responsibilities, including two babies and ageing parents, Hariri avoided political involvement in the Kingdom of Saudi Arabia. Times were sensitive, with Nasser fermenting trouble in Yemen and calling for the overthrow of the Saudi ruling family.

At the age of thirty-eight, Hariri had acquired the patience of the wise. He saw that development could only proceed in an orderly and peaceful environment. Fighting of the worst kind had destroyed the heart of Beirut and the spirit of well-educated Lebanese people. By 1982 the need for rallying energies and directing efforts to reconstruction was very strong, and Muslim Sunni leaders were very few.

The most outstanding Sunni leader, Saeb Salam, had given support to Bachir Gemayel in his bid to become president. Gemayel had promised to disengage from the Israelis, which he later did, and Salam felt at the time that Palestinian factions had dragged Lebanon to a pitch of fighting that nearly destroyed the country. He withdrew his support from Arafat and supported Gemayel, who was elected president of Lebanon after the withdrawal of Israeli troops from Beirut. On 14 September 1982 Gemayel was assassinated by a member of the Syrian Nationalist party, who believe in the inevitability of one nation including Syria, Jordan, Iraq, Lebanon and Palestine. After his assassination Lebanese parliamentarians elected his elder brother, Amine, as president. Once in office, Amine Gemayel concentrated his efforts on eliciting support from Arab countries and leading Muslim figures in Lebanon.

Hariri was called upon by Gemayel to help clear the rubble of destruction in Beirut, caused by Lebanese in-fighting, battles with Palestinian and Syrian armed factions, and the Israeli occupation of Beirut for nearly ten weeks. These calls for help persuaded Hariri to seek the support of King Fahd with whom he had developed close ties. Help was generously given and Hariri's teams worked hard to clear the rubble, restore electricity networks, secure water supplies and give the capital city a push towards self-sufficiency. However, in June 1982 Hariri's ambitious university centre that incorporated a modern hospital, an agricultural research centre, a nursing school, a technical university, and an advanced elementary and high school close to Sidon, was completely occupied by Israeli forces assisted by their Lebanese allies. Utilization and development of the centre's facilities were made impossible.

In 1979 Hariri launched the Kfarfalous project, so called after its location near to a village of that name situated at the intersection of roads leading to the Chouf district, the western Beqaa and Nabatieh in the south. He contracted with the leading French university in Lebanon to run the university faculties and the hospital, and agreed with the International College to run the high school. The project was to be completed over an area of 2 million square metres, and its cost was estimated at $100 million. Hariri funded the project, and drove his associates and family to complete it in record time. The development represented a promise of better educational possibilities for residents of certain administrative districts of Lebanon that were still highly underdeveloped, and by May 1982, students were registered at the high school and the first wave numbered over 150. However, Israeli occupation restricted movements between parts of Lebanon, and the Kfarfalous project, although ready in terms of structures and equipment, was not allowed to fulfill its role.

In 1985 the Israelis withdrew from Sidon and its periphery. Kfarfalous was stripped of all its equipment, and even most of its trees. In 1986 Lebanese collaborators with Israel tried to offer Hariri's equipment back to him at a discount, but he declined their offer. Kfarfalous, which was prepared as a technical university, an agricultural institute, a nursing centre and a general bilingual elementary and high school, was not to be.

With the Israelis occupying the new university centre at Kfarfalous, and destroying parts of his home town of Sidon, Hariri's nationalistic drive was whipped up by the challenge of restoring minimum services to Beirut and transcending the losses he had suffered. This young man with tremendous energy, great resources and boundless commitment to Lebanon plunged into the fray of reconstruction without hesitation. He became determined to rebuild Beirut to its former glory, and to launch Lebanon on the road to meaningful reconstruction.

Hariri knew that success in realizing reconstruction objectives depended on the availability and motivation of talented individuals, and that the selection of priorities and timing of objectives needed vision and intellectual perspicacity. To this end, the Board of Reconstruction and Development was established, steered by its chairman Dr Muhammad Atalla, a soft-spoken, well-trained and highly intelligent economist who came from Sidon, Hariri's home town. Hariri was attracted by Atalla's qualities as a professional as well as his personal integrity, and the two men became friends and allies in the effort to extract Lebanon from the precarious situation it faced after the Israeli withdrawal from Beirut in early September 1982. Hariri financed a major study of Lebanese reconstruction for the Board of Reconstruction and Development.

By 1983 Hariri was fully immersed in the economic and political future of Lebanon. His most ambitious programme for helping young Lebanese had started in 1979, in Sidon, with the formation of an Islamic educational foundation – that later became the Hariri Foundation – which provided thirteen students with scholarships. Before the mid-1980s, and as is discussed later in this book, the Hariri Foundation became the largest and most diversified donor of university scholarships on a worldwide scale.

Hariri realized his meteoric success through risk-taking, hard work, motivation of collaborators and, most importantly, ever closer ties with the ruling family in Saudi Arabia and with the centre of decision-making in Lebanon.

The process of getting closer to the power centre in Lebanon was not difficult. President Gemayel was open to cooperation with Hariri, yet the question was how long Gemayel would retain power whilst making major policy mistakes. Hariri did not want to be drawn into the cobweb of Gemayel's friendships and commitments. He had already started a friendship with Abdul Halim Khaddam, then minister of foreign affairs of Syria, and with the chief of staff of the Syrian army, Hikmat Chehabi. His company, Oger, already fully acquired from its former French partners, built a sophisticated international conference centre in Damascus with Saudi financing arranged by Hariri. The Syrian rulers did not trust Gemayel, and Hariri kept his distance from the Lebanese president whilst dabbling increasingly on the fringes of Lebanese political life.

In this, he was helped by being nominated as an assistant to Prince Bandar bin Sultan[1] and Prince Saud al-Faysal[2] when two national Lebanese conferences were held in Switzerland in 1983 and 1984 to try to resolve differences between Lebanese groups, but without success. In 1989 he assisted King Fahd in the context of the Tripartite Committee that was entrusted to resolve the Lebanese dilemma. This committee, nominated in 1989, included King Fahd, King Hassan II of Morocco, and Chadli Benjedid, the Algerian president. The Taef Conference in 1989 presumably crowned the efforts of the Tripartite Committee but, in fact, was first and foremost a Saudi initiative. Hariri expended tremendous efforts to make this conference a success and, in essence, Lebanon regained peace and adopted a new constitution at Taef in November 1989. I understand that the Taef Accord was written by Hariri, and I was informed by Hariri himself that the late Nasri Maalouf, an eminent politician, lawyer and linguist, helped edit the draft, which then benefited from a number of suggestions by different Lebanese politicians and groups, before being finally approved.

Between 1983 and 1988 Hariri developed strong relations with leading Lebanese diplomats such as Johnny Abdo, the former head of army intelligence in Lebanon who was accused of helping the election of Bachir Gemayel as president and maintaining contacts with the Israelis. Abdo had become Lebanon's ambassador in Bern, Switzerland, although this role stifled his ambitions, and he was closely associated with Hariri and for a number of years affected Hariri's political thinking. Also in close contact with Hariri was Suheil Shammas, Lebanon's brilliant and

1. Prince Bandar bin Sultan is the Saudi ambassador in Washington and the son of Prince Sultan, the minister of defence in Saudi Arabia.

2. Prince Saud al-Faysal is the son of King Faysal and the long-serving minister of foreign affairs of Saudi Arabia.

eloquent ambassador to the United Nations, and Dr Abdalla Abu Habib, a friendly and outspoken figure who was nominated by President Amine Gemayel to be the Lebanese ambassador in Washington. Habib had been a senior member of staff at the World Bank before assuming his diplomatic role and later rejoined the World Bank before moving to Lebanon as an advisor to the former deputy prime minister, Issam Fares.

Hariri's political involvement was orchestrated on a macro level as well as on a micro level. Most importantly he became the trusted Saudi emissary in respect of Lebanese affairs, and this trust enabled him to develop strong ties in Syria, particularly through Khaddam and Chehabi, who together supervised Lebanese-Syrian relations in the 1980s. Hariri also developed strong ties in France and the United States. In France, he maintained large offices for Oger, which included purchase centres for his projects, and employed hundreds of technicians. It was only to be expected that he would develop strong relations with Jacques Chirac, then the mayor of Paris, who later became president of France. The two men became close personal friends and Hariri could depend on Chirac's support within the European Union. The Paris II Conference, held on 22 November 2002 in Paris, at the invitation and urging of President Chirac, provided Lebanon with the biggest package of aid granted by the international community to a country as small as Lebanon.

In the United States, Hariri attracted attention through the activities and programmes of his educational foundation. By 1983 the Hariri Foundation had become the largest organization of its type, offering university scholarships to thousands of students in the US and Canada. The foundation established its offices in Washington and was efficiently run by Rafiq Bizri, another close ally from Hariri's home town Sidon.

The activities of the Hariri Foundation attracted public attention and, in turn, Hariri engaged a number of leading political and diplomatic figures as consultants. One such distinguished figure who helped Hariri better understand American foreign policy, as well as the structures of power in the United States, was Richard Murphy, the assistant undersecretary of state for Middle Eastern affairs from 1982–8. Murphy had also served previously as ambassador in Syria, and became a personal friend of President Hafez al-Assad.

In the 1980s Hariri's mission was to save Lebanon from the contrasting ambitions and affiliations of Lebanese leaders and to bring Lebanon's plight to the attention of the major world powers. In 1983 the French and Americans sent forces to help Lebanon after the Israeli withdrawal and both suffered massive human losses from suicide attacks, hence withdrawing their forces. Hariri persisted in his efforts to regain credibility for Lebanon with four countries, particularly Saudi Arabia, where resources were abundant as well as employment opportunities, and where the ruling family had an emotional attachment to Lebanon, and Syria, which had regained its military supervisory role in Lebanon after the first withdrawal of its forces under Israeli attacks in 1982. As of 1984, when government was split between East (Christian) and West (Muslim) Beirut, Syria's role had become far more important than before. A grand attempt at stopping fighting in Lebanon was made in 1985 with the signing of the Damascus Accord by practically all Lebanese warlords, but the accord was shattered upon the return of the Lebanese Christian delegation by an insurgency led by Samir Geagea, the military leader of the Christian Lebanese Forces faction. This insurgency took place in mid-January 1986.

The two other countries where Hariri concentrated his efforts in favour of Lebanon were the United States and France. In the US, Hariri could depend on the support of Prince Bandar bin Sultan, the ambassador of Saudi Arabia, who enjoyed excellent relations with President Reagan and President George Bush Sr, as well as the new Democrat president, Bill Clinton. In France, Hariri's friendship with Chirac, who by this time had become prime minister and was on his way to the presidency, served Lebanon well.

Hariri undertook a hectic schedule in the 1980s. He had to play not only a delicate political game, but also had to maintain the necessary material resources for travel, offices and staff, and for cultivating press and political relations. He became a heavy investor in France, the United States, Lebanon and Saudi Arabia, and before the end of the 1980s Hariri had become a major figure in Arab banking. Through his Mediterranean investment group, Banque Méditerranée in Beirut and Paris, he owned the second largest shareholding in the Arab Bank after the Schoman family, who had established the bank, and one-third of a Saudi bank owned jointly with the Arab Bank.

In the early 1980s Hariri recruited an effective and loyal team of collaborators. These were engineers, financial people, lawyers, diplomats and journalists. His primary condition was loyalty. If any of his assistants did not fully devote their time to Hariri's agenda, then their contracts would be terminated. By the mid-1980s, Hariri had become a leading business figure as well as an important political mediator. However, Hariri was also aware of the important role of the media in the practice of politics. He had an instinctive liking for the press and encouraged and supported the late Nabil Khoury to produce *al-Mustakbal*, a magazine published in Paris. Khoury was a talented and experienced journalist who befriended Hariri in the late 1960s in Saudi Arabia. Although Khoury was born in Jerusalem, he had been chosen by President Chehab to be director of the ministry of information in Lebanon in the late 1950s, and whilst fulfilling this function Khoury published several novels that attracted a wide readership.

Khoury faced serious financial pressures in Paris and Hariri stepped in to help sustain *al-Mustakbal*. At a later stage, the licence and trade name of *al-Mustakbal* (The Future) had to be auctioned by court order. Hariri acquired the name and started his own daily paper, *al-Mustakbal*, in Lebanon. This name now connotes Hariri's political movement, which is the movement with the largest number of parliament members in Lebanon.

While supporting Khoury and *al-Mustakbal*, Hariri also purchased from a young Lebanese, Ragid Shammaa, a fledgling radio station in Paris that started transmissions directed at the Arab world under the name of Radio Orient. In 1995 Hariri launched his television station of the same name, with both the television and radio stations reaching Lebanese emigrants almost worldwide.

In late summer 1983 Hariri's belief in the importance of media exposure led him to seek an interview with me on Lebanese Television, the only operating station in Lebanon at the time. I had a weekly economics programme and Hariri wanted to use it to express his views about the priorities of reconstruction and development in Lebanon. The scheduled one-hour programme generated a positive response and people wanted to know more about Hariri and his views.

Throughout the mid- to late1980s Hariri cultivated friendships with Lebanese and foreign press figures. Moreover, he hired a full-time media advisor, a young and intelligent journalist, Nuhad Mashnouk, who later became his senior political advisor during Hariri's first stretch of premiership, from autumn 1992 to autumn 1998.

After Hariri became prime minister in the autumn of 1992 he further developed his relationships with leading media figures. Hariri could always spare time for journalists. Moreover, he did not hesitate to show his appreciation of journalistic talent. This was obvious in his support of Nabil Khoury and, later, Talal Salman, the publisher of the *as-Safir* daily newspaper and a powerful writer and analyst. The Lebanese press baron, Ghassan Tueni (if indeed there was such a role in Lebanon), publisher of *an-Nahar* newspaper, became a friend of Hariri in spite of their age difference (Tueni was nineteen years older than Hariri) and their diametrically opposed political convictions. Numerous publishers benefited from Hariri's support over time, and he became a 36 percent shareholder in *an-Nahar*, a holding that was renegotiated in autumn 2004. Another of Hariri's close journalist friends was Imad Eddine Adib, an Egyptian journalist and famous talk-show host whose programmes on Orbit Channel 2 reached a worldwide audience. Adib interviewed Hariri more than once and achieved a privileged relationship with him, which was originated and cultivated by Machnouk.

Hariri was well received by critical press personalities. Although Hariri's mastery of English or French was never perfect, he was respected for his charm and for his readiness to listen and to argue. One such occasion was an interview with Hariri by Robert Fisk, the well-known

British foreign correspondent for *The Independent*, and Lara Marlow, who was writing for the *Financial Times*. Both Fisk and Marlow were readily critical of Hariri's style of government, his nepotism, etc. Yet after a lengthy interview with him, they both became friends of his. Marlow, who now corresponds for the *Irish Times* out of Paris, was the only journalist to whom Hariri related the threats to his person and his children by the Syrian intelligence security man in Lebanon, Rustum Gazale, in summer 2004, while requesting she keep this information unpublished. It was only following Hariri's assassination that Marlow published the information in the *Irish Times*, the particulars of which have helped the International Investigation Commission. Marlow was one of the speakers at the touching ceremony in memory of Hariri that was held in the square adjacent to Hariri's home in Paris just a few days after his death. Other mourners included Amin Maalouf, the famous Lebanese novelist living in France, and the internationally known Lebanese pianist, Abdul Rahman al-Bacha.

Hariri's ability to communicate with ordinary people was one of his great qualities and contributed very much to his successful relationship with the media. It was for this reason that journalists, once they had a serious one-to-one discussion with him, tended to warm to his outlook. Moreover, Hariri went out of his way to associate with journalists and TV personalities. It is useful to note two incidents, which show Hariri's easy interaction with the press.

In 1998 the Arab Journalists Union held their annual meeting in Beirut. I invited Hariri together with eleven editors and publishers of leading newspapers and magazines to lunch at my home. In preparation, the main table was set with eight seats and a smaller table for four was placed in an adjacent corner in the dining room. Conversation had warmed up before lunch, and as we entered the dining room, Hariri stood at his seat at the head of the table and said: 'Marwan, pull up the table with me so that we can put the smaller table at the other end and maintain the group together.' Thus we settled together to eat and the journalists present were both pleased and flattered.

Another example of Hariri's immense attraction to the press was provided in an interview in 2000 with Issa Ghorayeb, the then editor of Lebanon's prestigious daily French newspaper, *L'Orient–Le Jour*. Ghorayeb was well known and respected for his independence, clear thinking and elegant expression (and, indeed, he is still popular with the readers of *L'Orient–Le Jour* in his role as column-writer). Between 1993 and 1998, the first long stretch of a Hariri-led string of cabinets, Ghorayeb maintained a critical and cynical attitude *vis-à-vis* Hariri and his policies. Hounded by President Lahoud, Hariri spent the two years from 1998 traversing a political desert. Ghorayeb remained unsympathetic, yet still felt that Hariri's views should be heard.

Accordingly, in late 1999 Hariri contacted Ghorayeb and suggested he would like to be interviewed by him. While he was at first reluctant, Ghorayeb agreed to conduct an interview provided Hariri did not interfere in any manner or form with the text of the interview once prepared by Ghorayeb, and provided he answer all questions. The interview took place over three hours and was meticulously recorded. It was published on a full page in *L'Orient-Le Jour* on 3 January 2000, and its content was sympathetic to Hariri as a person and to many of his ideas. I inquired from Ghorayeb as to the interview's positive tone, and he answered in clear terms that Hariri had a warm and honest personality and that he kept his word not to interfere with the text. Ghorayeb was one of the most eloquent voices in lamenting Hariri's loss in 2005.

The 1980s were a period of intense and diverse activity for Rafiq Hariri. In the late 1970s he had instituted a scholarship programme for a limited number of students in Sidon. By 1983 this initiative had become the Hariri Foundation, which funded the university education of 35,000 young Lebanese from all religious sects in a number of well-known universities in countries such as the United States, Britain, France, Canada, Australia and Italy. The total outlay of funds on this unique charitable enterprise exceeded $1.5 billion. It was enough for Hariri that these young people were not fighting battles but acquiring skills and developing learning in peaceful and advanced societies.

Also in the 1980s, Hariri went through a major transformation on a business level. From construction and contracting, he moved into maintenance and advanced engineering techniques. In Saudi Arabia, he established a printing plant that produces two million copies a year of the Holy Qur'an, and which are essentially distributed to pilgrims. In Lebanon he moved into banking after having acquired Banque Méditerranée, which was active in Paris and had a network in Lebanon. Yet this bank had many problems and Hariri appointed Fuad Siniora, a close Hariri aide and former head of the Banking Control Commission, to deal with them while Hariri started another bank from scratch. Further, Hariri became a heavy investor in real estate, started his Kfarfalous project, and began studying the legal and technical requirements for rebuilding the commercial centre of Beirut that had been severely damaged during the war years.

Beyond Lebanon, Hariri invested heavily in real estate in Paris and transformed an aging block in the chic *seizième* district into a modern office complex. Moreover, in January 1987 he acquired 4.9 percent of the shares of the newly privatized Paribas Bank in Paris. His group was given a board seat on their international affiliate bank and later he acquired a significant holding in Crédit Agricole. One of his notable investments in France was the purchase of the residence of Gustaf Eiffel (the man who built the Eiffel Tower), a 3,000 squaremetre villa in the midst of a gently sloping terrain of similar area located opposite the famous tower across the Seine river.

Hariri reached further to the United States market and bought the Heinz Tower in Houston, which at the time – late 1986 to early 1987 – was one of the major developments in the capital city of the American oil industry. This foray was supplemented by purchases of land in a number of states and a sumptuous residence in Washington. To these investments were added a huge property for hunting in Rhodesia and a large farm in Brazil.

By the second half of the 1980s, Hariri had become a daring investor in industrialized countries. After his acquisition of 4.9 percent of the shares of Paribas Bank, he became responsive to investment projects proposed by them. In 1988 the bank proposed that Hariri invest in a 50/50 real-estate venture in London that required a total investment of £300 million. Although he was approached at short notice, Hariri responded positively to the proposal and took up an equal share with Paribas.

Before the end of the 1980s Hariri had invested heavily in prime real estate in Paris, London, Houston, Washington and Beirut. This pre-dated the formation of Solidere in 1993 – the company for rehabilitation and reconstruction of the commercial centre of Beirut – in which Hariri invested $183 million for the capped 10 percent shareholding by any individual, institution or group. Just prior to the 1990s, Hariri's portfolio of real estate holdings in the four countries was in the order of $1 billion. Banks shareholdings in France (Paribas and Méditerranée), Jordan (Arab Bank), Saudi Arabia (30 percent of the Saudi Investment Bank), and Lebanon accounted for $700–800 million. Together with his vast scholarship programme, Hariri had dispensed with over $3 billion in less than ten years. He was unique in this, and achieved stature of international recognition.

In order to achieve greater complementarity in financial services, in 1995 Hariri established MEDGULF, an insurance company that operates throughout the Middle East and North Africa. In 1998, Prince al-Walid bin Talal bin Abdul Aziz became a 30 percent shareholder. The Hariri family interests account for the majority of total shareholding whereas the vereran insurance specialist, Lutfi al-Zein, who runs MEDGULF, is a minority shareholder. Today MEDGULF is the second largest insurer in Saui Arabia, possibly the third largest in the Arab world and it owns and runs a re-insurance operation in London.

Together with all these initiatives, which placed Hariri at the forefront of the international business community, he worked continuously to bring about a Lebanese political rapprochement, and on maintaining public institutions and private educational institutions. The Lebanese army, which suffered a split in 1984 and was on the brink of falling apart because of lack of resources, was supported for a number of years by transfers of $500,000 per month from 1985 until 1988. General Michel Aoun, the then commander in chief of the army (and currently an important political leader in Lebanon), repeatedly acknowledged this help. Lebanon's two oldest universities, the American University of Beirut and the St Joseph University, were both about to close their doors in the mid-1980s, but Hariri's support kept them going. Today, both universities are thriving and are considered high-quality institutions in advanced fields of learning.

Also in the 1980s Hariri was involved in intricate and time-consuming political networking. He never tired of repeated failures at reconciliation. With help from the Saudis, Hariri finally succeeded in gathering a sufficient majority of Lebanese parliamentarians who met in Taef over twenty-three days to outline a new constitution commonly referred to as the Taef Accord. Fighting between warring factions stopped and a new president, René Mouawad, was elected to steer Lebanon in November 1989. On Independence Day, 22 November 1989, President Mouawad was assassinated by a massive roadside bomb that blew up his car – as happened to Hariri fifteen years later.

Deputy Elias Hraoui was elected president in November 1989, but could not move to the presidential palace in Baabda, which was under the control of General Michel Aoun. Aoun had been nominated prime minister by the departing president, Amine Gemayel in September 1988, and a schism came about with two governments: one in West Beirut headed by Salim al-Hoss, prime minister until the end of Gemayel's presidency, and Aoun's disputed government of three in Baabda.

Between 1989 and 1993 Hariri provided President Hraoui with living quarters and offices in two modern apartment blocks in Beirut. The location was considered suitable as it was close to the headquarters of the Syrian intelligence in Beirut (presumably aimed at protecting the president, especially after the assassination of President Rene Mouawad). In the first half of Hraoui's six-year term, Hariri greatly contributed to the cost of staff, accommodation, logistics, communications, armoured cars and security equipment.

President Hraoui maintained al-Hoss as prime minister until after October 1990 when Michel Aoun was driven out of Baabda. In December 1990 Umar Karame was nominated prime minister, and during 1991, the economy witnessed a boom in activity, transfers to Lebanon and government revenues. Growth recorded a 37 percent figure that was only possible because economic activity and investment were severely depressed in 1990. Karame assumed, mistakenly, that growth in the economy and government revenues would continue in 1992. Thus, at the end of 1991, the head of parliament Hussein al-Husseini approved 60 percent salary increases for government employees; when the impact on end-of-service indemnities is allowed for, the increase was in the order of 120 percent. Salary adjustments were backdated to the beginning of 1991, and government employees came into a lot of cash in February 1992. They rushed to purchase dollars, and the exchange rate for the Lebanese pound fell within three weeks, from LL880 to the dollar, to LL1,200 to the dollar. By the end of February 1992, the Central Bank declared that it would no longer support the exchange rate of the Lebanese pound. From then on, there was an economic free fall that resulted in LL2,800 to the dollar by August 1992.

In the meantime the cabinet nominated an eight-man committee of experts to develop and outline a plan for dealing with Lebanon's economic and financial problems. This committee, of which I was a member, after intense efforts and papers from all its members, submitted a report on 5 May 1992. The report recommended resorting to privatization, elimination of public authorities with little or no productivity, administrative reform and more developed techniques for bond issues, and interest rate charges, etc, by the Central Bank.

On 5 May 1992 there were public demonstrations against inflationary pressures, feverish speculation against the Lebanese pound, poor government services, etc. The demonstrations bordered on violence and involved the burning of tyres across streets in Beirut, which blocked traffic and increased public fears. Karame resigned the same day, accusing the opposition of artificially inflaming the masses. Yet, in fact, Karame never acknowledged the real reasons for public rejection of his policies.

Following this turn of events, a caretaker government was formed by Rachid al-Solh, an aging and agreeable figure, to supervise parliamentary elections during the summer of 1992. The last elections had been held in 1972, and twenty years without elections had seemed to doom the process. In fact, the Lebanese resumed their usual bickering and factional alliances. The elections were completed successfully and the time for rebuilding Lebanon had come. However, many Christians mistakenly chose to boycott these elections.

For his valued work and all that he represented, Hariri was the desired prime minister. As of late September 1992, when Hariri's nomination seemed certain, the exchange rate of the Lebanese pound improved drastically, from LL2,500 to the dollar to, by 31 December 1992, LL1,837 to the dollar. Hariri formed his first government in November 1992.

TWO

Hariri: the Man Behind the Name

Hariri was immensely strong physically and believed in regular exercise. He would spend half an hour in the morning on the treadmill or lifting weights. During this period he would be briefed about the press and listened to the BBC World Service.

During Hariri's first stretch as prime minister, from 1992 to 1998, his family (other than his daughter Hind) was rarely in Lebanon. The eldest son Bahaa was responsible for developing international business affairs; his son Saad was responsible for the business in Saudi Arabia, which was the original source of wealth for the family. Saad returned from the United States in 1993 after completing his business studies in Washington. Hariri's younger two boys, Fahd and Ayman, were still in high school and, later, in university: Fahd in France where he studied architecture and is currently an art dealer, and Ayman who studied computer science in the United States and started a business there, which became highly successful. Following his father's assassination, Ayman returned to Saudi Arabia to look after Oger Communications, a worldwide network of cellular telephone services and the largest of the Hariri family enterprises.

Hariri was a loving, family man. He was deeply affected by the untimely death of his second-born Hussam in a car accident in the United States in 1990. Yet he did not make it his occupation to speak regularly of his family. When he did, he was very proud of Bahaa's and Saad's achievements. On more than one occasion, he would say, 'I don't need to work as they (Bahaa and Saad) are outperforming me'. Hariri's only worry was for the safety of Hind, the youngest of his children, who chose to study in Lebanon and stay by her father's side. A gentle, intelligent young woman, Hind got her BA degree in June 2005, less than six months after Hariri's assassination.

Hariri witnessed the evolution of his four sons with pride. Bahaa, the eldest, has a generous and friendly personality, and has done well on international markets and in real-estate development. Currently, Bahaa is supervising a major development in the centre of Amman, Jordan. In Lebanon he is developing a major real-estate project in a prime location at the end of Beirut's Verdun Street, and is working on the construction of a five-star hotel at Raouche, an area overlooking the sea. The two projects in Lebanon are being developed with Kuwaiti partners.

Saad, who was chosen by the family to follow in his father's political footsteps, is known as a man of independent judgment. He looked after Oger Communications and its progress in South Africa, and succeeded in achieving inroads in other countries. He passed this responsibility to his brother Ayman, who returned from the United States to look after the family business out of Saudi Arabia. The youngest son, Fahd, studied architecture and started a career in Paris as an exclusive art dealer. Like his father, he is energetic, full of ideas and highly intelligent. All four brothers have learnt the value of money and are hard working, which is just as well, as by acting for Hariri's enterprises they are each involved in the largest conglomerate of Lebanese roots, with a yearly turnover of $5 billion and around 30,000 Lebanese employees.

Hariri kept in touch with his sons practically on a daily basis to enquire about developments, yet he would not interfere with his sons' decisions. He sought to be a guiding spirit rather than a firm hand. His daughter Hind he spent time with every day. Hariri's wife, Nazek, a gentle, attractive woman with a kind and generous spirit, hated politics for its intrigues and because it had consumed her husband's time and energy since the early 1980s. At about that time, Dr Ahmad Abdul Wahab, senior advisor to King Faysal until his assassination in 1975, advised Hariri to abandon Lebanese politics and live his life in comfort and close to his family. Hariri's response was 'Lebanese politics and the desire to participate in saving Lebanon are my dearest wish.' Politics became Nazek Hariri's rival for her husband's affections and made the telephone the trustee of their emotions and alliance: every evening, no matter where he was, Hariri would talk at length with his wife before she went to sleep. He would relate to her his triumphs and challenges whilst trying to calm her anxieties. He wanted most of all to bring his wife closer to his political life, and gradually his patient efforts bore fruit.

Hariri spent much of his time at home in Koraytem, a neighbourhood next to the old campus of the Lebanese American University (LAU), where he had built palatial quarters for his own personal residence, for the accommodation of his security people, and to serve also as operational offices. Fridays and Sundays witnessed hundreds of visitors. Frequently, during the period of launching construction projects in 1994–5, Hariri would drive to one or more site with associates following in their cars. In his early months in government, Hariri would often visit restaurants, particularly Italian restaurants in Beirut, or the Bourj al-Hamam restaurant that provides Lebanese specialties and is located a few kilometres to the north of Beirut. He would travel with very little official security, accompanied by his trusted bodyguard Abu Tarek (Yahya al-Arab) and his team. As of the late 1990s, Hariri added to his residences a complex at the top of Fakra, an exclusive winter sports and relaxation destination that is targeted by skiers from all over the region. Access to this residence was difficult: the trip from Beirut took at least one hour and required driving skills and a four-wheel drive vehicle; also, meeting with Hariri at Fakra on Fridays or Sundays was strictly regulated by appointment.

Hariri, like most successful people, had little time or patience to learn about social or personal problems. He delegated this task to close associates. Moreover, most of his instructions were verbal and he had a habit of reviewing progress every week on every major issue with the associates concerned. He would do this on weekends, Friday and Sunday, and whenever he was in Lebanon Hariri would see his associates and friends on these days with or without appointments. Normally, Hariri devoted two hours in the morning, between eight o'clock and ten o'clock, for meetings over issues requiring his immediate attention. His memory and attention to detail were astounding and he criticized any associates who fell behind schedule, whether due to time pressures or laxity. If their failure was thought intended to sabotage progress or suggested a whiff of political affiliation to the opposition, then Hariri would bring to an end the existing association no matter how important the terms of reference.

Hariri had a great need for capable and dependable individuals to handle various sections of his business and, later, public tasks after he became prime minister. He could not attend to all the details of running a government whose administrative structure was in shambles and overburdened by antiquated regulations. As an example of the administrative nightmare at that time: a director general of a ministry needed ten signatures to procure coffee for his visitors; a municipal truck in need of repair required sixty signatures.

The inefficiencies of Lebanon's public administration were made more difficult given that Hariri frequently had to travel, and had three separate work bases. During office hours, when in Lebanon, Hariri would be at the Grand Serail, where meetings were meticulously scheduled by his trusted assistant Lieutenant Colonel Wissam al-Hassan. Yet Hariri's senior assistants and associates often felt they were floating in vacuum before receiving an opinion or instruction and there was undue agitation between his associates to claim his ear. This fervent competition for Hariri's favour sometimes resulted in associates going home, or to opposition camps.

For a man who could mobilize teams that completed in five years $10 billion of construction work with furnishing and fittings, the Lebanese bureaucracy was stifling. For this reason, Hariri chose people who had his full confidence to fulfill important posts. A selective list provides a clear picture of his team at work.

Fuad Siniora was chosen to be Hariri's actual minister of finance. Siniora holds an MA from London University and had extensive experience in finance, banking and accounting. Before taking this responsibility, Siniora was chairman and general manager of Banque Méditerranée.

Mustafa Razian, a reclusive old-time friend of Hariri with a doctorate in economics from the US, was entrusted with running the affairs of Mediterranean Investment Group (MIG), which controlled Hariri's interests in the financial sector in Lebanon and abroad. This role he fulfilled from early 1985 to December 2004.

Bassil Yared, a lawyer who worked as legal advisor to the former chairman of Banque Méditerranée in Paris, was entrusted with follow-up of banking affairs in France and maintaining close contacts with Jacques Chirac and his team. He served Hariri as well as a board member of the international affiliate of Banque Nationale de Paris Intercontinentale (BNPI).

Dr Bahij Tabbara, an eminent lawyer and former minister, became Hariri's full-time legal advisor as well as a minister in all his governments. He is today the éminence grise of the Hariri parliamentary bloc.

For press affairs and political council, Hariri engaged Nuhad Machnouk, a young journalist who had achieved recognition in his profession and with leading political figures in Lebanon, including Takieddine al-Solh who was prime minister in 1973–4 and a man of moderation and wise leadership. Machnouk claimed his political education came about from working for Takieddine al-Solh.

In 1992, the pressures on the Lebanese pound necessitated appointment of a professional banker to take the helm at the Central Bank. In 1993 Hariri chose Riad Salameh, a successful investment banker with Merryll Lynch, as governor of the Central Bank. He is still serving in this capacity for a third six-year term.

The Banking Control Commission, which is the supervisory authority that reviews the adherence of banks to regulations and good banking practices, needed a new chief. Hariri secured the services of Dr Muhammad Baassiri who had specialized in accounting and finance and was gainfully employed in Washington DC. After serving as head of the Banking Control Commission, Baassiri has been nominated to head the group responsible for applying Financial Action Task Force (FATF) regulations against money laundering in Lebanon.

Finally, in the public sector appointments, Hariri chose engineer Fadel Chalak, who was working with him in Saudi Arabia, to head the Council of Reconstruction and Development. Chalak had supervised the operations for clearing the rubble from Sidon and Beirut and restoring basic infrastructure facilities. Chalak had also worked on developing the Hariri Foundation and its tremendous scholarship programme. From 1995 until September 1996 he was minister of telecommunications.

In respect of Solidere, the company responsible for rehabilitation and construction of Beirut's commercial centre, Hariri brought in as chairman of this enterprise Dr Nasser Chamaa. Like Hariri, Siniora and Razian, Chamaa originates from Sidon. He graduated from California and worked with Bechtel before joining Hariri in Saudi Arabia.

For financial matters relating to Solidere and Banque Méditerranée, Hariri appointed Abdel Hafiz Mansour to the board of both enterprises, a man with excellent abilities in finance and accounting and known to have exceptional integrity and application. He now manages Horizon Management, the company established in 2003 to oversee and develop the Hariri Group's real estate portfolio in Lebanon and abroad.

Another five professionals further supported Hariri's team on various projects. These were engineer Fadi Fawaz, who was Hariri's project trouble-shooter. Dr Daoud Sayegh helped in developing regional and international political scenarios whilst maintaining a regular intellectual relation with the Maronite Patriarch who considered Hariri a friend worthy of support. Dr Nadim Mulla, an economist and econometrician from Tripoli, supervised the computerization of the bank's requirements and offered help and studies as requested – he was designated as economic advisor to the prime minister in 1996, and in 1998 was asked to be chairman of Future Television (he is still the chairman of Future TV and the senior economic advisor to Saad Rafiq Hariri, leader of Lebanon's majority bloc in parliament). In 2000 Ghazi Youssef, a professor at AUB with a doctorate in economics, was appointed as the executive secretary of the Higher Council for Privatization.

Although Youssef worked hard on this task, little was achieved because of political bickering and, finally, he ran for elections in 2005 and is currently a parliament member. The fifth and youngest professional was Dr Bassel Fuleihan. He had been recruited by Mulla and left a senior post with the IMF to come to Lebanon. In 2000 he was elected as a member of parliament and later designated as minister of economy. He was the author of the programme for administrative and financial reform, which was submitted to the donors at the Paris II Conference held on 22 November 2002. Fuleihan died after fighting for his life for 64 days in a French hospital where he was treated for severe burns following Hariri's assassination – he was sitting next to Hariri at the time of the explosion.

In addition to this core team of professionals, Hariri often called on the expertise and opinion of close friends or individuals whose opinion he valued, or well-known journalists with capability to analyse regional developments. Yet it is impossible to provide a full enumeration of all close associates or friends of Hariri without failing to mention certain important characters. While I do not claim to know all Hariri's close associates, and have chosen to mention the few that were put in the forefront of Hariri's initiatives, mention must be made briefly of the following additional important figures in Hariri's career in Lebanon.

Abdel Latif Chamaa	One of Hariri's closest friends and a self-effacing figure.
Nabil al-Jisr	An outstanding engineer who headed the Council of Reconstruction and Development after Chalak, and later played a steering role in the affairs of Oger.
Hosni Majzoub (MD)	A medical doctor from Hariri's home town who was crucial to the success of the Hariri Foundation in its early years.
Rafiq Bizri	The man who ran the American chapter of the Hariri Foundation and who still continues to do so.
Sabbah al-Hajj (PhD)	An early recruit, who although an economist ran Oger Lebanon for a while and later the Saudi-Lebanese Bank.

Muhammad Kashli	A leftist intellectual who maintained Hariri's contacts with left-leaning politicians and union leaders.
Radwan al-Sayed (PhD)	He advised Hariri on matters of Islam in an international context. Dr al-Sayed is a distinguished Islamist who taught at Harvard and participated effectively in the Committee of Christian-Islamic Dialogue in Lebanon.
Salim Diab	A close associate, who handled election campaigns for Hariri as well as aid to social organizations, the needy, sports clubs and active leaders of communities. He is the heir of a well-known trading family in Lebanon.

When Hariri first assumed political responsibility, he thought that he knew the ropes and was impatient to achieve, but he could lose his temper and oversimplify solutions. On the whole, and in spite of his intelligence, he committed mistakes because of his lack of patience. In later years, his patience became legendary and there are many observers, including myself, who believe that his patience and tolerance contributed to his assassination. There were very few politicians who were trusted by Hariri after his long experience as prime minister. One member of parliament who had his full trust was his sister Bahia Hariri. She always had a special place in his heart. When she was first elected to parliament in 1992, Hariri was overjoyed and was continuously seeking her counsel in his early years as prime minister.

In spite of all the undercurrents, logistical difficulties and feverish petty struggles, Hariri was renowned as a man who was clear and concise, and always well prepared. He was affable, friendly, intelligent, and had a sense of humour. Working with him was enjoyable to the point of overcoming the tactical challenges that faced each and every one of his associates. On his official visits abroad, Hariri preferred to use a simple and clear approach, but he would stress possible areas for cooperation. He would not leave a country he visited without developing strong relations with its leadership. Yet, with all these qualities and resources, whether material or human, Hariri found the role of running the country – as head of the executive body – quite difficult and even frustrating.

President Chirac was asked to comment on Hariri in an interview on 14 February 2006, one year after Hariri was assassinated. He highlighted Hariri's two most important characteristics: his commitment to education and his belief in the improvement of higher education for young Lebanese of all denominations. Chirac also stressed that Hariri left a lasting impression of capability, care and compassion with all the world leaders with whom he had met and debated.

The Senegalese President, Abdo Diouf, emphasized the same characteristics and revealed that Hariri had helped him secure from King Fahd of Saudi Arabia the funds for completing a conference centre in Dakar to accommodate the Islamic Summit held there at the end of the eighties.

This centre, like that in Damascus, was built by Hariri's engineering enterprise and President Diouf stressed that it still represents an important centre for diverse activities in his capital city.

THREE

The First Six Years, 1993–1998

Hariri was prime minister over successive cabinets from November 1992 until November 1998. Although the summer of 1993 witnessed a massive Israeli thrust in southern Lebanon, which displaced hundreds of thousands of Lebanese, it was a year during which Lebanon regained its self-confidence. Lebanon started to function as a unified civil society – the country attracted back Lebanese talent and capital, and achieved significant growth. Yet by 1998, the picture was one of recession and gloomy expectations. It is not my purpose to draw a detailed historical description of these six years, but rather to broadly survey the major developments that turned expectations from rosy to gloomy, despite a great deal of work to the contrary.

The Lebanese economy attracted attention and investments in 1993. Major economic indicators were all positive.[1]

Year-on-year variations at the end of 1993, compared with the end of 1992, provide this picture.

---

1. All the financial and economic data in this book is taken from the *Annual Economic Reports* (M. I., Beirut, Lebanon), published yearly since 1980.

- A 6 percent real increase in national income, the highest such increase in the Middle East.
- Consolidated balance sheet of commercial banks increased from $7.9 billion to $10.99 billion.
- Capital base of commercial banks increased from the equivalent of $125.5 million to $260 million (core capital represented on both dates 85 percent of the total capital base).
- Balance of payments account showed a surplus of over $1 billion.
- Central bank reserves, other than 9.22 million ounces of gold, and deposits by commercial banks with the Central Bank amounted to $1.6 billion. Net purchases of dollars over the year by the Central Bank equalled $175 million, and the exchange rate of the Lebanese pound improved from LL1,838 at the end of December 1992 to LL1,711 by the end of 1993.
- Licence permits for construction, which are granted after payment of significant fees, increased to over 15 million square metres. This was not only a high figure, but represented the equivalent of 15 percent of the total built-up area in Lebanon.
- In spite of substantial increases in financial resources and an actual increase in national income by 6–7 percent, the cost of living index in Lebanese pounds increased by 5 percent. Due to a stronger Lebanese pound, and dependence on imports to cover 65–70 percent of total consumption, inflation could have been lower. Distribution inefficiencies, high profit margins, pockets of monopoly, and an unproductive government administration, all contributed to this situation.
- Budgetary earnings in 1993 amounted to LL 1,800 billion ($1.06 billion), and covered 60 percent of current expenditures including interest payments on accumulated internal public debt. Without these payments, revenues would have covered 85 percent of total expenditures.
- In December, the General Federation of Labour reached a settlement

over wage claims. Increases and benefits accorded added anywhere between 40 and 45 percent to the total wage bill. On a national level, the impact of increased wages and benefits was about $600 million, and yet there was no negative impact on the exchange rate of the Lebanese pound from these commitments as of 1 January 1994. In fact, the exchange rate of the Lebanese pound continued to appreciate, and the Central Bank was able to continue purchasing dollars with a continuous marginal improvement in the exchange rate of the Lebanese pound.

- On 31 January 1994, parliament finished voting on the proposed budget for 1994. For the first time in twenty years, the budget proposal was available to parliament members to study. Although over fifty deputies spoke out, the changes brought about were minimal and did not touch 1 percent of the overall total figure of 4,677 billion Lebanese pounds.

- Budgetary debates produced possibly the most important change desired in the attitude of parliamentarians. Questions of privatization were always shelved without discussion due to rigid rejection of the idea. Examples of privatization policies in neighbouring countries, and awareness of the need to speed execution of major income-earning infrastructural projects, brought about an unexpected change in outlook.

- Parliament, in fact, authorized three major projects to be financed on a private basis or by the collection of specific fees. These projects and their estimated financial costs were: the Beirut-Damascus Rapid Highway (estimated costs $600–650 million); expansion of Beirut International Airport (estimated costs $450 million); and a cellular telephone network of 100,000 lines (estimated costs $50 million).

If this outlook were to be more generalized and to include other projects, such as the expansion of refineries, collection and treatment of waste, public transport, etc, then the total borrowing requirements over the coming ten years would be much less and the net inflow of capital much more.

- The government was anticipating continuous stability in the exchange rate, further balance of payments surpluses, and enhanced banking resources, although the ordinary budget deficit was projected at 45 percent of the total, and developmental expenditures were projected at 2,000 billion Lebanese pounds ($1.168 billion) in 1994.

During 1995 and 1996, the progress on projects was restricted to the airport and the cellular lines. These turned out to be much higher figures for subscribers, and hitches with the two licencees started emerging. Granting cellular licences to publicly prominent individuals or groups raised a number of objections. At the time, however, cellular phone licences were still very new internationally and their value could not be ascertained easily. The technical dimension of operations was considered well covered by the majority participation of France Telecom in the ownership of one licence, and significant minority participation by Finnish Telecom in the second licence. Everything seemed experimental at the time, whether costs of installation, number of subscribers, users' charges, territorial coverage, etc. The one clear aspect was the great need for the service.

In the second half of the 1980s Messrs Taha and Najib Mikatti began a tentative and successful experiment with wireless telephone services. They introduced wireless telephone services with bulky units that were linked by satellite to New York numbers. Each telephone unit cost $4,400 and each minute of use cost $3. Over 15,000 such telephones were bought in a short period and the service continued until the start-up of cellular operations in the mid-1990s. Actually, subscribers to the previous service were automatically given access to the service provided by Cellis, the cellular operation in Lebanon, which was 67 percent owned by France Telecom and 33 percent by the Mikattis.

The most significant development in 1995 was the question of presidential elections. Hariri worked hard for the extension of the term of President Hraoui for three more years. This move was unpopular with public opinion and contributed to feverish speculation against the Lebanese pound. Some $2.7 billion had to be sold by the Central Bank, and net reserves fell to an all-time low of $150 million. To avoid further drainage, the Central Bank issued one-year and two-year government bonds in Lebanese pounds, which earned some 37 and 42 percent interest a year. The cost over two years, felt in 1996 and 1997, was practically equal to $2.2 billion, and budgetary deficits were in the order of 51 percent and 59 percent respectively. In essence, one could say that the extension of Hraoui's term for a further three years cost Lebanon $2 billion a year over this stretch. This was a heavy price to pay, and in later years, both President Haroui and Prime Minister Hariri declared that in retrospect this extension was a mistake.

Other than the financial cost, which is enormous and represents 15 percent of Lebanon's total indebtedness by the summer of 2005, this renewal of the term of President Hraoui paved the way for the renewal of the term of President Lahoud in early September 2005. The greater consequence of this move was Hariri's assassination on 14 February 2005.

Nomination of Hraoui in 1989 was not expected or enthusiastically endorsed by the Lebanese. It came about in consequence of the assassination of the president elect Rene Mouawad on 22 November 1989. Hraoui demonstrated a strong will to push the country forward, and being from the Beqaa, the Lebanese region that interacts most with Syria, he realized the need for maintaining strong ties with President Hafez al-Assad and worked hard to achieve this result.

The Taef Accord, concluded in 1989, had reduced the powers of the Christian president of Lebanon. At the same time, the sponsors of Taef, particularly the United States, Saudi Arabia, Algeria and Morocco, conceded to Syria the responsibility of supervising the implementation of the Taef Accord, or Lebanon's new constitution.

During the elections of Lebanese parliament members in the summer of 1992, important Christian factions abstained from participation in the elections. They were protesting against marginalization of their role, lack of progress on promised Syrian withdrawals to the Beqaa within two years of the signature, and lack of progress on forming the National Committee of Abolishing Religious Sectarianism in government administration, which was a principal condition agreed in Taef.

The choice of Hariri as prime minister in autumn 1992 served to calm Christian fears and to boost expectations of a fast economic recovery. In June 1991 Hariri, in his capacity as a trustee of the American University of Beirut, was invited to address the 778 graduates that year on the occasion of the 123rd Commencement exercise in the history of the university. Hariri spoke of the need for all Lebanese factions to cooperate in rebuilding the political institutions and infrastructure of Lebanon. He stressed that the rights of all factions were preserved in the Taef Accord and that no faction could mobilize political power and influence to the detriment of the rights of other Lebanese. He acknowledged that the objectives of Taef had not been realized and that political practices should be adjusted to better ensure realization of the spirit of Lebanon's new constitution. Hariri asserted: 'We should all work together on pulling Lebanon from its political malaise and physical damage. All factions must cooperate with the president, prime minister and speaker of the house to ensure a better future for our children.'

As to his own role, Hariri considered at that time that it should be confined to rebuilding at a fast pace the ravaged infrastructure, restoring life to the capital, and making Beirut an attractive centre for business and investment, and Lebanon the destination for Arabs and foreign visitors alike.

Hariri's speech was strong, reformist and optimistic. As of 1996, and the beginning of the impact of the costs of renewal for President Hraoui, growth faltered and the Lebanese economy lost steam. A turn to the worse was even more evident in 1997, which paved the way for mounting criticism of the government in 1998, as well as the election of Emile Lahoud as president, and the ousting of Hariri from his responsibilities. Had it not been for the April 1996 agreement, concluded by the end of April to protect civilians in the south, criticism would have been much stronger.

The April 1996 agreement was extremely important as is illustrated for the following reasons. Early in April 1996, President Chirac visited

Lebanon on an official visit that was very cordial and supportive to Lebanon. Israel had been protesting about attacks by Hizbullah, which were not particularly harsh at the time, but Israel was to have elections by the end of April and the extremist Benjamin Netanyahu challenged the moderate Shimon Peres who was favoured by the Clinton administration. The American secretary of state then, the elderly but elegant and aristocratic Warren Christopher, felt that the election of Peres would improve peace prospects in the Middle East.

Peres wanted to show that while he was a man of peace who had written extensively on the subject, he could wage war as well. As acting prime minister, he approved a widespread operation against Hizbullah bases in South Lebanon that was called 'Grapes of Wrath'. It turned indeed to wrath against Israel after its forces literally murdered 109 children, women and elderly people that had taken shelter in a UN compound in Qana.

The Israelis searched for excuses, claiming Hizbullah fighters had taken refuge in the UN compound, but UN officials denied this allegation. Later, they claimed it was a mistake in defining bombardment coordinates, but this pretence was shattered by photographic and audio proof provided by members of the Norwegian contingent of the UN peace-keeping units in Lebanon.

Norwegian UN troops' members saw an Israeli drone flying over the UN camp in Qana before the bombardment and during the bombardment, which took place on 18 April 1996. They filmed the drone and recorded the bombardment sounds. The soldiers were so shaken by the Israeli massacre of innocent civilians that they decided to turn the drone and its role in directing bombardment of a UN peaceful target into public knowledge.

The Norwegians concerned contacted the well-known British journalist Robert Fisk to deliver to him the incriminating film. A meeting was arranged along a deserted road in South Lebanon. Norwegian soldiers in a UN jeep stopped next to Fisk's car, verified his identity, threw him the film and drove on. Fisk, a veteran journalist well versed in Middle Eastern politics, succeeded in convincing the editor of his newspaper – *The*

Independent – to publish photos of the massacre and the drone. To avoid controversy, *The Independent* told its readers that it was ready to supply a copy of the video film to any reader with doubts about the veracity of Israel's activity. The film was made available to Boutros Boutros Ghali, the Egyptian secretary general of the United Nations. After his teams verified what happened on site, he called for the United Nations Assembly to hold a session. This was done, to the chagrin of the United States and Madeleine Albright, then the American Ambassador at the UN, who worked hard to prevent Ghali's renewal for a further five years as secretary general (his first five years' term was to cease at the end of summer 1996).

Hariri secured Chirac's undiluted help in responding to the tragedy, convinced John Major of the enormity of the butchery, persuaded Boris Yeltsin to champion the Lebanese cause and to chastise Israel at least verbally, and passed a convincing message to the German chancellor. In the United States, Hariri depended on the support of Prince Bandar bin Sultan, the Saudi ambassador who had developed close ties with President Clinton, as he had with George Bush Sr. Clinton was fearful of the loss of his Middle East peace initiative and therefore instructed his secretary of state, Warren Christopher, to do everything possible to address the impact of the Qana slaughter. The Lebanese president, Elias Hraoui, had addressed the UN General Assembly on 23 April, and on 24 April he visited President Clinton and passed him a copy of the video film.

Since the start of the 'Grapes of Wrath' operation on 8 April 1996, the French minister of foreign affairs, Hervé de Charette, a cultivated and honourable man, had not stopped conferring with all parties to achieve a lasting truce. He never left the area from 8 April until 26 April, when the so-called 'April Accord' was signed. Incessant efforts by de Charette were undoubtedly helped by Warren Christopher's intensive efforts. The Americans wanted an agreement at any cost before the end of April, in the hope that Peres' chances of winning the election would improve.

On 26 April 1996 Prime Minister Rafiq Hariri and Hervé de

Charette announced the April Accord in Beirut, while at the same time in Jerusalem the same announcement was made by Shimon Peres and Warren Christopher. The April Accord had four major provisions:

1. Lebanese armed groups (presumably Hizbullah) will not carry on Katyusha rockets attacks on Israel or other forms of attacks by armaments.
2. Israel undertakes, together with its Lebanese collaborators, to abstain from firing by any weapons against Lebanese civilians or civilian targets in Lebanon.
3. Both parties undertake to protect civilians, irrespective of circumstances, from armed attacks; and both parties undertake to abstain from launching attacks from heavily populated areas or industrial posts and electricity generation or distribution facilities.
4. Without abrogating this agreement, each party can exercise its right to self-defence.

An Observation Committee was formed to supervise implementation of the April Accord. The committee was formed of the United States, France, Syria, Israel, the UN and Lebanon. This accord was considered an important improvement on a verbal agreement reached for the same purpose in the summer of 1993, when Israel ravaged the south of Lebanon and blew important bridges and electric facilities. In fact, for Lebanon, this agreement constituted the first acknowledgment of its statehood since 1975 by the Americans, Israelis and Syrians. The combination of Hariri's efforts, Fisk's delivery of the video film to Ghali, and the emotive call on the conscience of the international community by President Elias Hraoui, all contributed to the signature of the April Accord. In this agreement, Hariri secured for Hizbullah an implicit recognition of their role and capacity to abide by international agreements.

After April 1996, Lebanon was no longer assumed to be under Syrian tutelage. Internationally, it could call on France or the United States to ease tensions with Israel in the future. To that extent, the shimmer of Syrian support in adversity was revealed to be an apparition.

1997 was a difficult year for most economic sectors in Lebanon. In particular, public sector finance did not achieve its targets and the projected budget deficit of 37 percent turned into a deficit of 59.3 percent. The president of the World Bank, who visited Lebanon in June 1997, pledged further facilities by the bank and the International Finance Corporation of $1.6 billion over four years, but warned that fiscal responsibility should be better manifested and exemplified in continuously declining budgetary deficit figures from a ceiling of 37 percent projected for 1998.

The prime minister became aware of slowing growth and increasing deficits and public debt. In late summer, he called for a three-day brainstorming review of economic conditions. The recommendations of the conference emphasized the need for controlling the budget deficit by better management of expenditures and increased revenues, particularly from an LL5,000 charge on sales of petrol per 20 litres, and the application of a sales tax of 5 percent. It was further recommended that an organization be set up with a capital of LL50 billion, subscribed by the Central Bank and the Bank Deposits' Guarantee Corporation, as well as commercial banks. This organization would facilitate long-term relatively soft loans to medium and small-scale businesses.

In September, discussions concentrated on raising $1 billion for urgent allocations in the budget, including significant sums for the displaced in Lebanon and for underdeveloped regions. This proposal was voted down in the council of ministers, and the government searched means and ways for borrowing $2 billion, over a long period, in order to avoid siphoning funds from the banking system and contributing to a liquidity crunch that had been restricting growth. The Parliamentary Finance Committee approved this recommendation and it was endorsed by parliament at the end of the budget debate concluded in late January 1998.

In September 1997, parliament voted down the request for $1 billion of allocations, which would be largely earmarked to the ministry of the displaced. This was due to the fact that the minister, Walid Jumblatt, had been accused of wasteful allocations and of favouring political allies.

In an unusual gesture of *mea culpa*, Hariri acknowledged to parliament that their criticism of wasteful expenditure was true. He emphasized that a task so big and so politicized could not be fulfilled without flaws. Moreover, he claimed that some of the waste was necessary to cement national unity considerations. A number of mature political observers, who were and remain opposed to Hariri's policies, acknowledged the validity of this agreement at the time.

In the meantime, two worrying developments emerged: Arab investors in government paper were unwilling, in October 1997, to renew their purchases of government bonds and, in consequence, settlements effected in Lebanese pounds were exchanged for dollars and sent out of the country. Within two months, Central Bank free reserves of currencies went down from $3.7 billion to $1.8 billion, and interest on government bonds had to be increased by 4 percent for two-year bonds. By the end of 1997, it was clear that the total net public debt exceeded the equivalent of $14.5 billion, and this figure included some $2.7 billion of foreign debt. The budgetary deficit was the highest in the past five years, at 59.3 percent of expenditures.

This level of public debt seemed to exceed 90 percent of the total value of the national product, and all indications suggested that it would reach $17.5 billion by the end of 1998. Even if projections in the proposed budget law proved accurate, and this was doubtful, as these projections had not proven to be accurate over the past four years, $3–$3.5 billion of additional public debt would accumulate in 1998. In fact, by the end of 1998, the total public debt equalled $18.3 billion.

Two conditions contributed to the conviction that in spite of adverse figures about the deficit, public debt and slower growth, Lebanon continued to enjoy international trust. In October 1997 rescheduling of $400 million of foreign public debt proceeded without a hitch, and Saudi Monetary Authorities placed $600 million with the Central Bank of Lebanon, for three years, on deposit for 5 percent every year. This deposit encouraged another $200 million of additional term deposits from Kuwait and the UAE in the first quarter of 1998.

Although the Lebanese government felt relief by the end of 1997, it was only short-term. The budget figures had to be bantered and voted on before the end of January and radical adjustments could not be brought about. Still, the end package indicated a projected deficit of 44 percent, seven points higher than the targeted 37 percent. Also, rating agencies, particularly Moody's and Standard & Poor's, had notched Lebanon's long-term credit standing downward.

An agreement on principles for administrative and financial reforms was concluded between President Hraoui, Prime Minister Hariri and Speaker of the House Nabih Berri. The details announced included the recommendation of a turnover tax of 1 percent, resorting to foreign borrowing instead of internal borrowing to improve general liquidity and lower average interest rates on outstanding debt, and numerous measures for better control of public expenditures and improved efficiency of government employees.

The lack of conviction in the success of the suggested measures to bring about the desired results – the reduction of the budget deficit to 37 percent and activation of the Lebanese economy – stemmed from the realization that all proposed reforms could have been done, and should have been done, five years earlier. Also, application of the 1 percent turnover tax proved difficult to crystallize, particularly in respect of earnings and charges levied by banks.

The budget, as approved, had to be recessionary. Allocations to projects were practically halved, and demands for adjustment of the salaries, wages and benefits of public sector employees were shelved until resources could be secured. By early June 1998, the government submitted a proposed law in this respect for approval by parliament. Any steps for implementation had to await 1999 and a new president and government.

Table 1: Major Economic Indicators

	1993	1994	1995	1996	1997
External Debt ($ millions)	327	772	1,291	1,769	2,351
Internal Debt ($ millions)	2,580	4,080	5,820	8,580	12,008
Net Public Debt ($ millions)	2,907	4,847	7,110	10,349	14,359
Revenues (LL billions)	1,855	2,252	3,033	3,533	3,752
Expenditures (LL billions)	3,017	5,204	5,856	7,225	9,155
Deficit	38%	58.8%	49.3%	51%	59%
Balance of Payment Surplus ($ millions)	1,170	1,130	256	786	400
Annual Growth	13.3%	9%	7%	4%	3%

When the debate over the budget figures was concluded in late January 1998, the government was holding the following problems in its hands:

- Projected higher budgetary deficit at 44 percent rather than the targetted 37 percent during 1998.

- Slower growth at 3 percent or less, which would not generate employment opportunities.

- Tightening of the crisis within the real estate sector, with possible adverse repercussions on the banking sector.

- Continued pressure for adjustment of salaries and wages in the public sector, without corresponding availability of revenues or broadening of the tax base.

- Anticipation of possible mounting internal political tensions due to scheduled municipal elections in May and June 1998 and presidential elections in September. Any noticeable increase in tensions would fuel speculation against the exchange value of the Lebanese pound, the stability of which had contributed to improving faith in investment in Lebanon and Lebanese instruments, whether government or private.

To avoid a speculation crisis and to ensure tranquility until the end of the year, the government encouraged and achieved the following objectives:

- Secured $800 million from Arab sources for intermediate deposits with the Central Bank at 5 percent per year. These resources strengthened the exchange pool of the Central Bank and its freedom of action.

- Issued $1 billion of five years bonds, which were covered practically instantaneously. Paribas, which handled the issue – for an average interest of 8.5 percent per year – did not have to search for funds, as Lebanese banks contributed $730 million. This issue could be soon supplemented by another of equal value, thereby contributing to a lower than average interest rate on outstanding public debt whilst enabling Lebanese financial and monetary authorities to combat speculation moves.

Realizing that a 44 percent budgetary deficit could be bad, although approved by parliament, the ministry of finance sought to restrict expenditures to the maximum extent possible. In the first four months of 1998, the deficit was limited within a ratio of 38 percent. However, many due and substantial payments were delayed, and the feeling of a slide into recession brought second thoughts about required measures for activation of the economy.

To prepare for the costs of increased salaries and wages as of 1998, and to limit deficits in 1998, the government increased all customs duties by 2 percent. Total customs duties in 1997 amounted to $1.1 billion and were practically 15 percent of the total import bill. The 2 percent across-the-board increase, approved in early April, represented a 14 percent increase on actual rates and was expected to raise $150 million over a full year. In 1998 it was hoped to secure $120 million of the total, as the volume of imports was not even on a monthly basis and tended to concentrate at the end of the year, which facilitated the achievement desired although the increase in customs rates was approved after three months of the year had elapsed.

Slow growth, a recessionary budget and higher import dues are a formula for a spin into recession. The government wanted most of all to avoid a prolonged period of little or no growth. Low growth in 1998 could perhaps be attributed to a number of political factors, but justification for continuity of the Hariri government had to be based on more rapid development in the near future. For this reason, the government initiated two programmes that could contribute to averting an impending crisis and to dynamize growth.

On the one hand, the government and the Central Bank devised a plan for using obligatory reserves by banks with the Central Bank, which earn no interest to finance medium and low-income housing requirements for the Lebanese people. Up to $100,000 could be provided for apartments in Beirut and $50,000 outside the capital. Interest rates would not be collected for the first ten years, and would be subsidized for the next ten.

Obviously this plan, declared before the end of May, would begin to bear fruit only by late summer when the procedures become clearer to beneficiaries (those who need loans) and providers (the banks). What is certain is that the financial base was substantial, as 10 percent of deposits in Lebanese pounds in the Lebanese banking system – which are allotted as obligatory reserves – equaled $1.3 billion and were increasing yearly.

The second programme aimed at fulfilling the decision taken in the economic brainstorming three-day conference held a year before by the prime minister. The formation of an organization with a capital of 50 billion Lebanese pounds, thus guaranteeing long-term loans to small and medium-sized businesses, was proposed. This recommendation was given on the basis of studies concluded by the Central Bank. The organization could not be operational before 1999.

Another area of potential economic and financial stimulation under evaluation by the government was that of putting in place long-awaited regulations and structures for activation of the Beirut financial market on a regional and possibly international level. Studies were prepared and refined dating back to 1993, and the Central Bank commissioned further detailed studies for regulations, procedures and activities. However, hesitation by the government concerning the endorsement of advanced regulations for the organization and activation of a financial market in Beirut, was due to fears about volume, diversity of instruments and overall preparation. Most importantly, the availability of funds in the banking system ($27 billion deposits and $2.1 billion capital resources at the end of March 1998) indicated that practically all financial requirements by the private and public sector could be satisfied by banks operating in Lebanon. The framework for investments and long-term facilities needed to be better defined.

Irrespective of measures taken and policies adopted, it can be said that concentration was aimed at short-term measures designed to avoid a crisis: higher revenues to stem a frightful deficit; subsidized loans to avoid a real estate and housing crisis; late activation of long-awaited moves for easing long-term loans to small businesses, etc. Efficiency in government administration, clear policies on privatization, control of monopolies, specialization in advanced services and other similar issues were shelved to await future developments. These same issues overshadow prospects in 2005.

Lebanon was in a position to reduce its budget deficit to well below 30 percent without further taxation. Resources in the order of $1 billion per year could result from improved collection of electricity bills, road taxes, profits tax and possibly higher petrol taxes. Also elimination of subsidies to sugar beet, tobacco and wheat would save $102 million per year. As of 1998, these steps could improve the budgetary balance by at least $500 million per year. If another $500 million or more were secured each year for two years from privatization of the government's share in Intra Investment Company, partial privatization and rehabilitation of Lebanon's antiquated refineries (two), and sale of electricity generation capacity to the private sector, it would have been possible to lower average interest rates on outstanding debt by 3–4 percent a year. One percent accounted for $160 million a year.

The rough approach outlined would have increased revenues and cut expenditures by $1.5 billion a year. This figure exceeded 25 percent of the total budget for 1998 and thus provides an image of what could have been achieved. Failure to achieve any of these objectives was due to political feuding and the tendency of political leaders to push for benefits for their sects, while forgetting or overlooking the national interest. This egotistic attitude strengthened during President Lahoud's first term and was compounded by direct Syrian interference and meddling in economic and financial affairs. One consequence of Hariri's assassination was that people overcame their fear of the security regime. Clear abuses were uncovered, including the draining of the national economy of at least $1–1.5 billion a year since 1999.

Much was achieved between 1992 and 1998. Electricity generation capacity had been enhanced; over 1,200 schools were rehabilitated; work on the airport progressed; a long-awaited plan for building a campus for the Lebanese university was launched; teachers – whether elementary, high school or university levels in the public sector – were engaged in abundant numbers; and significant progress was achieved in communications, whether the network of fixed lines or mobile telephones. Areas that were neglected were roads, bridges, traffic control, pollution and environmental care. The number of cars, trucks, buses and commercial vehicles had increased six-fold in twenty years, from 250,000 in 1976 to 1,500,000 in 1998, and it was not possible, whether in terms of resources or time, to meet the challenge of making improvements in these areas.

Rehabilitation efforts, as well as improvements in public education, including the start up of a major review of curricula and methods of instruction, were not sufficient to detract from growing political criticisms. These were further inflamed by a latent feeling that Syrian hegemony was sapping the energy of the Lebanese economy. This feeling was justified. Syrian officers under the supervision of General Ghazi Kanaan, who headed the Syrian contingents from 1980 until 2002, felt that they were given free sway over Lebanese affairs and citizens – as a result of the Taef Accord, and with Arab and American blessings. Syrian senior officers were given a free hand by their leadership provided that nothing serious was done to irritate American diplomats.

General Kanaan, who committed suicide on 12 October 2005, and his dependent team, always tried to please the Americans. As an example of this, Kanaan was involved in an embezzlement incident in which he provided protection to a Shiite member of Amal. The story goes as follows. In 1990, the

American University Hospital engaged a financial manager who happened to be a member of Amal, one of the two Shiite armed groups in Lebanon (the other being Hizbullah). This manager was caught issuing cheques for purchases of pharmaceuticals, which were not secured or inventoried by the hospital, and the embezzlement had reached $400,000 by the time it was uncovered. Judiciary police secured from the man a statement of his guilt and a commitment to pay back the money; he also resigned his post. However, as Amal was a close ally of Syria, the accused, who had confessed his guilt, returned to his job following his dismissal. Kanaan contacted the acting president of AUB, Dr Ibrahim Salti, to obtain the letter of guilt and resignation: this was a clear example of how Syrian officers could affect the judiciary in Lebanon, even in the private sector, but what Kanaan failed to consider was possible American official awareness of the incident and official response.

The chairman of the board of trustees, Dr Fredrik Herter, was so enraged by this incident that he communicated all its details to the American ambassador in Syria at the time, Edward Gerdjian, an American of Syrian extraction. Gerdjian was furious and communicated American dissatisfaction to Syria's top political officials. Later, on the same day, Kanaan visited Salti of AUB, apologized, handed back the letter of guilt and the resignation letter, and a cheque for $400,000.

This incident clearly demonstrates that senior Syrian officials could protect thievery and promote monopolistic practices, whether for political or material gain. Such practices were widespread in cross-border smuggling operations in an attempt to avoid customs dues on both borders, secure payments for eviction of displaced people, make purchases of fuel for electricity generation, secure contracts for public projects, tie up international calls through Syria, and even encourage the production and exports of illicit products. This type of insidious interference was rampant, particularly after 1991, and escalated to intolerable levels by 2000–02, as Brigadier Rustum Gazale was taking over from Kanaan and reporting directly to President Bashar al-Assad. The efforts of Hariri's governments were certainly weakened by Syrian interference and the greed of Lebanese politicians.

FOUR

Summer 1998: Vilification of Hariri

Although Hariri had regained a measure of international recognition for Lebanon, and could call on any leader in the world at short notice, he faced severe criticism in the spring and summer of 1998. It was obvious that his six years at the helm had irritated his partners in government and set a significant proportion of the population against him.

In spring 1998, criticism of Hariri centred on a number of issues of which the following two were the most important. First, he was accused of giving priority to construction of infrastructure rather than development of social welfare. The man who coined the phrase '*al-hajar qabl al-bashar*' ('construction before human concerns') was Dr Salim al-Hoss, a respected economist and political figure who had been prime minister for long stretches between 1976 and 1990. In fact, he had exercised the powers of prime minister for a total of eleven years, the longest period of leadership (although not continuous) by any prime minister since independence.

Second, in April 1998, Najah Wakim, a parliament member who has clearly stated in numerous lectures and articles his excellent relations with Libya, and who has never denied his ties with Syria – and a populist who thrived on drumming up public issues – published a book entitled *Black Hands*. He accused Hariri, Nabih Berri (the head of the chamber of deputies), and President Hraoui of profiteering and mismanagement of public funds. His primary target, however, was Hariri – Wakim attempted to ruin his image as a leader – in essence arguing that all Hariri's initiatives were linked to expected benefits for himself and his team members. Hariri's choice of a team for running important organizations such as the Reconstruction and Development Board, the Fund for the Displaced, the Central Bank, the ministry of finance, and the ministry of communications, was portrayed as a sinister manipulation of power to secure personal benefits. Yet, by contrast, it could be argued that without good and capable people in these positions, little could be done. In fact, judging by the performance of some institutions after severe changes were brought about by President Lahoud's new team – which had been installed in autumn 1998 – one could easily judge that Hariri's team functioned better on a national scale.

Wakim's wild accusations concerning Hariri's supposedly shady international relations, were slanderous, to say the least. In any country that provides protection against slander, Wakim could have been taken to court. He was not, it seems, for three reasons: in Lebanon, as a parliament member, he enjoyed immunity from prosecution; he was an avowed ally of Syria and its designated emissary, Ghazi Kanaan; and his venture to publish a clear condemnation of Hariri in April 1998 was clearly linked to Hariri's declared opposition to the election of General Emile Lahoud as president of Lebanon. The Syrians' choice had become clear by that time, and Hariri's resistance had to be weakened. Wakim's book was a diversion intended to cast doubts about Hariri's character in the public arena and to preoccupy Hariri with defending himself. Hariri reacted coolly and continued to resist Lahoud's election until the last few days.

It must be remembered that in spring 1998, Hariri's leadership as prime minister could be criticized objectively. On the one hand, his support of a renewal of three years for President Hraoui was proving very unpopular. Hraoui's bravado, sprinkled with vulgar jokes, had worn thin after nine years of his presidency. Hariri was held responsible for the last three years of Haroui's presidency and such renewals of presidential terms could not be written off in the future.

In addition to this grievance there were real fears on two other fronts. First, public debt was increasing at a fast pace, from less than $2 billion at the end of 1992 to $17 billion by the beginning of summer 1998, and all indications showed that cumulative public debt would reach over $18 billion by the end of that year. The budget deficit in 1997 had reached a record 59 percent and growth rates had fallen from 13 percent in 1993 to 3 percent in 1998. Second, emigration of young and educated Lebanese was on the increase and expectations of progress had dimmed to a large extent. At the beginning of the summer of 1998 Lebanon seemed badly in need of a change in its political climate and leadership.

Leading figures in international development and finance expressed concern about Lebanon's future and its urgent need of reforms. The president of the World Bank had spoken of Lebanon as a 'sinking ship' because of leakages (waste of financial resources), and the head of the European Commission also stressed the need for administrative and fiscal reforms. At the same time, the World Bank, the European Union and Arab funds all declared their readiness to help Lebanon overcome its difficulties, on the condition that the Lebanese adopt reform programmes in respect of government and administration, control of expenditures and selection of priorities. All this concern about and for Lebanon had emerged during Hariri's stretch as prime minister, from 1993 to 1998. He had developed excellent relations with James Wolfensohn of the World Bank and Romano Prodi of the European Union. Hariri paid particular attention to their delegations in Lebanon and maintained a consistent and continuous involvement of these delegations in Lebanese economic and reconstruction efforts. Hariri and his team looked after relations with Arab funds, particularly Fuad Siniora as minister of finance, and Fadel

Chalak and Nabil al-Jisr, as the successive heads of the Reconstruction and Development Board.

Hariri, because of his close contact with regional and international organizations and developments, sensed that the 21st century was going to be a time of change. In spite of progress achieved on different levels in Lebanon over five years, he recognized that fundamental changes had to be brought about in the political body and system of the country if it were to succeed in meeting new challenges and expectations. Europe was becoming a unified and seamless market with a unifying currency, the US was witnessing advances in biology and electronics that were beyond the scope of our imagination, and China was re-setting the balance of economic performance on the world scene. In 1998 these monumental changes pushed Hariri to seek serious political change and improvement. He declared that Lebanon could not match the pace of advanced countries with its antiquated and prejudiced political system. He called for reform of the electoral law, administrative organization and selection of senior government employees, and modern standards of service to the Lebanese. He called upon all nominees for the presidential elections to publish their programmes and encourage debate.

To the camps supporting election of General Lahoud, Hariri's proclamations seemed slanted against their hopes. Lahoud, as head of the army, could not come up with a programme. In fact, without a constitutional amendment, he could not run for elections. Hariri's call for reform was portrayed by his detractors as an attempt to put himself above all others, including the president and the head of the chamber of deputies. Criticism of Hairiri became consistently more widespread and poisonous.

In June 1998 a parliament member submitted a query requesting to know whether or not trips by Hariri to the Vatican, France, England, Brazil, Poland, Turkey, etc were conducted with the prior knowledge and approval of the cabinet and, moreover, whether or not Hariri was paying for his trips. The answers to both questions were in the affirmative: the cabinet and president knew and approved of Hariri's schedules, and Hariri was paying for his trips and not the Lebanese treasury. Still, political criticism continued. Hariri hoped presidential elections would bring a change for the better, but he was to face a bitter disappointment.

However, by contrast with internal criticism levelled against him, which culminated after election of General Lahoud as president in easing him out of his premiership, Hariri enjoyed significant support by visiting foreign dignitaries. Prime Minister Dr Kamal Janzouri of Egypt, who visited Lebanon in September 1997, spoke very highly of achievements realized by Hariri. Janzouri himself had steered the Egyptian economy towards privatization and reduction of the role of the public sector. He did this over a period of five years during which the public sector's share in the GNP (gross national product)[1] fell from over 60 percent to 35 percent while achieving strong rates of growth and reducing the birth rate from 3.5 percent a year to 2.5 percent. Egypt had achieved great progress and yet the Egyptian prime minister considered that Lebanon had achieved even more.

Dr Mahatir Muhammad visited Lebanon in 1998 and was impressed with the progress achieved in upgrading infrastructure, restoring educational institutions, and rebuilding the commercial centre of Beirut. He had transformed Malaysia over sixteen years from an underdeveloped country to a prosperous society that ranked as a leader in the circle of Far Eastern countries called the 'Asian Tigers'. Muhammad felt that Lebanon had achieved significant progress but that its bureaucracy was too heavy, complicated and lethargic. He told Hariri that the Malaysian government, in order to give responsibility to capable individuals, recruited managers to fulfill the roles of directors general of various ministries and paid them private sector salaries. Such individuals could receive $200,000 or more per year to work as hard and efficiently as they do in the private sector. Moreover, Malaysia was moving towards a paperless government, as the use of computers and advanced software substituted for tedious procedures.

---

1. Gross national product (GNP) is the term used to describe the total production of goods and services by all those working in Lebanon, plus net transfers.

One of the by-products of this policy was the fast development of the computer hardware industry in Malaysia as well as electronics in general. Hariri repeatedly visited Malaysia and developed strong ties with Mahatir Muhammad. He felt that their model could serve Lebanon but not necessarily in industry, as Lebanon did not have a disciplined labour force in great numbers.

Positive evaluation of Hariri's outlook and performance was also enjoyed by diplomats. Richard Murphy, an American career diplomat, the former ambassador to Syria and assistant undersecretary of state for Middle East affairs from 1982–8, closely followed developments in Lebanon (he helped in the preparations for the Taef Accord). One of his assistants at that time was David Satterfield who served as American ambassador to Lebanon as of 1998, and later assumed responsibilities as the assistant undersecretary of state in the Middle East up to March 2005.

During a recorded interview that I conducted with Richard Murphy in Washington in April 1998, he had much to say in evaluating Lebanon's progress under Hariri's leadership in the nineties:

> Lebanon achieved important steps in regaining its health as an organized society ... I am confident that Lebanon today is better placed in foreign affairs than it has been in the past thirty years which passed since the signature of the Cairo Agreement in 1969. That agreement with the Palestine Liberation Organization compromised the integrity of Lebanon as a state and weakened its relations and freedom in dealing with a number of countries, particularly Arab countries ... These achievements were realized during five and a half years of three governments under Hariri. There are still important internal problems. Debates about developmental and reconstruction efforts, although important, are less important than Lebanon's establishment anew in the community of nations ... Lebanon is now capable of achieving continuous and sustainable growth. Critics who allege that more attention is given

to construction than human conditions must realize that they themselves are the instruments of change. Whether the critics are ministers, parliament members or private citizens exercising their rights to vote, they must realize that they have been charged with the responsibility and burden of bringing about change in a positive manner. Criticism, although necessary in an open society, is not enough. Work on improvement of conditions and the business climate is a societal responsibility. It should involve all thinking and mature Lebanese.

By 1998 Hariri was aware of failure to improve the political scene in Lebanon. He was also aware of monopolistic and profiteering practices by well-placed politicians in the oil products market, public contracting, cellular operations and numerous public or semi-public services. While Hariri was by temperament and experience tolerant of profiteering attitudes and behaviour, when faced with inefficiencies and delays in the execution of urgent projects such as roads, the airport, electricity generation and distribution networks, he began to feel anxious about future prospects.

In 1993 and 1994 Hariri witnessed a euphoric return of capital and entrepreneurship to Lebanon. There was widespread belief in the example he set and in anticipation of significant advancement in a short period of time. By late 1995, and certainly by summer 1996, the evaporation of positive expectations was clear and scathing, and Hariri could not ignore this turnaround in expectations and application. He started calling for fundamental reforms, whether in the electoral law or public administration, or in the working relations between the president, the prime minister and the head of the chamber of deputies. Hariri had become a pundit of change as against his image as a quiet and patient figure of transformation. Time was running out for Lebanon, and for Hariri as well in his leadership role.

The last six months of 1998 witnessed a lull in the economic activity but intense political efforts. During June and July, elections for municipal councils were held in Lebanon for the first time for thirty-five years. With newly elected councils, municipalities could fulfill their duties better and the objective of decentralization of many public services endorsed by the Taef Accord had a better chance of implementation. By the end of the summer, Lahoud was elected as president, and together with Nabih Berri, the head of parliament, he delayed a process for exploring nominations by members of parliament for the prime minister, which, to say the least, was unclear and unfair. Hariri was forced not to accept the nomination, as doing so under a shadow of doubt would have left him in a position of power behind that of the president. Hariri felt the whole process was an abrogation of Taef and withdrew.

Dr Salim al-Hoss formed a new cabinet, which included a number of clearly anti-Hariri figures, particularly the ministers of finance and telecommunications. Within weeks of its formation, the new cabinet levelled serious accusations, often so unjust that Lahoud and al-Hoss appeared as characters seeking political vengeance rather than reformists. This manifestation was clear in most cases, but four cases in particular shall be discussed briefly. It is important to stress, however, that all Hariri nominees who were accused of wrongdoing or were imprisoned were later declared innocent by Lebanese courts.

The first case was that of Fuad Siniora, minister of finance in Hariri's governments and one of his closest associates (Siniora is currently – at the time of writing – prime minister). Siniora was accused of wasting financial resources in the form of a loan by the Italian government for the erection of an incinerator in a densely inhabited suburb of Beirut, Bourj Hammoud. As it turned out, Siniora was the only minister to object to the deal and the payment of repatriation money for work that was never done. He had recorded and signed his objection in the council of ministers' 'record of proceedings'. Yet over a period of months, Siniora underwent questioning by a magistrate. He and his family were put under great stress, but finally the judge pronounced that Siniora was not only innocent of the accusation but was the only minister who did not participate in a wrong and wasteful decision. Had there been a law for seeking damage from the Lebanese government for slander, Siniora could have raised a good case, accusing one or two ministers of al-Hoss's cabinet of spreading accusations against him.[1]

Minister Hagop Demirjian, a close friend of Siniora, was urgently persuaded by him to join the first government of Hariri and to leave behind a prosperous business. Demirjian held a number of portfolios in the first three cabinets of Hariri. Lahoud's government tried to raise a case against him but failed to provide evidence of his guilt or responsibility. Although charges failed to materialise, Demirjian's life and that of his family was made miserable for several months. Only when the Demirjian family, who were in control of huge business interests, declared their intention to leave Lebanon – which would have encouraged other prosperous Armenian-Lebanese families to do the same – was the pressure of meaningless accusations withdrawn.

The third example related to Dr Abdel Moneim al-Youssif. With a doctorate in electronic engineering and experience in modern communications technology acquired in France and the United States, al-Youssif joined Hariri's team to take on the responsibility of supervising investments and technical services in the telecommunications sector. This capable, honest and creative man (he has nine registered inventions to his name) was hounded and imprisoned by the government. After two years, his innocence was declared and Prime Minister Siniora has given him back his previous responsibilities.

The fourth case relates to Muhib Itani. Itani is an engineer who was nominated by Hariri to be director general of the Port of Beirut in 1997. At the time, the Port of Beirut was still suffering from ships sunk during the fighting in Lebanon. A debris cleaning contract had been given to a company (Sarmolin), presumed to be British and represented in Lebanon by Wissam Hajj, a cousin of Hariri's top security man, Ali Hajj (who

---

1. It should be noted that the disputed contract was signed in 1988, four years before the first Hariri government was formed in November 1992. Moreover, the Italian company concerned had received its payments from the Italian organization for export insurance. The remaining dispute was between the Italian and Lebanese governments.

later became director of the interior security forces). The said company undertook to complete the job in six months, but by the end of that period had done nothing. After a written extension for commencement of clearing works in two months, supplemented by a further tolerance period of two months, but with no results, Itani gave the contract to an Armenian-Lebanese contractor, Harout Sofian, who scuttled and lifted the shell of a 1,300-ton freighter that was blocking the pier (next to the grain silos at the port that constitute an important facility). Itani became a target for the Lahoud-al-Hoss tag team. He was imprisoned for seven months and four days, and released in January 2000. Together with Sofian, the Armenian contractor, Itani was absolved of the fabricated fable that they had misplaced or appropriated $3,700 of steel cables.

Beyond these personal vendettas there were many more. Senior people could be accused of misdeeds, their reputations tarnished, and whenever the truth became clear and they were declared innocent, they could not ask for compensation and moral retribution. Such was Lebanon's condition by the end of the 1990s.

At this time, the al-Hoss government wanted to implement a reform programme for reducing budgetary deficits, starting payback of outstanding debt and achieving higher rates of growth. Two young economists were entrusted with the task of developing the corrective programme, Charbel Nahas and Makram Sader, the former trained as an engineer and the latter with extensive experience in banking and finance. They set up shop with a number of assistants and came up with a coherent programme that aimed to realize the following objectives over a five-year period:

- Reduce the budget deficit from a projected 40 percent in 1999 to 19 percent in 2003.
- Increase the rate of growth from 2 percent in 1999 to 6 percent in 2003.
- Reduce dependence on transfers and capital inflows to cover up current account external deficits. They argued that opportunities for

work abroad, particularly in oil-rich Arab countries, would dwindle for the Lebanese, and that transfers would begin to shrink.

- They called attention to the dangers of bank deposits, which are a multiple of national income figures and primarily devoted to financing public deficits.

They suggested corrective measures aimed at increasing government revenues from the equivalent of 18 percent of GDP (gross domestic product)[1] to 24 percent in five years. These measures included:

- Increase of income tax rates on salaries and profits.
- Imposing a tax on real estate profits realized by individuals; in fact, they recommended a tax on capital gains.
- Unifying sources of revenue and choosing family revenue as a base for taxation.
- Imposing a tax on interest from banking deposits without abrogating the Banking Secrecy Law adopted by Lebanon since 1956.
- Defining what residence means for Lebanese people in order to tax their realized income abroad if they qualify as residents.
- Improvement of verification and collection procedures for eliminating possible tax-evasion practices.
- Adoption of the Value Added Tax system as of 2001.

These were the most important elements in the programme and were supplemented by various other recommendations regarding privatization and improved government administration. This programme was, in fact, a well-conceived programme that, however, glossed over two important considerations. First, taxation of Lebanese on income earned abroad, if they were classified as residents in Lebanon, could not be applied

---

1. Gross domestic product (GDP) is the term used to describe the total value of final goods and services produced within a country's borders in a year. It is one of the measures of national income and output.

without driving enterprising Lebanese individuals and corporations to seek residence abroad. This recommendation could have caused damage to levels of production and employment in Lebanon. The al-Hoss government did not endorse it.

The second consideration related to opportunities for work and attracting transfers. In fact, these prospects increased tremendously because work opportunities for Lebanese increased in the UAE due to strong growth generated by liberalization of work conditions, ownership rights and residence terms by many members of the UAE, particularly Dubai, Sharja and Abu Dhabi. Also, oil and gas revenues in the region increased considerably with the development of Qatar's tremendous gas potential and the increase in oil prices and incomes, which seems likely to continue.

The pertinent question in relation to both points is: will young, educated Lebanese professionals return to Lebanon after working abroad for a number of years, particularly in the Gulf? Attracting the resources, and later the Lebanese professionals back to Lebanon, depends not only on economic prospects, but far more on the rule of law, the spread of real democracy and preservation of the environment in Lebanon.

The al-Hoss government diluted the programme of Nahas and Sader and operated during the first six months of 1999 without endorsing a budget. The budget voted in late June of that year projected a 43 percent deficit and was recessionary by its provisions. Due to suggestions of taxing income earned by Lebanese abroad, higher tax rates and severe collection and assessment practices, many Lebanese abstained from expanding their work in Lebanon or increasing their investments in the country. In 1999, for the first time in eight years, the Lebanese economy witnessed negative growth as the GDP shrank by 1 percent instead of growing by 2 percent as Nahas and Sader hoped. Thus 1999 ended on a sad note; there was neither an improvement in financial performance nor more effectiveness in government departments. Added to this, there was the real sense of the country's lack of freedom for expression of opinions.

The year 2000 started badly for the al-Hoss government and

Lahoud's regime. Public debt had increased by $3.4 billion to $21.7 billion, the budget deficit was high (over 43 percent), and confidence was low, particularly with the recessionary atmosphere that prevailed. Moreover, accusations against numerous Hariri assistants had not been substantiated. On top of all this, parliamentary elections were to be held in early summer 2000 and Hariri's prospects seemed very promising. Yet instead of assessing the reasons behind the growing sympathy for Hariri, the Lahoud-al-Hoss tandem increased their frenzied public criticism of Hariri and his practices. The official Lebanese television network devoted much of its airtime to criticizing Hariri, and the arguments used were often inaccurate and in many instances rude. It was this atmosphere – combined with lack of efficiency in government, continuous large deficits, and overt signs of subjugation to Syrian directions[1] – that served to strengthen Hariri's chances of success in the 2000 parliamentary elections.

When these elections were held, Hariri achieved sweeping gains in Beirut and significant gains with his allies in other districts. Hariri's list was elected in its totality in Beirut, and al-Hoss – the prime minister, ardent critic of Hariri, and ally of Lahoud – was defeated by an immense margin by a young female university professor of computer science, Ghinwa Jaloul. This result was possibly the most telling development of the popular resistance to the Lahoud-al-Hoss policies between November 1998 and late summer 2000. After the results of the elections, Hariri was the *de facto* nominee for the premiership, and returned to the prime minister's seat just two years after being tricked out of it. But he did not take into account Lahoud's latent resentment.

In May 2000 Israel started to withdraw from South Lebanon where its forces had been entrenched since 1978, and cultivated an army of collaborators under the leadership of the Lebanese general, Antoine

---

1. An example of undue Lebanese subjugation to Syrian wishes and whims was made clear with the death of King Hussein of Jordan. Salim al-Hoss was in Saudi Arabia and could have flown directly to participate in the king's funeral. However, Syrian-Jordanian relations were tense and both Lahoud and al-Hoss first wanted a sign from Syria. When President Hafez al-Assad went to the funeral, the next day al-Hoss flew to present the Lebanese government's condolences.

Lahd. The withdrawal had been announced and it was clear that the Israeli prime minister, Ehud Barak, who had stated this objective at the beginning of the year, wanted to avoid further human losses. Mothers of Israeli soldiers had been protesting the loss of their children; and after the April 1996 agreement, which gave protection to civilian targets on both sides of the border, continued occupation was useless.

There is little doubt that Israel was driven out because of resistance by Hizbullah fighters. President Lahoud and Prime Minister al-Hoss tried their best to claim a role for the state and visited liberated areas but, beyond these visits, they failed to marshal a programme for aid and development. The minister of finance wanted to hold a donors' meeting in July or August 2000, but the best he could muster was a tepid reaction from ambassadors.

Rafiq Hariri concentrated his efforts on devising a programme for averting continuous high deficits, reducing public debt and regaining the thrust of growth. Personal conflicts were suppressed for the purpose of achieving good results. During his long and bitter experiences with politicians, and close aides in Lebanon and abroad, Hariri had become infused with surprising tolerance levels: he concentrated on expected results and overlooked hints of resistance to his premiership and personality.

Hariri resumed his powers in autumn 2000 and was confident of bringing about improvements. Lahoud was resentful and seemed confident of his ability to obstruct Hariri's progress. This struggle continued for four years, until the re-election of Lahoud on 2 September 2005, for a three-year term, unleashed the torrent of international political protests, further inflamed by Hariri's assassination on 14 February 2005.

FIVE

2000–2002: Period of Challenge, Change and Chagrin

The last stretch of Hariri's premiership extended over four years, from 2000 to 2002, and 2002 to 2004. These were distinct and important periods and will be discussed in successive chapters.

Hariri was happy with the results of parliamentary elections in the year 2000. In spite of efforts to tarnish his image, question his achievements and strangle his decisions, Hariri received overwhelming support, due in part to the ridiculous public defamation campaign launched against Hariri by President Lahoud and the al-Hoss government. Al-Hoss, in a book he published about his experience during 1998–2000, admits that he was ashamed of some aspects of the smear campaign against Hariri:

> During the election campaign the official Lebanese television conducted an ugly smear campaign against the person of Rafiq Hariri. This campaign was launched by security agencies. I felt that it contradicted my political stance and that I did not need this kind of malicious propaganda to win a seat in parliament ... I stopped

this campaign too late, however, to change the popular impression
that I was behind it.[1]

For whatever reasons, Hariri's success left Lahoud and Berri no option
but to cooperate with Hariri as prime minister, although Hariri took on
the reigns of government with considerable burdens. Nasser Kandil, a
Syrian sponsored figure who had been nominated as head of the Audio
Visual Commission in 1996, was imposed on Hariri as one of two
Shiite nominees for parliament in 2000. Until less than a week before
elections, Hariri's list carried the name of Ghazi Youssef, a distinguished
economist and university professor, but under pressure Kandil was
elected on Hariri's list. The other Shiite nominee on Hariri's list was
chosen by Hizbullah and taken on willingly by Hariri. From 2000 until
the end of 2004, Hariri was at pains to rid himself of obligations *vis-
à-vis* Kandil. The Syrians tried to place him as minister of information
but his apparent links to Syrian intelligence did not help at the time.
Many other informers had become ministers and taken on important
ministries but Kandil could not advance. A few months after the
elections and certainly as of 2001, Kandil was not invited to attend
Hariri's parliamentary bloc meetings. Hariri was still angry at his being
forced to lose a good associate such as Youssef for the company of such
an unreliable member.

As a parliament member but not accepted in the ranks of Hariri's
cabinet, Kandil was frustrated and devoted efforts to undermine Hariri.
On television he was particularly prolific in singing the attributes of
Syria and President Lahoud. This was the kind of tax on viewers' nerves
particularly enjoyed by General Jamil al-Sayyed, who often imposed
interviews on major talk shows and, in particular, invited incoming calls
for comments by supporters of the regime.

At the time of forming a new government in late 2000, Hariri
underestimated important difficulties, not least the death of President

1.   Salim al-Hoss, *For Truth and History: Governing Between 1998–2000*, Beirut, 2002,
      p. 311.

Hafez al-Assad and the election of his son Bashar as president in early summer 2000, and the latent grudge of President Lahoud, who insisted on appointing a young and unknown engineer, Jean-Louis Kordahi (head of the municipality of Byblos) as minister of telecommunications, and later, Karim Pakradouni (the leader of the Phalangist party) as minister of administrative reform. Both men were charged with sabotaging Hariri's efforts and raising disputes in cabinet proceedings. Further, Hariri had to face up to criticisms by the heads of security organizations.

Hariri had taken on two agitators in his government, but felt that he could overcome their negative manoeuvrings. He assumed that the Syrian leadership would support his efforts towards administrative reform and his plan for salvaging a deteriorating financial position. The Syrian regime, however, had shifted in its allegiance. Bashar al-Assad, the new Syrian president, did not like Hariri and did not feel indebted to him. In fact, Bashar al-Assad resented the fact that Hariri helped arrange for him his first visit to a Western power, France. For the young Syrian president, pride came ahead of prudence.

By contrast, Bashar's father, Hafez al-Assad, recognized Hariri's potential and felt a measure of gratitude for his help in completing the construction of an ultra-modern conference centre in Damascus with Saudi financial help and help from Hariri himself. Hafez al-Assad inaugurated the $85 million centre in early March 1989. Moreover, Hariri worked hard on improving relations between Syria and Saudi Arabia and, in consequence of this improvement, Prince Bandar bin Sultan, the Saudi ambassador to Washington, helped to organize the meeting between Hafez al-Assad and President Clinton in Geneva in April 2000. As Clinton indicates in his book *My Life*, he had found al-Assad to be truthful, intelligent and strong-willed. Clinton blames the Israeli prime minister, Ehud Barak, for the failure of the Shepherdstown negotiations between Syria and Israel. By April, when Clinton met al-Assad in Geneva, the Syrian president was aware of his deteriorating health and very concerned about transferring power to his son Bashar. He did not want hardliners in Syria to undermine Bashar's presidency, and Hafez al-Assad was very disappointed with Barak's lack of determination to finalize a peace agreement.

Bashar al-Assad came to power under the cloud of the failure of negotiations with Israel, as sponsored by the United States. His sense of appreciation for contributors to the process of Syrian-American rapprochement was certainly less acute than his father's. Hariri was not on Bashar's list of close allies and the age difference between the two men was not helpful. Moreover, Abdul Halim Khaddam, the Syrian vice president and Hariri's close friend, was distanced from the power centre. Hariri did not realize that his backing in Syria had been buried with the late President Hafez al-Assad.

Although accusations levelled against senior Hariri aides by Lahoud's team had crumbled one after the other, Hariri was still harangued about two matters. First, his son-in-law's ownership of one of the two cellular phone operations: both companies, LibanCell (owned by Hariri's son-in-law) and Cellis, partly owned by the Mikattis and largely by France Telecom, declared yearly profit growth of 55 to 60 percent, and this performance was held against Hariri as a form of private profiteering through nepotism. Second, the issue of accumulated public debt that exceeded $25 billion by the end of 2000 and $28 billion by the end of 2001. To the critics, it did not matter that the al-Hoss government had added $7 billion to the debt in just two years.

When Hariri took office in 2000, he was intent on achieving reform and restoring growth. He wanted to live up to the criticisms he had made of the process of government in 1998 and again in a book he published about his experiences and perceived needs of reform. In his latest cabinet, Hariri had two key nominees that were entrusted with conceiving and implementing reforms. These were Fuad Siniora, the unjustly accused minister of finance who was subsequently restored to his post, and Bassel Fuleihan, who was entrusted with the ministry of economy.

The ministry of telecommunications became of pivotal importance for the Lahoud camp. This is obvious from reading the Detlev Mehlis report, which was submitted on 21 October 2005 and is analysed in a later chapter. Surveillance of telephone communications was a major objective as well as disbursement of benefits by allotting rights for sales of prepaid telephone tickets, issuing free numbers which could be used commercially to the great advantage of the beneficiary ($2 million a year in one case) and concluding international tariff agreements with countries from which calls originate or terminate and link up countries such as Syria.

Jean-Louis Kordahi, the then newly appointed minister of telecommunications, and a protégé of President Lahoud, undertook from day one to pester Hariri. After numerous debilitating clashes between Kordahi and the Higher Council for Privatization, headed by the prime minister, over procedures and laws for privatization of this sector, Hariri decided to suspend the two BOT (Build-Operate-Transfer) licences in June 2001, four years before their expiry date. He wanted to prove to Lahoud that he was not protecting any private interests. This wholesome attitude, however, did not lead to the desired results as Kordahi kept altering his strategies while pleading concern for the public good. Hariri's act of bravado reflected his growing assurance about Lebanon's future role. Already, he had finalized plans for an Arab summit in spring 2002 in Lebanon, and for the Summit of the Francophone countries, delayed from a year before, scheduled in Beirut for autumn 2002.

The saga of approaching privatization of the telecommunications sector with a view to impose efficiency, reduce charges and enhance Lebanon's attraction as a business centre proceeded on a dramatic and painfully haphazard path as is clear from the following outline of events.

Highlights of the Mobile Conflict

- In August 1994, the ministry of telecommunications (MOT) signed two Build-Operate-Transfer (BOT) contracts with Global System for Mobile Communications (GSM) operators LibanCell and Cellis, enabled by Law 218 dated 13 May 1993, and the decisions of the Council of Ministers dated 26 May 1994. It is interesting to note that the US issued legislation for regulating cellular operation as late as 1996.

- Problems started to emerge between the state and the mobile operators as early as 1996, mainly over the sharing of revenues from value-added services.

- In 1999 the Audit Bureau of the Lebanese government issued a report accusing the mobile operators of breaching the BOT contract. Among the main issues at stake were:

  - The 'cap' over the number of subscribers allowed in the contract for each operator. It is to be noted that the contract states: 'The programme will contain a mandatory initial phase with a capacity for at least 300,000 subscribers. Further expansion of capacity will be performed according to actual demand'.

  - Revenues from value-added services, the operators argued, are exempt from revenue-sharing with the government. Article 3.1 of Attachment 1 of the BOT contract states: 'The revenue sharing due to MOT in respect of Special Services shall be applied only to airtime charge of such services'.

  - Avoiding payment for the use of microwave frequencies.

  - Not providing the geographical coverage as stipulated in the contract.

- In 2000, LibanCell and Cellis offered to pay $1.35 billion each, of which $900 million each was up-front payment and the rest in annual payments, in order to convert their contracts to 20-year licences that cover mobile and data communication services. The Lebanese government rejected this offer. The minister of telecommunications instead sent each of the two companies a debit note for $300 million for presumed infringements of the BOT contracts.

- On 14 June 2001, three years before the end of the ten-year period, the Lebanese government unilaterally cancelled the BOT contracts with the two GSM operators. This was an initiative by Hariri, later criticized by Kordahi.

- The government announced its decision to privatize the two GSM networks and to award mobile licences. HSBC was hired as the financial advisor to the transaction.

- In September 2002, the government issued an ownership transfer agreement that transferred the ownership of the two networks to the Lebanese state. As part of the agreement, the government offered the two firms $179 million ($118.6 to Cellis and $60.48 to LibanCell) in compensation for the premature termination of their contracts.

- The transfer of the operators' networks to the government was finalized during December 2002, when LibanCell and Cellis agreed to sign the ownership transfer agreement. According to the agreement, LibanCell and Cellis would continue to manage the two networks based on performance standards stated in the agreement. The two operators would also have to report to a technical and financial auditor (KPMG), which in turn had to report to a supervisory board appointed by the ministry of telecommunications.

- The government published a call for expressions of interest for a simultaneous auction for the sale of the networks and award of licences, and a tender for the management of the two GSM networks in July 2002.

- On 28 November 2002 the Lebanese government decided to suspend its $600 million claim against LibanCell and Cellis for alleged contractual violations, and to submit the dispute to international arbitration.[1]

- After many delays, mainly due to disagreements over which option to favour, pre-qualified bidders were announced in May 2003.

- The auction/tender process for the two GSM networks was launched in October 2003 amidst a barrage of accusations traded between

---

1. International arbitration will be applied with FTML (France Telecom owns 67% of its shares), and the decision would apply to both FTML and LibanCell.

the ministry of telecommunications and the Higher Council for Privatization's secretariat, which was in charge of handling the day-to-day preparations of the transaction.

- The GSM auction/tender was a flop. Only two bids were accepted: LibanCell and Investcom Holding (a shareholder in Cellis). A third bid from France Telecom was disqualified because it did not fit the auction and tender requirements. Other pre-qualified firms pulled out because of unease about the process as well as the draft licence and contract. The firms also complained that they did not receive responses for the questions they raised with the Higher Council for Privatization, and that observations were not taken into consideration.

- The government decided to reject the outcome of the GSM auction/tender. A ministerial committee[1] established to review the auction and tender announced that the process had failed and recommended that another tender for a management contract be held. The Council of Ministers empowered the minister of telecommunications to relaunch a tender process to award contracts for the operation of the two mobile networks. Naturally, the two qualifiers felt their rights were abrogated and went for arbitration.

- The minister of telecommunications and the ministerial committee revised the old tender documents and the bidding process was re-launched on 20 February 2004.

- The qualification criteria were revised to disqualify LibanCell and Cellis from participating, the value of the bank guarantee was reduced from $100 million to $30 million, and the arbitration clause was modified to allow arbitration on the outcome of the tender to take place overseas. The revised tender documents for the management of the two GSM networks stipulated that any firm that wished to take part in the bidding process should have at least three years of

---

1.   The committee is composed of five members: three appointed by MOT and two by HCP.

experience in operating a mobile network, and a minimum of 500,000 existing subscribers.

- Twelve companies acquired the tender documents: Orascom Telecom (Egypt), Worldtel (Sweden), TIM (Italy), Bouygues (France), Orange (France), Telenor (Norway), Detecon (Germany), Digicell (Ireland), ATG (USA), Link Cell (Lebanon), Megaphone (Russia), MTC (Kuwait).

- The deadline for submitting proposals was set as 29 March 2004.

- Detecon presented the lowest bid, followed by MTC, which gave the second lowest bid for LibanCell, and Orange, which gave the second lowest bid for Cellis.

- Detecon was selected to operate the Cellis network and opened the way for MTC to operate the LibanCell network.

At present, both cellular management companies are under severe criticism for deteriorating services and lack of expansion plans. Both companies plead that their terms of operation do not allow major investments. Even current maintenance charges were not settled by the MOT. To make matters worse, arbitrators in Switzerland ruled in favour of Cellis and LibanCell, according each $256 million compensation. The Lebanese lawyers who represented the government had little experience in arbitration and were ridiculed by their French colleagues representing both companies. Nevertheless, the ministry of telecommunications paid 6.5 billion Lebanese pounds ($4.3 million) in arbitration fees.

The Lebanese government, instead of continuing with the review of its case with France Telecom and LibanCell, opted to settle $96 million to France Telecom, to be paid in three equal instalments over three years, without interest. This agreement is still subject to approval by the board of the French company as well at its Lebanese partners. The decision was declared in mid-November 2005. By contrast, settlement with LibanCell cannot automatically proceed on a similar basis. Originally, LibanCell had received half the compensation already paid by the government to both companies, $60 million as opposed to $120 million. Moreover, France Telecom could probably charge the uncollected funds of the compensation decided by the court against profits in its consolidated balance sheet. Owners of LibanCell could claim that, in their case, the damage has been greater as the Lebanon operation was the backbone of their enterprise.

However, during this period of Hariri's government, much more important events took place than squabbles over privatization of telephones, and I now want to turn my attention to the events of 11 September 2001.

This terrorist attack pushed President George W. Bush at speed into the conservative camp of political thinkers and paved the way for a build-up of American and British forces to attack Iraq. It is beyond the scope of this book to consider the ramifications of the subsequent military manoeuvres to overwhelm Iraq's Ba'athist regime, and the capture and trial of Saddam Hussein. My concern here is to look at what came about in consequence of American and British measures *vis-à-vis* individuals of Arab extraction, and the fact that both powers adopted the alarming principle of the right of pre-emptive strikes and detention of suspects.

Saudis, Kuwaitis, UAE nationals, Syrians, Iraqis and, to a certain extent, Lebanese, were subjected to strict security measures on their visits to the United States and Britain, as were those who were in fact residents of either country. The freezing of bank accounts, holding people in detention until proven innocent, subjecting Arab diplomats to stringent security controls, etc were measures that persuaded well-to-do Arabs to stay away from the United States as visitors, students, residents or investors. The same attitude prevailed in Britain, and the flood of Arabs in the summer to the south of France was stemmed for at least three years.

Dramatic and tough measures adopted by the United States, Britain and eventually Russia, opened a window of opportunity for Lebanon. Arab investors sought to return most of their money to the Middle East, and this has contributed to the real estate and stock market boom in the Arab Gulf countries. This surplus of cash was further enhanced by much higher oil prices achieved in 2004 and 2005. Wealthy Arabs searched for investment opportunities in Lebanon, Syria and Egypt, the number of visitors from Arab countries to Lebanon was on the increase, and banking resources started to exceed local requirements even after allowing for borrowing needs by the Lebanese government, which showed no signs of slowing down.

Other than the financial and economic window of opportunity that opened for Lebanon, concentration on the activities and movements of terrorist groups seemed to serve Lebanon as well. There was no longer tolerance for state encouragement of terrorism, and countries like Syria were subjected to pressure and scrutiny. The Syrians, wanting to avoid confrontation with the Americans, cooperated in matters relating to terrorism to a limited extent and helped with information and the actual hand-over of two or three significant terrorist figures.

Lebanon was in no way implicated in the 11 September attacks, and Hariri soon realized the economic and financial prospects of the return of Arab money to the region. Due to his stature as a businessman and politician, he was consulted on a regular basis about important investments in Lebanon. He wanted to develop this potential and to bring about significant long-term assistance, which would help Lebanon overcome the yoke of inordinate indebtedness. Hariri started to exploring development possibilities with his friend Jacques Chirac and was surprised to be advised to draw up a convincing programme of reforms that involved self-help and discipline, and had political support – once this was established then Chirac would do everything possible to help.

Hariri gave the task of preparing the government programme to Bassel Fuleihan. This young, energetic and liberal economist set to work on a meaningful, convincing programme. He was primarily responsible for the document presented to the Paris II Conference held on 22 November 2002 in Paris at the invitation of President Chirac. In essence, the objectives of the programme were outlined to President Lahoud in the summer of 2002, of which he approved and promised to help in securing approval for executive decisions needed to facilitate and implement the programme. Fuleihan had benefitted from input by a number of experts including the minister of finance, Fuad Siniora, his assistant Dr Jihad Azour, Dr Nadim Mulla, and Dr Ghazi Youssef, the executive secretary of the Higher Council for Privatization. On the Lebanese president's team, Domianos Kattar and Dr Elie Assaf reviewed Fuleihan's draft and approved its arguments and recommendations. Kattar later served in the Mikatti government, which played a pivotal role from early April 2005 until the end of June. Kattar was the dynamic minister of finance for this stretch.

By September, the usual month for the IMF-World Bank yearly meetings, Lebanon had not achieved much on any of the test marks indicated. Rating agencies and the IMF both warned against weakening the private sector by neglect of fiscal control. There was no Paris II in 2001 and this factor stimulated efforts in 2002 to meet at least partially the tests of the international community. However, end-of-year statistics for 2001 showed that it was not a year of achievement. The most optimistic government sources spoke of a growth of 1 percent, whereas most economists considered there was no growth whatsoever. Total credit facilities did not increase; the balance of payments showed the largest deficit in its history – over $1.17 billion; and factory closures multiplied.

By contrast with negative indications and conclusions, the Lebanese economy did nevertheless witness some important steps that helped strengthen its future prospects. Government legislation was promulgated to combat money laundering, and the relevant procedures were activated. Pressure by FATF relaxed, and Lebanon's banking system was no longer threatened with punitive international measures. There was progress on the implementation of free trade agreements with Syria and Egypt, and steps taken toward the realization of a pan-Arab free trade area. Negotiations with the European Union proceeded positively and led to the initializing of the agreement terms with the community in early January 2002, and a date for final signature in June. Serious work on improving electricity production, distribution and collection of bills commenced late in the year. This thrust, it was hoped, could produce a significant reduction in government deficits, as cash drainage in this sector was over $1 million per day. At least six more months were needed for clear results to emerge, and then presumably by mid-2003 electricity could be privatized. Support for the costs of transport of quality controlled exports of fruits and vegetables started yielding good results and these exports increased by 40–50 percent in 2001. For the first time in years, Lebanon's official exports approximated $1 billion. When exports of the informal economy are added, the result is quite in excess of this figure. Preparations for implementation of the value added tax (VAT) law approved in 2000 were completed in 2001. The law provided for a uniform 10 percent rate applied to most purchases, but excluding fresh food, pharmaceuticals, school tuitions, books, newspapers, insurance, residential rents, etc. As of February 2002, application of VAT commenced and was expected to yield $550 million over the year. In fact, it yielded over $700 million.

Nevertheless, the tragic events of September 11 impacted strongly on Lebanon. Preparations that were well advanced for holding the international conference of heads of state of French-speaking countries in Beirut in October came to nothing. The conference was delayed for one year and was held in Lebanon in October 2002.

By the beginning of 2002 much of what would happen in the near future seemed to depend on the ability of political leaders to work together, and progress in the privatization and improvement of government administration. It was hoped that 2002 would prove to be the year of long-awaited breakthroughs, yet it began with pessimistic expectations. Political disputes seemed to cloud economic expectations, and before the end of 2001, rating agencies had downgraded Lebanon and its outstanding debt. Debate over the budget figures for 2002 reflected scepticism about realization of its objectives. Moreover, the start of the application of the VAT as of 1 February 2002 was protested against by the trade sector, which is the largest in the economy. Fears of pressures against the Lebanese pound escalated, and deposits made in American dollars increased to over 70 percent by the end of 2001.

In early 2002, the Euro-Med Association Agreement was initialized, although this result had been targeted for December 2001. February witnessed the introduction of VAT with minor reservations about the process. In March Lebanon successfully hosted the Arab Summit, during which Prince Abdullah, Crown Prince of Saudi Arabia, presented his project for re-starting Palestinian-Israeli negotiations and overcoming widespread violence. The plan was well received in Western circles, and Lebanon came out of the summit with broader recognition of its status as a peaceful and developing society. The summit was a great success for Hariri and, contrary to the claims made by his critics, showed that Prince Abdullah held Hariri in great respect.

As of May, the drain on foreign exchange resources had reversed. The balance of payments started to achieve surpluses, and exchange reserves with the Central Bank improved. The inflow of visitors was encouraging, and before the year ended there were signs of manifest interest in real estate holdings by wealthy Arabs. Fears of failure of banking enterprises receded.

In June, the law for privatization was approved by parliament, and the Euro-Med Agreement was signed and came into force immediately, with trade waivers for Lebanon that eased its fulfillment of requirements over five years.

In October the Francophonie Summit was held in Beirut and President Chirac, the prime minister of Canada, and other French-speaking nations expressed considerable support for Lebanon. Beirut had successfully hosted two summits, and Lebanon's credibility was no longer an issue with international leaders.

In November, the Paris II Conference took place, which gave Lebanon a tremendous boost. President Chirac invited European leaders, Arab leaders and international financial institutions to offer financial aid to Lebanon. However, expectations of success were weak, particularly because of the fact that, at that time, American pressure for confronting Saddam Hussein was having a knock-on effect on Lebanon and Syria; had the United States been opposed to an aid package to Lebanon it was in a position to sabotage the proceedings. Nevertheless, contrary to opinion, the conference succeeded beyond the expectations of opposition groups in Lebanon. Italy asked for approval of the programme by the IMF before making commitments, but the Saudi delegate, Prince Saud al-Faysal, stated that the Lebanese government's paper provided a convincing programme of action and pledged $700 million. He suggested that the IMF could review progress in their routine six-monthly missions to Lebanon, and most conference members endorsed this stand, with Italy participating with $100 million in the package and promising a further $400 million if the IMF review proved positive. France made a commitment of 500 million euros, which proved to equal more than $500 million by the time this commitment materialized in February 2003.

At the Paris II Conference Lebanon secured pledges for $3.1–3.5 billion in subscriptions to Lebanese government bonds for fifteen years with a two-year waiver at low rates of interest (5%). Before the end of 2002, approximately $1 billion were received, and the Saudi and French participation increased the total to $2.2 billion by the end of February 2003. For once, an Arab and international commitment for aid to Lebanon was translated into concrete results (earlier pledges in 1979 and 1989 had never materialized). In addition to the immediate loans of $3.1 billion, Lebanon secured commitments for development loans from the European Investment Bank, the Arab Fund, and the World Bank for $1.3 billion.

Upon declaration of the Paris II Conference results, a number of positive developments emerged.

- Speculation against the Lebanese pound seemed futile and $1 billion of deposits were exchanged for Lebanese pound deposits in one month.
- Interest payments by the Lebanese government for outstanding bonds in foreign exchange were expected to fall by $165 million a year in consequence of substituting long-term low-interest bonds for short-term high-interest paper.
- The schedule of redemption of part of the government debt improved

in terms of interest payments (as mentioned above) and duration.

- A number of large banks with substantial holdings of government bonds could expect redemption rather than extension of maturities in 2003. In essence, Lebanese banks could expect to receive $1.5 billion in settlements by the government in 2003.

- Interest on new government bonds dropped by between 2 and 3.5 percent, due to improved credit worthiness. Interest savings on this account could be even greater than the direct savings on the equivalent of $3 billion of government bonds, which could be transformed into long-term low interest issues as a result of the Paris II commitments.

- Most important of all was the message conveyed by the international community of its interest in salvaging the Lebanese financial situation before it became an actual rather than potential crisis. Inevitably, Lebanon's rating by international agencies was expected to improve, as it did.

Immediately after the Paris II declarations, the Bankers Association in Lebanon expressed its interest in providing the equivalent of 10 percent of total deposits in the form of non-interest bearing loans for two years to the Lebanese government. As deposits at the end of 2002 equalled $37 billion, this initiative meant that interest savings by the public sector could equal $370 million a year on this account. By the end of March 2003, total deposits had reached $40 billion in the banking system.

Worked out arithmetically, interest savings could account for a total, in millions, of over $800 per year ($165 + $250 (due to reduced interest on new issues and renewed issues) + $400 = $815). This would equal nearly 30 percent of the total deficit recorded in 2002. As this deficit amounted to 42.3 percent of the budget, the deficit would fall to 29.6 percent in 2003 before accounting for higher revenues from VAT and compression of expenditures by 10 percent. The government projected for 2003 a deficit of only 25 percent.

For the purpose of ensuring its budgetary targets in 2003, the government introduced a 5 percent tax on all interest earned from bank deposits. This measure was estimated to yield the equivalent of $100 million in 2003.

When these measures were approved and became practical parameters, it was soon evident that their effect would be recessionary. Banks could not reduce debtor interest and maintain profitability. Moreover, with a total increase in deposits in 2002 of less than 10 percent, banks could not increase their facilities to the private sector in 2003 unless deposits increased by well over 10 percent. The likelihood of this eventuality became more remote after the introduction of the 5 percent tax on interest earned on deposits.

Total loans to the private sector did not increase in 2001 and their increase in 2002 was only 2.7 percent.

Due to the developments noted above, it can be said that Lebanon improved its international financial standing, and avoided a financial crisis, but went too far in adjusting financially at the cost of reduced growth. For these reasons, Lebanon's challenges at that time could be summarized as follows. First, moving ahead with privatization schemes, particularly with respect to communications and electricity, to fulfill two objectives: the reduction of public debt, which had exceeded the equivalent of $31 billion by the end of 2002; and improving the efficiency of public services. Second, to effectively utilize the $1.3 billion for development projects secured at the Paris II Conference, and allocating resources to projects with significant economic and social benefits. Third, to improve productivity of the public sector and achieve a rate of growth of 3–4 percent per year in order to improve expectations and employment opportunities. Fourth, to secure Lebanon as a destination for Arab visitors and Arab capital: this could be justifiably anticipated after the war on Iraq produced fears of Western hegemony throughout the Arab world.

SIX

The Lebanese Economy Since 2003

At the beginning of 2003, the success of the Paris II Conference held on 22 November 2002 was still colouring the expectations and hopes for 2003. It seemed that finally Lebanon was to begin improving its economic performance and reverse the growth of debt.

In principle, the Paris II Conference approved the extension of $3.1 billion in long-term low-interest loans (fifteen years at 5 percent) that would contribute to the restructuring of the country's public debt. Another $1.3 billion was pledged by major international and regional development agencies for financing socially and economically beneficial projects in Lebanon.

In return, the conference delegates requested Lebanon's commitment to the principle of privatization, an active administrative reform project, structural initiatives for improving productivity, and easier bureaucratic procedures. All the requests from the Lebanese side were, and still are, considered to be essential requirements to achieve a satisfactory rate of growth and inflow of investments.

The restructuring of public debt, due to the Paris II Conference and its aftermath, affected over $10 billion – or 30 percent – of total public debt by the end of 2003. Approximately $1.8 billion was offset against paper profits that accrue to the government due to variations of gold prices. This move was more of a side-step than real improvement, particularly because sale of government gold in Lebanon has been subjected to parliamentary approval from 1988, and the Central Bank, which is the custodian of the gold, has no role in this respect. This type of rigidity is purely political and speaks of the ignorance of parliament members about trade in metals.

Beyond the monetary re-engineering of public debt, and calculation of profits or losses on account of gold policies, the economy showed a very sluggish performance. The rate of growth, claimed to equal 2 percent by the Central Bank and the ministry of economy, is disputable. There were obvious signs of growing activity in three sectors only: first, tourism reflected an 8–9 percent growth with visitors exceeding one million for the first time in recent history. Also, expenditures exceeded $1 billion. Second, the total financial resources of the banking system increased by 9–10 percent, thus leading to a situation of excess liquidity over borrowings by $5–6 billion. Also, Lebanese banks started to explore regional activities in Syria, Jordan and beyond, and international activities. Third, interest in prime real estate by Arab investors and Lebanese emigrants increased, as was clearly demonstrated in purchases of luxury apartments, as well as large areas for development outside Beirut.

Although Lebanon achieved a high balance of payments surplus, and accumulated substantial resources in the banking system, it did not create a positive chain reaction. If anything, the country continued to pay the ever-increasing toll of government inefficiency.

Loans to the private sector had not increased over four years, whereas loans to the public sector increased by 25 percent and now exceeded loans to the private sector by at least 30 percent, as most of the available financial resources were going to the public sector and some of its most inefficient enterprises – such as Electricité du Liban (EDL). Productivity and growth became very hard to achieve; only massive private investment in diversified activities could compensate for the drag on performance that the public sector represents in Lebanon. Activity by the private sector required administrative facilities, tax incentives, financing at reasonable costs, and short take-off periods. Possibly, only the subsidized financing of tourism, and industrial and technical projects, could offer a window of opportunity. Over the past few years, total subsidized loans have increased to around $1 billion, or 7 percent of the total loan portfolio of the private sector in Lebanon.

Industry and agriculture, the two sectors that traditionally contributed 25–27 percent of the GDP, suffered from serious competition. In particular, energy costs, labour charges and financing charges hinder the progress of both sectors (over 9,000 jobs were terminated in 2003). The pressure for subsidies for agricultural production increased significantly and a subsidy was re-instated in favour of sugar-beet farmers, although local production of sugar costs $1,000 per ton, which equals five times as much as the cost of imports.

Whatever increase in economic activity came about was the result of an improved inflow in the number of visitors, manifest interest in expensive or expansive real estate, and a certain measure of optimism after the Paris II Conference. This optimism could have mushroomed had Lebanon been able to progress in its efforts towards privatization of the cellular and fixed telephone networks or electricity production and distribution. While such moves were promised in the paper submitted by Lebanon to the Paris II Conference, political resistance prevailed, and lack of progress began to affect expectations. By late summer 2003, the World Bank as well as the European Union criticized Lebanon for lack of progress in promised initiatives. Accordingly, the residual of the Paris II commitments ($700 million) could not be expected to materialize. By early 2004, President Chirac of France, who had played a central role in organizing the conference and urging his European partners to support it, expressed disappointment at the lack of progress.

At about this time, early 2004, Hariri felt that the aim of this obstruction was to leave Lebanon at the mercy of Syrian initiatives and conditioned reflexes by Lahoud. He became a confirmed believer in the need of Syrian withdrawal from Lebanon and expansion of liberties. Without this result, Lebanon could not hope to pull out of its predicament. Hariri, in his quiet way, relayed his conviction to a small number of close associates and family members.

Serious problems, which cast a shadow over positive expectations, were of varying severity. Irrespective of Lebanon's appeal and latent dynamism, the only factor pushing the economy was represented by substantial transfers from Lebanese emigrants and capital inflows from Arab investors. Transfers by Lebanese for their families, or for investments, have been the main reason for the balance of payment surpluses in Lebanon. According to the Bank of International Settlements' estimates, transfers by Western Union and similar facilitating agents to Lebanon were in the order of $2,400 million in 2003. Bank transfers added a further $1 billion and an equal amount was probably brought in cash by Lebanese emigrants coming home for a visit or permanently. A tragic airplane crash in Benin (West Africa) on Christmas Day 2003 resulted in the death of over 130 Lebanese and a loss of $20 million that was being carried in cash. This is a reflection of how dollars reach the country: the law in Lebanon does not restrict the amount of cash carried by any Lebanese or any visitor. Only when a bank account is opened would there be enquiries about the source of funds for any account in excess of $10,000.

With a level of transfers of $4.4 billion to Lebanon, a country of 3.4 million people, the average per capita volume of transfers is in the order of $1,300/capita. This is a higher figure for income per capita than is the case for total income per capita from all types of sources and activities in most developing countries. Lebanon could achieve balance of payment surpluses while having a balance of trade deficit in the order of $5 billion, only because of these transfers. Moreover, considering the impact of these transfers on consumption and investment, it can be claimed that this inflow is what contributes to a crawling rate of growth, which is achieved whilst the total population is shrinking in number.

Direct investments by Arabs are increasing and reflect in some cases disenchantment with Western economies. This alienation has come about in the wake of the 11 September attacks, and subsequent restrictive practices *vis-à-vis* Arabs in many Western countries, particularly the United States, Britain and Australia. Direct investment is a prime mover of growth. It creates jobs and leads to diversification of economic activities. In 2002 direct investment exceeded $650 million, whereas in 2003 this figure was probably closer to $800 million. Most investments by Arab individuals and corporations are still directed at real estate and, in certain cases, merchandising. The Habtoor Group, responsible for building the Metropolitan Hotel, completed a major mall and multi-activity centre adjacent to the hotel with a total cost in excess of $100 million. Another UAE leading business figure, Majid al-Foutaim, who holds the Middle East rights for the Carrefour chain of hypermarkets, purchased property for over $50 million to develop a huge store and two five- and four-star hotels that, when completed, would cost well over $300 million (with land purchases).

Indications seemed to suggest that general interest in Lebanon as a business destination remained strong. This was the case in spite of stalling in the decision-making process. Yet even the prime minister admitted in public that political differences were having an effect on the willingness to invest in Lebanon. This was a rare declaration from Hariri, who had adopted optimism as his banner and encouraged business and financial conferences in Lebanon. The completion of the BIEL facilities and rehabilitation of the Phoenicia Intercontinenetal Hotel, and Le Vendome, owed a lot to his encouragement. Hariri's expression of disappointment was thus acutely felt.

Considering Lebanon's indebtedness, there is only one way to break out of the vicious circle that thwarts growth: investment in diverse activities. Massive, diversified and productive investments presume efficient administration in government and productive organizations in the private sector. Both thrusts require modern laws in which the procedures are simplified to enable investors to proceed with speed and assurance. Also, litigation in Lebanon in regular courts requires too much time, and costs are extremely high. This factor is percolating in the minds of investors and is becoming a serious deterrent to long-term investment commitments, particularly in projects that require multiple partners.

Lebanon is in need of expanding the scope of arbitration in business disputes. Moreover, by law this should become a final point for resolution of differences. Up until now, decisions of arbitrators have to be ruled upon and approved by Lebanese courts. Consequently, this method involves payment of fees twice instead of once, and the time required for final resolution of disputes is further extended, thus enhancing reluctance of investors due to legal delays and costs.

During 2003, the al-Madina Bank cast a shadow across the Lebanese banking scene. Hariri was a friend of the chairman of al-Madina Bank and was attacked in the Lebanese press for the possible cover-up of the bank's misdeeds. Although this accusation was false, the bank came under scrutiny by investigators assigned to uncover the perpetrators of Hariri's assassination. For this reason, affairs at al-Madina Bank will be discussed here at some length.

Al-Madina Bank

In the early 1980s, the Iraqi Mehdi Bahr al-Ouloum ran al-Madina Bank. Al-Ouloum had previously worked with the Arab Monetary Fund, which had been established in Abu Dhabi, but it was later revealed that al-Ouloum and a former Iraqi minister were involved in the embezzlement of hundreds of millions of dollars from the Arab Fund. In 2004 he was serving a sentence in Abu Dhabi.

The Abou Ayash family acquired shares in al-Madina Bank in 1984. The purchasers were Ibrahim and Adnan Abou Ayash. The latter brother had graduated from the University of Texas at Austin in 1974. While studying there, he became a close friend of Nasser Rashid, a Saudi engineer who became consultant to the Saudi royal family for all their construction requirements in Saudi Arabia and to a certain extent abroad, particularly in Spain. Adnan Abou Ayash went to Saudi Arabia directly

Muhammad al-Amine Mosque

Hariri's funeral procession

The Rafiq Hariri shrine

French president Jacques Chirac and his wife Bernadette with Rafiq Hariri's family at the shrine

Rafiq Hariri with his family

Hariri's mountain villa at Faqra

Pope John Paul II's open-air address, 1997

Grand Serail, the prime minister's offices

The ESCWA building

Detlev Mehlis, head of UNIIIC until the end of 2005

The demonstration of 14 March 2005

Religious Distribution of Voters in Lebanon by Province

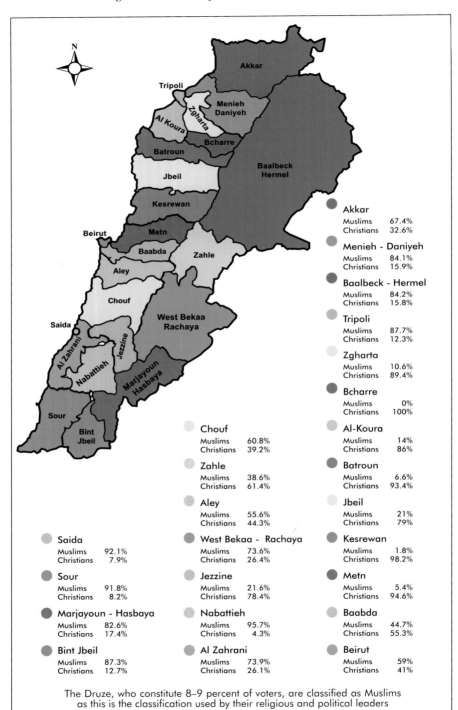

Akkar
Muslims 67.4%
Christians 32.6%

Menieh - Daniyeh
Muslims 84.1%
Christians 15.9%

Baalbeck - Hermel
Muslims 84.2%
Christians 15.8%

Tripoli
Muslims 87.7%
Christians 12.3%

Zgharta
Muslims 10.6%
Christians 89.4%

Bcharre
Muslims 0%
Christians 100%

Al-Koura
Muslims 14%
Christians 86%

Batroun
Muslims 6.6%
Christians 93.4%

Jbeil
Muslims 21%
Christians 79%

Kesrewan
Muslims 1.8%
Christians 98.2%

Metn
Muslims 5.4%
Christians 94.6%

Baabda
Muslims 44.7%
Christians 55.3%

Beirut
Muslims 59%
Christians 41%

Chouf
Muslims 60.8%
Christians 39.2%

Zahle
Muslims 38.6%
Christians 61.4%

Aley
Muslims 55.6%
Christians 44.3%

West Bekaa - Rachaya
Muslims 73.6%
Christians 26.4%

Jezzine
Muslims 21.6%
Christians 78.4%

Nabattieh
Muslims 95.7%
Christians 4.3%

Al Zahrani
Muslims 73.9%
Christians 26.1%

Saida
Muslims 92.1%
Christians 7.9%

Sour
Muslims 91.8%
Christians 8.2%

Marjayoun - Hasbaya
Muslims 82.6%
Christians 17.4%

Bint Jbeil
Muslims 87.3%
Christians 12.7%

The Druze, who constitute 8–9 percent of voters, are classified as Muslims as this is the classification used by their religious and political leaders after graduating from the US. He started working with the Rashid Engineering Consulting Company, and by the early 1980s had become a junior partner in the enterprise as well as the acting general manager.

During the period 1974–82, Saudi revenues increased exponentially and construction boomed. The Rashid company prospered immensely, supervising billions of dollars' worth of construction works. By 1982 Adnan Abou Ayash had over $300 million of private wealth. He remained reclusive and lived modestly in a private villa in Riyadh.

Ibrahim Abou Ayach, the brother who followed in the business affairs of the family in Lebanon, adopted more overt attitudes to living. He was a spendthrift, and within a circle of close friends lived the life of the wealthy and famous.

In the summer of 1998, Ibrahim convinced Adnan that they should expand al-Madina Bank's role. They purchased ten branches of the Foreign Trade Bank's portfolio, and a bank with two branches, the Commercial Facilities Bank, the name of which was changed to United Credit Bank (UCB).

In 1998 al-Madina Bank started to expand aggressively. Ibrahim had assumed the role of chairman-general manager, as Lebanese law dictates, and Miss Rana Koleilat was employed as Ibrahim's personal assistant. Yet Ibrahim spent a lot of time living a luxury lifestyle – more interested in his boats and cars than in the affairs of the bank – and Koleilat was given a great deal of latitude. Al-Madina Bank, with an absentee majority shareholder (Adnan Abou Ayash was living and working in Saudi Arabia) and an extravagant local helmsman, started to drift into dangerous waters.

The period 2001 and 2002 witnessed flagrant and profligate waste of financial resources. Most often, it was associated with high profile purchases of land plots or hotels by members of the family of Rana Koleilat, particularly her brother Taha. Such purchases included the plot of land of the house of the late Michel Doumit on the seafront before the Summerland Hotel, as well as the Coral Beach Hotel (which was placed under Sheraton management) and Hotel Emilton in Maameltein on the shoreline going north from Jounieh. By early 2002 it was obvious that al-Madina Bank was in serious trouble. The governor of the Central Bank wanted to either apply strict measures to correct the situation or solicit a commitment by Adnan Abou Ayash regarding liabilities.

Some time in the spring of 2002, the governor and Adnan Abou Ayash were both dinner guests of Prime Minister Hariri. The prime minister in his work in Saudi Arabia had often cooperated with the Rashid Engineering Consulting Company, which was run by Adnan Abou Ayash. He had great respect for the man and knew that his means were considerable. At dinner, both the prime minister and the governor urged Adnan to restrict his brother's powers and to dismiss Rana Koleilat. Adnan assured them that Rana Koleilat was a capable employee who had integrity, and confirmed that he would guarantee all losses and debts of the Koleilat family.

As of 1998, Adnan Abou Ayash made a number of transfers of funds to the al-Madina bank, either to the account of his brother Ibrahim or to his own account (account number 69911). It was later revealed that no such account number existed.

Table 2 (pages 137–8) provides a summary of transfers made by Adnan from 14 November 1997 until 13 March 2003. It should be noted that transfers as of 29 November 2002 were made to the account of al-Madina Bank with BDL (Central Bank of Lebanon). Over four months (29 November 2002 to 13 March 2003) these amounted to $440 million. In total, the transfers amounted to $1.25 billion, and yet on 19 February 2003 the Banking Control Commission estimated that Adnan Abou Ayash needed to guarantee the equivalent of the following sums for each bank:

Al-Madina Bank	LL700 billion, of which LL450 billion were debts owed by Rana Koleilat personally ($465 million)
United Credit Bank	LL209 billion ($133 million)

By contrast, total facilities granted by al-Madina Bank to regular clients, i.e. clients who had nothing to do with the Koleilat clan or the Abou Ayash family equalled:

$56 million or LL85 billion	Al-Madina Bank
$17 million or LL26 billion	United Credit Bank

Considering the liabilities *vis-à-vis* regular clients, it is obvious that ordinary commercial loans, even if lost in total, were not the cause of lack of liquidity or accumulated losses, which exceeded $1.25 billion of transfers.

How could al-Madina and its affiliate lose so much money? In fact, the funds were not totally lost but grossly misused or misplaced. Assets were bought for much higher than actual values, and Messrs Ibrahim Abou Ayash and Taha Koleilat spent money without consideration for value. Ibrahim had eight yachts, varying in size from 12 metres to 24 metres; Koleilat had two yachts, one 22 metres in length, the second 35 metres. The collection of cars exceeded 150, including Range Rovers, Mercedes, Ferraris and Maseratis. Even Bassel Koleilat's seven-year-old son had a Ferrari registered in his name.

What seem to be trivial figures, in the context of the overall picture, possibly demonstrate the degree of flagrant misuse of bank funds. In December 2002 Rana Koleilat's cellular phone-bill was $14,539, her brother Taha's $14,189 and her brother Bassel's $9,374. Rana's credit bill for that month amounted to $1,088,692.

It is possible to provide various statistics about real estate purchases that exceeded hundreds of millions of dollars, involving properties that range from prime land to hotels and luxury buildings and apartments. In 2003, both the Abou Ayash family and the Koleilat family gave up all their holdings to the Central Bank. However, this initiative did not include over fifty apartments that were bought for people close to Rana Koleilat, whether relatives, employees or senior staff who worked under her direct supervision. Between December 2002 and January 2003, during which period Adnan Abou Ayash transferred $130 million to the account of al-Madina Bank with the Central Bank, Rana Koleilat issued cheques worth $150 million to third parties, which included purchases of a number of apartments for friends and relatives. Irrespective of all adverse developments and practices, and although alerted about imminent closure of the bank's doors by the Central Bank, Adnan Abou Ayash provided a notarized undertaking on 17 February 2003 which included the following:

> Transfers by me to the Central Bank have been intended to cover liquidity deficits of al-Madina Bank as per the Central Bank's requirements.
>
> The transfers of 14 February 2003 [which must be the transfers made from Switzerland on 11 and 12 February amounting to $90 million] are intended to cover credits provided to Miss Rana Koleilat by both banks.
>
> I hereby guarantee payment of any additional sums due to depositors and other rights' holders, undertaking on my responsibility all obligations registered in both banks. I will transfer all sums due to the Central Bank by both banks.
>
> This undertaking particularly covers any sum charged against Miss Rana Koleilat at both banks.
>
> I request that you withdraw all procedures undertaken by the Central Bank against Miss Rana Koleilat and others to raise responsibility from them and defreeze all accounts frozen by the Central Bank with all banks and to eliminate all claims by the Central Bank against their movable and immovable properties.

This blanket guarantee by Adnan Abou Ayash, one of the wealthiest figures in the Middle East and already chairman of the board, presented the governor with a dilemma. He could accept it at face value or reject it and liquidate both banks. He chose an intermediate and practical approach.

A general manager, Paul Choufani, was appointed to work directly under Adnan Abou Ayash, and two Central Bank nominees were appointed to review and approve all operations, Usama Sultani in al-Madina Bank, and Saadallah Hamade in Allied Bank. Moreover, both banks were not to accept deposits any longer. A clearing and restructuring operation was supposed to be launched. These efforts, however, did not stem the crisis and, by summer 2003, a veteran banker and former member of the Banking Control Commission, Andre Bandali, was appointed as interim general manager for eventually liquidating all rights and obligations.

After Adnan Abou Ayash issued his guarantee, as stated above, he accepted full responsibility for all deficits in both banks and the burden of debts by the Koleilat family *vis-à-vis* other banks in Lebanon as well. The last recorded transfer by Adnan Abou Ayash to the Central Bank for the account of al-Madina Bank was for $50 million received on 13 March 2003.

Managers nominated by the Central Bank of al-Madina (Sultani) and Allied Bank (Hamade) were not happy with the lack of progress at both banks, and they finalized a report on 24 April 2003 in which they estimated the shortage of liquidity at both institutions to equal $302 million. Rana Koleilat and Ibrahim Abou Ayash went by private plane to Jeddah, together with the al-Madina Bank's in-house lawyer, Michel Helou, to secure coverage by Adnan Abou Ayash. He succumbed to pressure and issued a cheque for $310 million in the name of his brother Ibrahim Abou Ayash, who was instructed to deposit it only when a cheque drawn by Rana Koleilat on Credit Suisse for $400 million was cashed by Adnan Abou Ayash. This cheque bounced and Adnan's cheque for $310 million was endorsed by Ibrahim Abou Ayash, favour Rana Koleilat, even before the plane left Jeddah. Later, Rana Koleilat gave this cheque to the Central Bank's governor, and the head of the legal department went to Paris to secure the funds, but the cheque had no corresponding funds.

As of summer 2003, the Central Bank raised cases against Adnan Abou Ayash and Rana Koleilat and sought to secure assets that would cover this amount. Real estate properties were assigned by the Koleilat family and the Abou Ayash family to the Central Bank, and creditor accounts in their favour in both banks were given up, which left around $30–40 million of uncovered exposure. By mid-summer 2003, Adnan Abou Ayash had raised a case of embezzlement and misrepresentation against Rana Koleilat, and the search for other assets continued. By early 2004, some fifty-two apartments belonging directly or indirectly to the Koleilat clan were put under seizure, as well as a number of yachts and at least 150 luxury cars.

By early summer 2004 the al-Madina Bank's débâcle had petered out. Small depositors had been paid in full and large depositors had received 80 percent of their deposits with interest. Before the end of September 2004, these depositors were fully compensated.

The whereabouts of Miss Rana Koleilat, principal culprit of the al-Madina Bank debacle, have been disclosed. She was arrested on 12 March 2006 by the Brazilian police in Sao Paulo for attempting to enter the country with a forged British passport and bribing the arresting officers.

Lebanese authorities had helped in identifying a location for a meeting between her and one of her former collaborators in Beirut. The Lebanese judicial authorities submitted an extradition request to the Brazilians. According to current agreements between both countries, extradition is not obligatory. Brazil, however, has to cooperate with the UNIIIC, which by Security Council Resolution 1595 can request assistance from all UN member countries in respect of Hariri's assassination. Any information Rana Koleilat may have is of primary importance to the UNIIIC and an interview with her is sought by the Commission.

Nevertheless, a number of issues and questions remain. First, how could a girl employed in an insignificant job with the bank in 1984 become a moving force in two banks whose shares were owned by Adnan Abou Ayash, a successful man living and working in Saudi Arabia? Second, numerous financial dealings would appear to suggest Rana Koleilat had strong ties with Syrian intelligence officers. As a consequence, both Patrick Fitzgerald, the deputy commissioner of the Irish Police Force dispatched to Lebanon, and Detlev Mehlis, commissioner of the Security Council, indicated the need to study al-Madina accounts.

Beyond the al-Madina Bank débâcle, of which the consequences are still to be incurred in full, the year 2004 was Lebanon's best year since 1996. Estimates of growth by the World Bank and Lebanon's Central Bank indicated a 5 percent growth. Activity increased, notably in tourism, banking, real estate and the launching of major projects.

Realization of the Paris II commitments, however, had hinged on implementation of structural and administrative reforms by the Lebanese government. These reforms were not realized due to political divergences, particularly between the president of the republic and Prime Minister Hariri. The setback represented by non-availability of a further $700 million of soft and long-term loans and $1.3–1.5 billion of project finance was partially compensated for by a subscription for two years by Lebanese banks of 10 percent of their total deposits, for no interest, to Lebanese government bonds. Some $4 billion were mobilized in this manner, saving the government $800 million in interest over two years. The full impact of this initiative was felt in 2004. For this reason, the budget proposed for 2005 projected interest payments in the order of LL4,000 billion instead of LL4,400 billion in 2004.

Lebanon's greatest achievement in 2004 was possibly the reduction of the ratio of total public debt to GNP by 3 points, from 185 percent to 182 percent. This result came about from two sources. On the one hand, the budget deficit fell by LL 900 billion or 23 percent, from LL3,938 billion to LL3,026 billion. The other contributing factor was represented by a more accurate evaluation of GNP figures by the French institute for statistics and economic studies, INSEE. In all previous years, the impact of transfers by Lebanese working abroad was understated. Figures provided by the Bank of International Settlements (BIS) of Basel, Switzerland, indicated total transfers in 2003 in the order of $4.5 billion.

When transfers are taken into consideration, the GNP figure increases to between $22 billion and $24 billion. This is due to the fact that nearly 35 percent of working-age Lebanese in the past ten years emigrated to Arab Gulf countries, Africa, Canada, the US, western Europe and formerly east European countries. This emigration was associated with expansion by Lebanese or Lebanese-owned enterprises in the Gulf region, Africa and eastern European countries. No less than five Lebanese enterprises achieved sales ranging between $200–$5,000 million per year. The internationalization of Lebanese enterprises in recent lean years in Lebanon has been more impressive than the expansion of Lebanese banks abroad, which has been important.

In early September 2004, following renewal of the term of Lahoud, it was expected that the cabinet be changed. This is normal practice, and Hariri resigned. He was asked to form a new cabinet and, in the meantime, the old cabinet continued to function. Hariri was under the impression that his task would not be made difficult, because he had opted against his previously declared position to support the renewal for Lahoud. Yet instead of cooperation he met with obstruction. He personally told me that his nominees for ministerial responsibility were repeatedly refused, and that he had become tired of it. He submitted his final resignation, thus opening the door for the Karame government.

Umar Karame was nominated as prime minister after Hariri's resignation on 20 October 2004. Karame's team included a number of ministers with experience in economics and finance: Adnan Kassar as minister of economy, Maurice Sehnaoui as minister of energy and water, and Elias Saba as minister of finance. This government was expected to function as a coherent team until the 2005 elections, scheduled for June.

Considerable work was undertaken towards the rescheduling of debt instruments due in 2005, and outlining the particulars for a sensible budget. The rescheduling efforts were successful and the minister of finance presented a budget that cut back expenses in the order of LL200 billion, and anticipated an increase in revenues, particularly from VAT in the order of LL800 billion. The deficit was projected to fall to 26.3 percent from an actual realized ratio of 32.4 percent in 2004. With these projections and continued growth of 4–5 percent, Lebanon could hope to reduce the ratio of total indebtedness to gross national income again in 2005. The general outlook seemed favourable. In 2004 the number

Table 2: Bank Transfers Made by Adnan Abou Ayash to al-Madina Bank

Source Bank	Date	Account No.	Account Holder	Amount Transferred
1997				
Credit Suisse	14 Nov. 1997	1–49	Ibrahim Abou Ayash	$2,500,000.00
			Total 1997	**$2,500,000.00**
1998				
UBS-Zurich	26 Jan. 1998	1–49	Ibrahim Abou Ayash	$15,000,000.00
Credit Suisse	9 Feb. 1998	1–49	Ibrahim Abou Ayash	$500,000.00
Credit Suisse	14 Apr. 1998	1–49	Ibrahim Abou Ayash	$35,000,000.00
UBS-Zurich	30 Sep.1998	1–49	Ibrahim Abou Ayash,	$4,000,000.00
UBS-Zurich	20 Nov. 1998	1–49	Ibrahim Abou Ayash	$6,000,000.00
			Total 1998	**$60,500,000.00**
1999				
UBS-Zurich	11 Feb. 1999	1–49	Ibrahim Abou Ayash	$400,000.00
UBS-Zurich	22 Apr. 1999	1–49	lbrahim Abou Ayash	$3,000,000 00
UBS-Geneve	30 Jul. 1999	1–49	Ibrahim Abou Ayash	$4,000,000.00
UBS-Zurich	3 Aug. 1999	1–49	Ibrahim Abou Ayash	$1,200,000.00
			Total 1999	**$8,600,00.00**
2000				
UBS-Zurich	17 Feb. 2000	1–49	Ibrahim Abou Ayash	$3,000,000.00
UBS- Zurich	10 Mar. 2000	1–49	Ibrahim Abou Ayash	$12,000,000.00
UBS-Zurich	10 May 2000	1–49	Ibrahim Abou Ayash	$1,500,000.00
Credit Suisse	4 Oct. 2000	69911	Adnan Abou Ayash	$10,000,000.00
UBS-Zurich	9 Nov. 2000	69911	Adnan Abou Ayash	$10,000,000.00
UBS-Geneve	30 Nov. 2000	69911	Adnan Abou Ayash	$5,000,000.00
UBS-Zurich	4 Dec. 2000	69911	Adnan Abou Ayash	$5,000,000,00
			Total 2000	**$46,500,000.00**
2001				
UBS-Zurich	7 Feb. 2001	69911	Adnan Abou Ayash	$30,000,000.00
UBS-Zurich	23 Mar. 2001	69911	Adnan Abou Ayash	$40,000,000 00
Credit Suisse	28 Mar. 2001	69911	Adnan Abou Ayash	$50,000,000.00
Credit Suisse	3 Apr. 2001	69911	Adnan Abou Ayash	$20,000,000.00
UBS-Zurich	27 Aug. 2001	69911	Adnan Abou Ayash	$150,000,000.00
UBS-Zurich	27 Dec. 2001	69911	Adnan Abou Ayash	$200,000 000 00
			Total 2001	**$490,000,000.00**

Table 2: Bank Transfers Made by Adnan Abou Ayash to al-Madina Bank (continued)

Source Bank	Date	Account No. (except *LCB = Lebanese Central Bank)	Account Holder	Amount Transferred
2002				
Solidere/ Méditerrannée	2 Jan. 2002	69911	Adnan Abou Ayash	$16,260,000.00
BDL Provisions	–	69911	Adnan Abou Ayash	$18,000,000.0
UBS-Zurich	3 Oct. 2002	69911	Adnan Abou Ayash	$30,000,000.00
Credit Suisse	8. Oct. 2002	69911	Adnan Abou Ayash	$100,000,000.00
UBS-Zurich	11 Nov. 2002	69911	Adnan Abou Ayash	$5,000,000.00
UBS-Zurich	22 Nov. 2002	69911	Adnan Abou Ayash	$10,000,000.00
UBS-Zurich	29 Nov. 2002	*LCB	Adnan Abou Ayash	$20,000,000.00
UBS-Zurich	12 Dec. 2002	*LCB	Adnan Abou Ayash	$80,000,000 00
			Total 2002	$279,260,000.00
2003				
Credit Suisse	8 Jan. 2003	*LCB	Adnan Abou Ayash	$25,000,000.00
UBS-Genève	8 Jan. 2003	*LCB	Adnan Abou Ayash	$25,000,000.00
Arab Bank Paris	6 Feb. 2003	*LCB	Adnan Abou Ayash	$10,000,000.00
UBS-Genève	10 Feb. 2003	*LCB	Adnan Abou Ayash	$50,000,000.00
UBS-Genève	11 Feb. 2003	*LCB	Adnan Abou Ayash	$24,000,000.00
Credit Suisse	12 Feb. 2003	*LCB	Adnan Abou Ayash	$66,000,000.00
UBS-Zurich	5 Mar. 2003	*LCB/# 8	Adnan Abou A ash	$15,000,000.00
Saudi British (Riyadh)	5 Mar. 2003	*LCB/# 8	Adnan Abou Ayash	$42,000,000.00
Saudi British (Riyadh)	5 Mar. 2003	*LCB/# 8	Adnan Abou Ayash	$10,000,000.00
ANB (Riyadh)	5 Mar. 2003	*LCB/# 8	Adnan Abou Ayash	$3,000,000.00
ANB (Riyadh)	5 Mar. 2003	*LCB/# 8	Adnan Abou Ayash	$10,000,000.00
UBS-Genève	7 Mar. 2003	*LCB	Adnan Abou Ayash	$40,000,000.00
Saudi British (Riyadh)	13 Mar. 2003	LCB	Adnan Abou Ayash	$50,000.000.00
			Total 2003	$370,000,000.00
			Total transfers, 1997 to 2003	$1,257,360,000.00

of visitors increased by 27 percent, inflow of capital reached $1 billion, and transfers exceeded $4.5 billion. Banking resources increased by 13 percent and consolidation initiatives in the banking sector indicated better expectations in 2005. The change of government did not cause expectations to change, provided the process of elections proceeded smoothly.

At this time, Lebanese banks with resources beyond local needs explored regional prospects. A number of Lebanese banks started operations in Syria after the facilities provided for establishment of banking institutions became law. Other banks established operations in Jordan and Sudan, and one major bank, which had become predominantly Lebanese owned, acquired a billion-euro bank in France.

At the start of 2005 expectations were positive and Arab attitudes favouring investment in Lebanon were strong. This outlook was linked to increased revenues and liquidity in oil-producing Arab countries. Oil prices had increased in 2004 and continued to increase in 2005. Previously, deficit budgets in Saudi Arabia and Kuwait became budgets with important surpluses. Oil-price increases that contribute to capital inflows to Lebanon, and transfers by Lebanese, however, have a negative impact as well. Lebanon imports all its fuel products, which exceed 5.3 million tons a year. If prices remain high in 2006, the import bill for these products alone would exceed $3.4 billion. During 2005 the cost of fuel imported for electricity, which represents over 55 percent of total oil-products imports, contributed to a cash deficit in the EDL of $900 million as compared with half this figure a year before. The cost of energy is going to play a large role in determining Lebanon's prospects.

Also at the start of 2005, regional considerations seemed favourable with increasing capital inflows and strong demand from Iraq for products and services. In 1982 Iraq had been Lebanon's largest market, and it was once again becoming an important destination for Lebanese exports and re-exports. Equity and bond markets were more active than in previous years, particularly in the case of foreign currency denominated shares and bonds. In particular, shares of Solidere more than doubled in value and

GDRs of leading banks improved by 30 percent. The Beirut stock market had its best year to date and its capitalization increased considerably, due to higher prices and an increase in listed bonds in the order of $2 billion.

At the beginning of 2005 Lebanese expectations were positive. Interest margins had narrowed, making profitability targets for banks more difficult, but the economic and financial base was expanding. Banking profits increased by 14.5 percent, although balance sheets increased by 13 percent. Lebanon's ability to service debt and maintain a balance of payments surplus seemed assured, in spite of a tremendous increase in the value of imports by over $2 billion. This increase was occasioned by the strong increase in oil prices.

There was concrete evidence of significant improvement in economic performance in 2004 to justify expectations of the ability to grow whilst reducing the ratio of total debt to the national income. In large part, this expectation was due to the positive impact of the Paris II Conference and complementary steps in Lebanon. In addition, steps taken in 2002 to improve economic performance were bearing fruit and, finally, the results of earlier international and regional efforts by Hariri were playing a positive role. It is important to add a few further comments on this aspect as it has a long-term bearing on Lebanese prospects.

Hariri strongly believed in developing trade and investment ties with regional economies and international emerging economic centres. In 1998, he travelled to Egypt to urge signature of the Arab Free Trade Zone Agreement between Syria, Lebanon and Egypt, which was implemented as of that date. In December 2000, two months after taking the reins as prime minister again in Lebanon, he urged the signature between Lebanon, Syria, Jordan and Egypt for construction of a natural gas pipeline from Egypt. The project would benefit each of the four countries. Due to Hariri's efforts and international support, this project is nearing finalization. In 2003, President Luis Inacio Lula Da Silva of Brazil visited Lebanon and Hariri took the opportunity to remind him that in 1994, on a visit to Brazil, Hariri called for greater cooperation between both countries, particularly with an important and active community of Lebanese descendants in Brazil. Agreements signed during President Lula's visit contributed to a significant increase in trade between both countries. China, as an emerging economic force, also attracted Hariri's attention, and he visited China more than once in the second half of the 1990s. He whipped up interest on both sides. Lebanese imports from China increased by 40 percent in 2004, and China indicated willingness to join the donor countries' ranks in the Aid to Lebanon Conference in February 2006.

The drive by Hariri to establish Lebanon firmly in the awareness and appreciation of the community of nations concentrated on economic and financial prospects, drawing on Lebanon's tradition of free trade, exchange, financial services and tourism. He spared no efforts to develop this angle and succeeded significantly in spite of delays and slow progress in Lebanon. Nevertheless, there were serious worries about the yearly deficit associated with electricity generation and distribution, estimated at $500 million, and the financial health of the National Social Security Fund. Serious efforts were devoted to the electricity problem, whereas the question of the National Social Security Fund awaited a political decision. A report of the social security system was finally commissioned and completed in October 2005. Still, the electricity problem, as has been indicated, has become enormous.

This whole picture was changed drastically by the assassination of Rafiq Hariri and his security team on 14 February 2005. Initial concerns were about speculation and the exchange value of the Lebanese pound. Moves made by the Central Bank contained speculation at the cost of higher interest rates on three-year foreign currency bonds, and higher interest rates on the Lebanese pound.

SEVEN

Immediate Consequences of Hariri's Assassination

Syria's role in Lebanon had become of international concern and, on 2 September 2004, the Security Council issued Resolution 1559; soon afterwards, under Syrian pressure, the term of President Lahoud would be extended for three years.

Resolution 1559 called for Syrian troops and intelligence personnel to be withdrawn from Lebanon. Also, it called for the disarmament of Lebanese militias (implicitly referring to Hizbullah) and Palestinian camps, and the restoration of democratic practices, particularly proceeding with elections to parliament without interference by Syria. This resolution was at first ridiculed by Syrian officials and most Lebanese politicians with an overt stand supporting Syria's role in Lebanon.

Hariri's assassination gave Resolution 1559 an urgency, which pushed the secretary general of the United Nations to dispatch a fact-finding team to evaluate the circumstances of Hariri's assassination and to recommend a future course of action. The deputy commissioner of the Irish Police, Patrick Fitzgerald, led the team. The mission spent a month in Lebanon, from 25 February to 24 March 2005. During this month, there were momentous popular demonstrations that turned the tide against Syrian dominance of Lebanon, and against the Lebanese authorities' apparent lack of interest and efficiency in respect of carrying out the investigation into Hariri's assassination.

The funeral procession of Hariri, called for by the family as they refused a state funeral proposed by the cabinet of Umar Karame, Hariri's successor as prime minister, took place on 16 February 2005. Hariri's final resting place was Martyrs' Square in the heart of the city, which he had rebuilt, and next to the Mosque Muhammad al-Amine, which he had financed. No less than 200,000 Lebanese of all creeds joined the funeral procession, with around 100,000 onlookers from balconies. There was a strong feeling of injustice, and the predominance of the Lebanese flag became the rallying symbol of unity.

Parliamentary speaker Nabih Berri responded to calls for a session to discuss Hariri's assassination. This was held on 28 February 2005. Calls for a protest march against the government for not showing enough initiative in unveiling the truth behind the assassination brought a torrent of Lebanese people to the heart of the city, carrying Lebanese flags and calling for Syrian withdrawal from Lebanon, and for the dismissal of heads of the security services in Lebanon, as well as the attorney general who had become minister of justice.

Two important developments took place on that day. First, army units entrusted with searching the demonstrators, and with creating diversions to delay a massive presence in Martyrs' Square – which was popularly re-named Liberty Square – gave in with grace to the flood of people. Army members kissed children, accepted white roses, and generally showed care and concern for the demonstrators. Second, Rafiq's sister, Bahia Hariri, made a brave speech in parliament: she called for the truth about Hariri's death to be revealed; for the elimination of the heads of security branches; for restoration of liberties; and the resignation of the Karame Cabinet. Her words and attitude were echoed with thunder in Martyrs' Square where no less than 200,000 people denounced inefficiencies and complicity with repressive security agencies, whether Lebanese or Syrian.

Marwan Hamade, a close associate of Hariri, was also among the deputies who addressed parliament on the morning of 28 February. Hamade nearly lost his life when a car bomb exploded 200 metres from his home on 1 October 2004. An eloquent and emotional speaker, Hamade accused Syrian and Lebanese senior officials of plotting to kill Hariri. Other Hariri bloc deputies, notably Farid Makari, spoke with fervour and courage.

The most important shock for Karame's government came from the address of Deputy Robert Ghanem. This mild-mannered deputy, a lawyer who successfully practised in Paris and Beirut, comes from a district in the Beqaa Valley with massive Syrian military presence. While it was expected that he would have mild criticism to make, his accusations aimed at the government and Lebanese and Syrian security agencies were severe. Thus, Karame realized that he was losing the support of deputies who had accorded his cabinet a vote of confidence. During the lunch-break recess Karame drafted a resignation letter, which he did not discuss in full with either the president or the speaker of parliament. This was a serious setback for the government.

On the evening of 28 February 2005, when Karame resigned, the American ambassador in Lebanon gave a dinner – at which I was present – in honour of David Satterfield, a former ambassador in Lebanon and assistant undersecretary of state for Middle East affairs. There were four Lebanese cabinet members at the dinner – Leila Solh Hamade, the minister of industry; Adnan Kassar, the minister of economy and a prominent business leader in the Arab world; minister Jean-Louis Kordahi, a close supporter of President Lahoud; and minister Yassine Jaber, a close ally of Nabih Berri, the head of the chamber of deputies. Ambassador Satterfield, well known for his directness, stressed four objectives for 2005: the withdrawal of all military and Syrian intelligence personnel from Lebanon before the end of April 2005; the launch of a UN-sponsored international investigation to reveal the perpetrators of Hariri's assassination; free elections for parliament around the end of May, with international observers recording infringements; and, finally, the exchange of diplomatic representation between Lebanon and Syria before the year's end. The first three requirements have been met despite expressed fears about Syrian reactions.

Minister Adnan Kassar said that he had just come back from a business conference in Abu Dhabi, and that important Syrian business figures warned that a forced Syrian withdrawal without dignity would lead to vengeful actions, such as closing the borders to traffic from Lebanon. Ambassador Satterfield indicated that Syria had to consider that its own exports to Iraq would be treated in a similar manner, and that it would be advisable that Syria avoid such moves. Minister Leila Solh asked Ambassador Satterfield: 'How can we be sure that the US will not change its position and soften its demands of Syria once some demands are met, particularly in respect of Iraq?' Satterfield responded by saying: 'Syria has been treating us as if our need for improvement can be quenched by a drip system. This is no longer the case; the world is changing fast and the Middle East is witnessing tremendous evolution. Syria has to catch up with the community of nations and the drip style is no longer satisfactory.'

In July and early August 2005, Syria blocked commercial land traffic from Lebanon. The pretence was specified as the need to make sure that trucks were not carrying bombs or armaments. Relaxation of Syrian restrictions only came about when Syrian trucks faced similar delays on the way to Iraqi destinations and on returning to Syria. Iraq's imports from Syria have been extremely important to the Syrian economy, which suffered greatly from the shrinkage of transfers by Syrian labour in Lebanon and evaporation of illicit benefits from dealings with the Lebanese.

The response of the pro-Syrian camp in Lebanon came on 8 March 2005. On that date, which is also the anniversary of the move by the late Hafez al-Assad to purge the Ba'athist movement, Hizbullah and Amal called for a public demonstration to express thanks to Syria for its role and efforts to stabilize Lebanon and protect so-called civil peace. There were possibly over 300,000 participants in this demonstration, predominantly carrying the Lebanese flag but also with a sprinkling of Hizbullah black flags and the green flags of Amal, as well as thousands of pictures of al-Assad. Hasan

Nasrallah, the spiritual leader of Hizbullah, denounced Resolution 1559 and said it served Israel and the United States whilst creating discord in Lebanon. At the time Nasrallah was passing these judgments, Syria declared its readiness to abide by the requirements of Resolution 1559 in respect of its withdrawal from Lebanon. President Bashar al-Assad had given this assurance to Terje Roed-Larsen, special envoy of Secretary General Annan, entrusted with following up on the implementation of Resolution 1559.

Nasrallah, in his address, pointed at the huge crowd in Riad al-Solh Square and declared: 'This is democracy.' Karame, who had resigned, was charged again with the mission of forming a government and he claimed clearly that he had a majority in parliament as well as in the street, as was demonstrated on 8 March.

Three leaders failed to hear the message of the ordinary Lebanese: President Bashar al-Assad, Hasan Nasrallah and Umar Karame. All three thought that popular demonstrations before 8 March had exhausted the will of Lebanese opposition members. What they did not realize was that most Lebanese, and certainly an overwhelming majority of young Lebanese, felt that Hariri's assassination was a great injustice, that they could not hope for freedom and good government as long as Lebanese leaders submitted without question to Syrian decisions. Twenty-nine years of Syrian control of Lebanon, or much of its area, became an intolerable condition. The international community was saying so, and Hariri's murder highlighted the need for change.

On 14 March 2005, one month after Hariri's death, the Lebanese people took to the streets to call for unity, independence and truth, and to express their rejection of practices by an antiquated government. Over 1.2 million Lebanese people, some 30 percent of the total population, headed for Martyrs' Square in the centre of Beirut. Hundreds of thousands were unable to reach the site of the demonstration because of traffic jams. Following this demonstration Lebanon could not revert to political compromise, and 14 March 2005 was the date of rebirth of a free Lebanon with a modern and humane outlook. The imperceptible decline towards a third-world status of standards and practices, dominated by intelligence agencies, was forever swept away.

This cataclysmic change in attitude and positioning of a whole population was brought about by the assassination of Hariri and his companions. Hariri's character was steeped in positive aspirations for Lebanon and its people. He had contributed greatly to education, and to restoration of Lebanon's credibility as a member of the community of nations, and he had regained the heart of Beirut for its inhabitants and visitors. Possibly his greatest contribution was his life, which served to purge Lebanon from its social and political afflictions.

The report of the fact-finding mission to the UN's General Secretary Annan underlined in no uncertain terms that Lebanese security services were unable, unwilling and lacking the credibility necessary with public opinion to conclude a thorough and objective investigation of Hariri's assassination. Moreover, the report submitted on 25 March 2005 stated the following:

> After gathering the available facts, the Mission concluded that the Lebanese security services and the Syrian Military Intelligence bear the primary responsibility for the lack of security, protection, law and order in Lebanon. The Lebanese security services have demonstrated serious and systematic negligence in carrying out the duties usually performed by a professional national security apparatus. In doing so, they have severely failed to provide the citizens of Lebanon with an acceptable level of security and, therefore, have contributed to the propagation of a culture of intimidation and impunity. The Syrian Military Intelligence shares this responsibility to the extent of its involvement in running the security services in Lebanon.[1]

The extent of Syrian control in Lebanon, particularly over intelligence services, is well illustrated in *Inheriting Syria: Bachar's Trial by Fire*. The author, Flynt Leverett, a Senior Fellow at the Saban Center for Middle East Policy at the Brookings Institution, was previously a Senior Director

---

1.   Patrick Fitzgerald, the deputy commissioner of the Irish Police, headed the Fact-Finding Mission.

for Middle East Affairs at the US National Security Council under Condoleeza Rice. Before that he was Senior Middle East Analyst at the Central Intelligence Agency. In January 2004, he interviewed Bashar al-Assad at length. In his book he outlines Hafez al Assad's program, and in respect of Fitzgerald's summary above the following excerpt of the book is very relevant:

> A second tool for maintaining Syrian hegemony in Lebanon has been the deployment of an extensive apparatus of Syrian intelligence officers throughout the country. For many years, under the command of Syrian military intelligence brigadier general Ghazi Kanaan (1982–2002), this apparatus and its extension, the Lebanese intelligence and security services allowed the Assad regime to keep tabs on and influence all important aspects and sectors of Lebanese political, economic and social life. (p.43)

Developments proceeded fast during April. Syrian withdrawal was achieved for both military and security personnel. By 26 April an international team was sent by the UN to verify Syria's withdrawal and later make sure that elections could proceed on time and without interference. On 19 April Najib Mikatti, a modern political figure with close ties to the Hariri family and President Bashar al-Asssad, was charged with the task of forming a new cabinet. He selected fourteen distinguished figures with no intention to run for elections, and the Mikatti cabinet received a vote of confidence on 27 April, and was intent on conducting elections during the last week of May.

On 25 May 2005 members of the International Investigation Team, entrusted by the Security Council to unveil the planners, perpetrators and executors of Hariri's assassination, started to arrive in Lebanon. They enjoyed wide powers of interrogation and detention of any Lebanese or Syrian officials that had criminal responsibility in this affair. The chosen head of the team, Detlev Mehlis, is a German prosecutor with a success record in uncovering terrorist acts of violence. He and a growing number of his team, which amounted to nearly 200, were very busy verifying evidence, applying advanced scientific tests, etc. Their work started before the end of May, and an executive summary report was provided to the secretary general of the United Nations on 25 August 2005. Following that date, four senior officers, all heads of security organizations and well-known allies of Syria, including the head of the presidential guard, were incarcerated and accused of plotting to assassinate Hariri. Nothing as cataclysmic had ever happened in post-independence Lebanon, i.e. over the past sixty years.

The domino effect started before the actual imprisonment of the four accused. Jamil al-Sayyed, the pro-Syrian head of internal security and the most arrogant of the four officers, was forced to submit his resignation, as did practically all the heads of military intelligence and internal security forces. Further resignations were expected, and the Lebanese government gave in to all international decisions for verification of the perpetrators of the crime as well as for assurance of proper, timely and fair elections.

The impact of Hariri's death on Lebanon's economic life was soon felt and is intensifying as time goes by. It is impossible to assess the losses incurred; all that can be attempted is an assessment of clear indicators and certain trends and events.

The first indicator of losses incurred is clear from the number of days of public demonstrations that followed the assassination. Over a period of forty working days after Hariri's murder, the Lebanese economy functioned at no more than 50 percent of its capacity, which meant the equivalent of the production of twenty days had been lost. For a country that works around 240 days a year, this already constituted a loss of 8 percent of annual labour. INSEE, the French institute for statistics and economic studies, which was employed by Hariri in late 2000 to estimate the GDP and GNP of Lebanon, had reported an estimate of GNP in the region of $22–24 billion by 2003. Previous estimates had been around $16–18 billion.

On the basis of macro-estimates, by the fiftieth day following Hariri's death, Lebanon had lost permanently 8 percent of its GNP, or at least $1.76 billion. This was not the only loss but it was the most comprehensive. Other losses could be recorded, but it must be noted that it is impossible to quantify them with any precision, as some losses would be recorded under the national income figures.

Financial pressures, deriving from fears about the exchange value of the Lebanese pound or the Lebanese banking system, were clearer to observe. Central bank gross reserves fell in fifty days by $4.5 billion, but issues of debts for longer terms in foreign currencies recouped $2.7 billion. Moreover, some $500 million was made available to the Central Bank from Arab sources before the end of March. Still, the reduction in reserves was no less than $1.5 billion in a short span.

Roving explosions in commercial, industrial and tourist establishments in the heart of what is termed as Christian areas, suggested vindictive actions by groups that resented Syria's forced withdrawal from Lebanon. These explosions and acts of terror, if continued, could certainly stall further decisions for investment in or visitors to Lebanon. Since summer 2005 three explosions occurred; in September 2005 in a poor section of East Beirut predominantly inhabited by Christians; again in September a car bomb injured and mutilated the well-known opposition television personality May Chidiac; and in January 2006 a car bomb exploded east of Beirut, killing the renowned journalist and parliament member Gebran Tueni and two of his aides.

The longer the uncertainty continues in Lebanon, then the greater the losses. The nature of the Lebanese economy, a service-based economy par excellence, makes it vulnerable to acts of sabotage and terrorism. In 2004, which witnessed the full benefits of the Paris II package, the World Bank, IMF and the Lebanese Central Bank estimated growth at 5 percent. It is to be noted that this rate of growth had not been witnessed since 1996. Moreover, it was achieved in spite of obstructionist policies followed by the anti-Hariri camp, which aimed to abort the benefits of the Paris II Conference and complementary initiatives undertaken in Lebanon.

Without obstruction, Lebanon could have achieved greater growth. Even more to the point, had Hariri been allowed to form a cabinet in September 2004, after extension of Lahoud's presidential term by three years, better results could have been achieved. The last three months of 2004 were non-productive.

Initially, President Lahoud's camp, essentially members of parliament aligned with Syria, ridiculed Resolution 1559, as did the Syrian minister of foreign affairs. Lebanon's opposition parties made political capital of this situation and intensified their opposition. Rafiq Hariri, the single most important political leader who had faced isolation and rejection by President Lahoud's camp, chose to remain distant from the fray. He was accused of being instrumental in the formation and passage of Resolution 1559, such accusations emanating from his strong ties to President Chirac who originally sponsored the Resolution. Only when Marwan Hamade, a Druze deputy and former minister in Hariri's government, barely escaped an assassination attempt, was Hariri moved to criticize the authorities. The year 2004 ended with tension, and the best growth performance in years, which could be built upon in 2005 and beyond, provided rational economic practices were adopted and political reforms made after the Syrian withdrawal.

Hariri's assassination took the steam out of the economic thrust of 2004. All aspects of growth were severely damaged. Tourism shrank and Arab visitors became reluctant to come to Lebanon; recurrent bombs frightened away visitors. Direct foreign investment receded as investors wanted to assess the climate, and were weary of the causes for obstruction of Hariri's initiatives by the ruling class. Exports and re-exports are still active on a lower scale but far more exposed to Syrian whims than before. It is very important to maintain good Syrian-Lebanese relations. This goes beyond the calls for withdrawal, and accusations against the Syrian and Lebanese authorities that fermented the tense political climate that facilitated Hariri's assassination.

To explore future possibilities, one has to imagine the flow of changes induced by the military, diplomatic and political moves affecting Syria and Lebanon. In the broader context of major historical moves, it is possible to detect positive elements deriving from Syria's withdrawal, and international Arab and western aid to Lebanon. Once Syrian withdrawal was confirmed before the end of April, attitudes about Lebanon's future improved considerably. The Central Bank issued $2 billion of ten-year papers for 10 percent and covered the issue in full in two days. At present, these bonds are trading for 106 percent of the par value.

It should be rememberd, however, that the legacy of Rafiq Hariri is an aspect of potential aid in itself, and should be examined before turning to evaluate the positive consequences of Syrian withdrawal from Lebanon. Hariri was instrumental in preparing the groundwork for the Taef Accord, which was concluded in autumn 1989. The Taef Accord, which became Lebanon's new constitution, had a number of additional agreements. One such agreement related to the establishment of a $2 billion fund for helping Lebanon with its reconstruction efforts. Financing of this fund was expected from Arab and Western sources including American, French and European assistance. This fund was left unattended, particularly after Saddam Hussein unleashed the second Gulf war by attacking and occupying Kuwait in early August 1990. That episode, which lasted until mid-February 1991 when allied forces pushed Iraqi forces out of Kuwait, cost the Gulf countries over $100 billion, and plunged Saudi Arabia and Kuwait into borrowing. Consequently, the Taef Fund for Lebanese reconstruction was forgotten.

At present, all Arab countries, including Syria and Lebanon, are calling for implementation of the Taef Accord. This agreement, which was shelved in 1991, suddenly regained its focal importance essentially as a face-saving device *vis-à-vis* the international community's (i.e. the UN's) insistence on implementation of Resolution 1559. If the Taef Accord is to be truly put to good use, as it should, the Fund for Lebanon's needs must also be mobilized.

This task, the rebirth of the Taef Fund for Lebanon, might be easier to achieve than it seems. The Americans have hinted at their readiness to assist Lebanon in the post-election period, provided free and fair parliamentary elections are held. European readiness for assistance has been repeatedly asserted and would be forthcoming, provided the Lebanese draft a programme of action that is rational and constructive. Arab funding is now much easier than in 1990. Oil prices have increased in the past two years, and Saudi Arabia and Kuwait are enjoying a surplus instead of deficit. Income per day for Saudi Arabia, Kuwait and the UAE, assuming a $30 per barrel increase in their export prices for 13 million barrels per day, yields additional revenues of $390 million per day. Total resources of the Taef Fund, which include Western contributions, were to equal $2 billion, or the equivalent of the increase in income for Saudi Arabia, Kuwait and the UAE over five days. Considering the significance of Western, i.e. American, presence in the Gulf countries, it is possible to assume that this sum or more could be made available to Lebanon shortly after the elections.

In addition to development funds due to Lebanon in consequence of the Taef Accord, Lebanon received pledges for financial assistance amounting to $3.2 billion at the Paris II Conference, of which $2.5 billion materialized before the end of January 2003. The remaining $700 million of long-term low-interest loans (15 years at 5 percent interest and two years' grace period) can be secured if Lebanon starts to execute certain structural improvements, as promised in a paper submitted by the Lebanese delegation to the conference.

Structural improvements could serve to better identify long-term investment projects, which contribute to development and social welfare. If a set of projects were identified and shown to be beneficial, then a further $1.3–1.5 billion of long-term project financing would be available from international and regional development agencies that participated in the Paris II Conference. This expectation was confirmed to Prime Minister Siniora in New York where a meeting was held on 19 September 2005, and which underlined the willingness of the international community – spearheaded by the United States, Britain, France, Saudi Arabia, Russia, Japan and China, together with leading international specialized agencies – to help Lebanon achieve growth and reduce its debt burden. Rational and long-awaited structural improvement measures are required of Lebanon and its people.

As part of Hariri's legacy to Lebanon, there are open opportunities for securing financing for long-term development provided sensible government policies are followed. Until 30 April 2005 – the date set for the withdrawal of the last Syrian soldiers and intelligence officers from Lebanon – the Lebanese government could still expect Syrian hegemony over development plans. Since that date freedom of the decision-making process has been restored, but the question remains, can the Lebanese as a people develop democratic ways of voting?

The picture is partly clarified when the consequences of Syrian withdrawal are properly evaluated. Evaluations of the Syrian-Lebanese economic, trade and technical relations were distorted by estimates of benefits derived by Syria at the expense of the Lebanese. Some of the comments made are lacking in accuracy and rational judgment. This was clearly demonstrated in respect to estimating transfers by Syrian labour from Lebanon. We shall identify false trails and attempt to clarify more important issues.

Economic relations between neighbouring countries can be very beneficial to both if trade relations are truly liberalized, even if only gradually over a number of years. What ruins benefits from exchanges and movement of labour is tampering with market conditions by conceding advantages to one country at the expense of other countries. In the European single market, such distortions between trading partners of differing sizes have been avoided by adopting equitable rules to be adhered to by all members, or resolved by a European court set up for that purpose. In this manner, Belgium could prosper while liberalizing its trade with France and Germany; and Portugal could achieve fast growth whilst liberalizing its exchange with Spain, Italy and France.

Trade relations between Syria and Lebanon could only be beneficial to both countries provided exchange rules and charges were uniformly applied. The same could be said about labour flow between the two countries. In fact, had there been proper regulation of exchanges between both countries, Lebanon and Syria would have become the future nucleus of an emerging Arab common market. This did not materialize because of distortions in the application of the rules of liberalization and practices of profiteering by border customs or security officials on both sides. As the Syrians were the dominant force, they could dictate the pace of profiteering, which they did in favour of Syria and its lackeys in Lebanon.

Huge fortunes were achieved from exporting all types of products from Lebanon to Syria. The same applied in respect of products imported through Syrian ports and delivered to the Lebanese market, without payment of any kind other than charges for conducting and transporting this illicit trade. These practices sabotaged the meaningful use of customs duties to regulate trade between both countries. It is possible that customs losses in Lebanon exceeded $250 million a year, whereas in Syria the figure would have been higher because of higher rates on practically all imports and exclusion of some imports. Syria must have faced losses in the order of $400 million per year and the larger part of these amounts went to officials who controlled entry points and transportation routes in both countries.

Labour relations were practically unilateral, i.e. a flow of Syrian labour to Lebanon and a trickle of Lebanese technicians and investors to Syria. According to official Syrian figures published recently, the number of Syrians working in Lebanon in recent years varied between a minimum of 350,000 and a maximum of 500,000. Many Lebanese commentators jumped to conclusions such as that Lebanon pays out $1 billion a year, assuming Syrian laborers work 250 days each year for an average pay of $10 per day, of which they save and transfer $2,000 every year to their home country. This could well be true, but these Syrian labourers were saving Lebanon much more. Their participation in construction, agriculture and basic services made possible all these activities at cheaper costs. Lebanon could well have transferred a billion dollars a year to Syria but one should bear in mind that Lebanon was saving one billion dollars in labour costs.

Exchanges of labour between the two countries have to be upgraded and better organized. There is little doubt that the Lebanese have exploited Syrian labour, particularly in construction and agriculture. At present, with growing fears about their safety in Lebanon, Syrian labour is very hard to find and therefore construction activity has nearly come to a standstill. Sales of steel and cement are a trickle of their previous levels and the move towards normalization of labour exchanges in a normal political climate is an urgent objective.

It is noteworthy that the extent of Syrian labour in Lebanon provides proof that unemployment could be much lower than the often-quoted figure of 25–30 percent. With at least 300,000 Syrian labourers out of the country, the Lebanese could fill the vacant jobs. Moreover, at least 150,000 Asians and Egyptians are working primarily in home and cleaning services as the Lebanese do not want to undertake menial jobs. However, rather than explore the forms and types of Lebanese-Syrian exchanges and cooperation, it is important to acknowledge the essence of the distortion in this relationship, which is multifaceted.

The Syrians, and particularly their army and intelligence officers, were the controllers. They had come from a central planning system, with no freedom of monetary exchange, to a country with a liberal trading tradition and complete freedom of currency exchanges. Opportunities for profiteering were exploited to the maximum possible degree over a distinct period of time. There was close cooperation between the Syrian controllers and active traders, businessmen, politicians and Lebanese officials. The network of corruption kept on expanding until it became the norm.

In a free market, formation of monopolies could prove very profitable (for the monopolists, that is, as monopolies are detrimental to the rest of the economy and to society as a whole). The practices of oligopoly and monopoly, favoured in centralized economies such as the Syrian economy, were grafted onto the Lebanese economic system. Symptoms were clear in communications, fuel imports, transit, trade, etc. Lebanon's economic system was distorted to serve the few who developed entrenched interests with senior Syrian officials. This harmful situation could not continue without feeding on itself.

There is no way to accurately assess the benefits derived by Syria through interference and control by its intelligence officers of trade routes, major contracts, profitable activities, etc. Regular sources of income, which varied in importance over years, included the following (the figures are not accurate, but indicative of orders of magnitude):

- Illicit drug activities including cultivation and processing, particularly in the years 1988–91: $200 million per year.
- Avoiding payment of customs duties in the period 1983–2004: on average $200 million a year, increasing to $300 million.
- Tampering with transit trade by delaying or facilitating flows yielded: $100 million a year.
- Overcharging for sales of high sulphur fuel oil over a period of at least ten years: no less than $250 million in total.
- Benefits from contracts secured for construction works, roads, schools, power facilities etc: possibly $100 million.
- Regular benefits secured from the tie-up of international calls with services of Syrian-controlled operators, the Casino du Liban, and quarries, especially during the five years 2000–04 amounted to no less than $200 million per year, i.e. $1 billion over the period. The benefits from the quarries seem to be continuing at present.
- Payments by al-Madina Bank, whether in cash or goods, to Syrian officials: $100 million.

The grand total of these estimates, which must be less than actual benefits derived as many other forms of payment (such as payments by political figures for benefits) cannot be evaluated precisely, and add up over the years to an astounding $800 million from drugs; $2,400 million from avoidance of customs duties; $500 million from tampering with transit trade; $250 million from sales of high sulfur fuel; $100 million from public works contracts; $1,000 million from international calls, Casino du Liban and quarries; $100 million from al-Madina Bank: the grand total being $5,100–5,500 billion.

The $5 billion average figure is an estimate of illegal or politically extracted benefits. To assess Syria's total benefit from Lebanon, one should add the perfectly legal transfers of Syrian labour. It was indicated before that these could have reached $1 billion or more per year. Consequently, as of 1990, Syria has probably secured from the Lebanese economy $20 billion of legal ($15 billion) and illegal ($5 billion) earnings.

There is little wonder that the Syrian regime, which benefitted from these illegal and non-conventional returns, as well as from regular transfers, is angry with the loss of control over Lebanon. This anger was clearly exhibited in the address of the Syrian president to his people on 11 November 2005.

The need to break away from profiteering and distortion of economic activities became clearer to Lebanon and Syria as both countries negotiated cooperation agreements with the European Union. Try as they might, both countries realized the futility of accumulating bad practices in a world getting more liberalized and globalized every day. Lebanese-Syrian profiteering and distortion practices have to be abandoned, but those involved in the process could not accept the inevitability of the changes lying ahead. They kept refusing reforms, and held on to exploitative powers until Resolution 1559 made them face up to reality.

For all the above reasons, and because of the intricate cobweb of illegal and profiteering practices that hurt both countries, Syrian withdrawal will prove of great economic benefit to Lebanon. Reluctance to invest in Lebanon because of fears from practices of a Syrian socialist regime will evaporate. Visitors will come without having reservations about a prevalent atmosphere of nervous and primitive intelligence networks. Launching enterprises and initiatives will not be hindered by the shadow of interference and profiteering. And, most importantly of all, the Lebanese decision-making process will be liberated from the duty of informal consultation with Syrian authorities. Decisions will be made more quickly and will be taken independently and based on rational considerations.

Lebanon's horizons will no longer be drawn at the Syrian border, but can extend to embrace modern developments worldwide. A healthier relationship has to emerge between both countries, and if Syria chooses to liberalize its economic system and free its political processes, it can achieve greater benefits than Lebanon.

Syrian anger at having to leave Lebanon has permeated every public address given by President Assad since Hariri's death. In addition, Syria's loss of foreign exchange due to the drying up of transfers from Lebanon and repayment of some Iraqi deposits contributed to a drop of 8 percent in the exchange rate of the Syrian pound versus the dollar.

By contrast, Syria speeded up its liberalization measures to attract investments, particularly from Arab oil-rich countries flush with cash due to higher oil prices. This influx of capital substituted, to a large extent, for lost transfers from Lebanon, and the capital influx included investments by six Lebanese banks, which exceed $200 million.

Whereas economic and financial exchanges between Lebanon and Syria proceeded on a lower threshold, political relations continued to be tense. Between November 2005 and February 2006 pro-Syrian political groups in Lebanon increased their pressure for normalization of relations between both countries and various crude attempts were made to cast doubts on the work of the UNIIIC Commission.

Lebanon's leading bloc of parliament members elected in May and June 2005, which is led by Saad Hariri, pushed strongly for implementation of UN resolutions relating to Lebanon and the UN-led international investigation of the crime.

By 14 February 2006, one year after Prime Minister Hariri, Bassel Fuleihan and their security entourage were assassinated, Lebanon was in political turmoil. The call for freedom, independence and liberty on 14

March 2005 was gradually eroded by bickering between various Lebanese groups. Frustration at the new parliamentary and cabinet majority's lack of performance diverted efforts towards the removal of President Lahoud, whose re-election for a period of three years, ending in September 2007, is alleged to be unconstitutional. The UN Security Council's Resolution 1559 of 3 September 2004 deems Lahoud's extended term unconstitutional.

Lahoud cannot be removed without the consensus of all political parties. Hizbullah are eager to keep Lahoud in power as they proclaim their alliance with Syria and Iran and their rejection of Resolution 1559, particularly with respect to disarmament. General Aoun, who has returned from fifteen years of political exile, aspires to be president of Lebanon and opposes any moves that will jeopardize his presidency.

Walid Jumblatt, the Druze leader and prominent figure during the 14 March youth demonstration for political liberty, is now fully in favour of implementing Resolution 1559. Saad Hariri, ultimately the pivotal political leader of the majority, was forced to leave Lebanon, for security reasons, from early July until 12 February 2006, when he returned to lead a public demonstration on 14 February, the first year's anniversary of the assassination.

Saad Hariri, Walid Jumblatt, Samir Geagea and their political supporters regained strength from the impressive turnout in Martyr's Square, calling for the truth about the assassination and the elimination of Syrian influence on Lebanon's political system. Over one million Lebanese from all districts converged on Martyr's Square, waving the Lebanese flag.

Political leaders of the parliamentary majority felt triumphant and turned their attention to the removal of President Lahoud as a strategic objective in the effort to rid Lebanon of Syrian influence. This determination had driven the country away from finalizing preparations for an international aid conference that was scheduled for February 2006, and later delayed because of political bickering in Lebanon.

I believe Lahoud's removal depends on there being evidence of his direct or indirect involvement in the assassination of Rafiq Hariri. The new head of the UNIIIC, the Belgian judge Serge Brammertz, has been working in total secrecy. When the US Secretary of State, Condoleeza Rice, visited Lebanon on 23 February 2006, Brammertz and a team of investigators were in Damascus. It was clear that the Syrians had decided to cooperate with the UNIIIC, as requested by Resolution 1644. President Mubarak, King Abdullah of Saudi Arabia and the Qatari Minister of Foreign Affairs, who has been acting as political broker between Syria and the United States, all urged President Bashar al-Assad to cooperate.

Rafiq Hariri was assassinated at the western periphery of the Beirut central commercial district, which he hoped to rebuild according to a coherent plan and excellent specifications. The company formed to fulfill this task – the Lebanese Company for the Development and Reconstruction of Beirut's Central District (Solidere) – was incorporated at the end of 1993. Since that date and until the end of 2004, Solidere overcame high costs for eviction and administrative obstacles to the souk's development – which is a project for finalizing gold and jewellery shopping areas as well as traditional pedestrian souks that were famous in previous years.

By 2004 Solidere seemed to have preparations well under way: sales of real estate construction rights reached $169 million, and these were supplemented by $11 million of sales in Saifi Village, which is a development completed by Solidere with narrow cobbled streets and shaded squares reminiscent of chic areas in Paris. Authorization for development of the souks was obtained in November 2004, a development that will add an upmarket mall, cinemas, a gold and jewellery market, etc, in over 160,000 square metres of built-up area. Profits or net income for 2004 stood at $54.1 million compared with $16.4 million achieved in 2003.

Much more important than these figures and data is the feeling that the reconstruction of the centre of Beirut had become a project of central importance in the region. Infrastructure works are already 90 percent completed. What remains to be completed are a few public parks and the installation of telephone booths, public benches and water fountains. The seafront area extending north of the Phoenicia Intercontinental Hotel contains the most sought-after seafront apartments in the Middle East. At the northern corner of this stretch, Beirut's Four Seasons Hotel is being completed.

Developments in the Beirut central district have attracted outstanding names in design and execution, whether Lebanese, Arab or foreign. The variety of developments is impressive and includes residential units and blocks, hotels, headquarters for contractors and designers, banks, furnished suites, training centres, a medical centre, religious prayer places, diplomatic quarters, international agencies and important government ministries and agencies.

Total possible built-up areas in the Solidere zone could reach 4.6 million square metres. Of this total, 600,000 metres are already dedicated to use by government ministries and agencies, such as the prime minister's offices, the ministry of finance, the Reconstruction and Development Board, the ministry of communications, offices of parliament members, etc.

Sales to developers so far amount to 700,000 square metres, to which must be added 150,000 square metres of developments by Solidere including the United Nations Economic and Social Commission for Western Asia (ESCWA) building and Saifi Village. Over the next four years, Solidere will build another 160,000 square metres in the souks. Of total permissible areas for construction, only 3 million square metres remain open on Solidere's books, with half this potential in landfill areas that require further treatment and compaction until the end of 2007 or mid-2008.

Existing stock of suitable construction areas, at present 1.5 million square metres (3 minus 1.5 million square metres landfill), could fetch at current prices – $1,200–1,300 per square metre of authorized above-ground construction – $1.95 billion, which exceeds the total capital of the company. Moreover, sales cannot eat up all available potential space, except over time. As was indicated in 2004, the year of the turning point of Solidere, sales for construction of 150,000 square metres amounted to $169 million, which implies an average sale price per square metre of construction rights of more than $1,100.

Enthusiasm for property ownership and development in the Solidere zone brought about significant changes in 2004. Sales, which previously could be paid for in instalments over seven years, now have to be settled in three years, which improves cash flow considerations. Loans to Solidere are now provided at lower interest rates, and the share value has practically doubled in recent months. From a low of $4.4 dollars in October 2004, the share price reached $13.5 in early October 2005 with heavy demand for it on the Kuwaiti exchange where it was recently listed. By mid-January 2006 the share price was $20, with yearly profits of $80 million anticipated.

Solidere has introduced an incentive system for payment of purchases of land by Solidere shares with an implicit increase in the estimated value of the shares by 15 percent. It is possible that out of total purchases of $169 million in 2004, half were affected according to this formula. If so, and if the price of shares holds or improves, Solidere could achieve a $20–25 million non-recurrent profit.

In spite of drastic events in Lebanon since the assassination of Hariri, the guiding spirit behind the reconstruction of the Beirut commercial centre, sales have proceeded at a brisk pace in 2005. Already by early October 2005, over 150,000 square metres have been contracted for, with a value in excess of $180 million. It is still possible to anticipate that 2005 could set a new record of interest in the Solidere zone. Hariri envisioned a rebuilt and rehabilitated centre of Beirut as his teams worked to clear the rubble following Israel's invasion of the capital in September 1982. What we see today is but a partial picture of the canvas Hariri started weaving for Lebanon by early 1983.

The prospects for Solidere as a company seem to have improved considerably in the past two years. Expectations of continuous improvement in infrastructure, facilities for enjoying a healthy life, the evolution of schools and small communities: all are factors that will contribute to higher prices for Solidere shares and an amiable and animated centre of Beirut in the decade ahead. The future development of Solidere will need great attention to parking and circulation issues, as well as finalization of treatment works in the landfill area and greening of the same. Possibly another ten years could pass before Beirut's centre is fully developed and inhabited in its various corners. Nevertheless, what has happened so far is very promising and there is no capital city in the Middle East that can compete with Beirut's charm and services.

There are works to be completed in the landfill area which relate to clearing of methane gas, compaction, extension of roads and attendant services, and eventual greening with the development of a second marina north of the one currently operating. It is tempting to assert that these improvements will be completed in three years' time, but it is much more realistic to estimate that five years are required.

Another area, which needs more attention, work and planning, is Martyrs' Square, with its open extension towards the sea. One block in this area is dedicated to the construction of the headquarters of the Lebanese Canadian Bank. Other plots can be developed without blocking the view or axis to the sea. There is a great deal of work to complete in this area, but most of the work relates to planning, with the exception of the need for completing underground parking facilities.

The centre of Beirut is evolving into coherent clusters of one predominant characteristic or another. There are commercial clusters in Foch and Allenby, and soon in the souks and the complex planned for Riad al-Solh Square. The governmental and diplomatic cluster is well defined, extending from the Serail to Parliament Square, and residential clusters have emerged in Saifi north of the centre of Beirut and are emerging in Wadi Abu Jamil to the southwest of Beirut's centre. The development of parking facilities, one or two important cultural institutions perhaps including a modern art museum, and reliable electricity and water supplies will make the centre of Beirut the unrivalled quarter in a modern city in the Middle East.

A fully operational, vibrant, interconnected and active centre of Beirut will be in evidence before 2010. Already, significant developments have been achieved, and certain delays have been overcome, and the full blooming of the centre of Beirut could be achieved before the decade ends. Some twenty-seven years will have elapsed since the conception of the project by Rafiq Hariri in 1983. La Defense took more than thirty years to achieve its own identity outside Paris, whereas Beirut's centre is regaining and improving its identity and role in a slightly shorter time.

EIGHT

Why Hariri Was Assassinated

Later on in the book we shall review the most relevant indications that will be provided in the report of Detlev Mehlis to the secretary general of the United Nations about the perpetrators of Hariri's assassination. Here, we shall deal with speculative evaluations of possible causes. It is my conviction that at least three main factors contributed to the development of the plot to eliminate Hariri. Further, it is my conviction that the perpetrators thought their act would be forgotten amid the chaos that would follow it. Heads of security affairs had become so accustomed to controlling political reactions by frightening ordinary citizens, that they assumed this is all it would take to contain reactions to Hariri's assassination. How wrong they were.

In my view, the three most credible reasons for wanting to eliminate Hariri are as follows. First, his role in changing Sunni Muslims from a passive and defeatist attitude – one that came about from supporting causes that appeared to diminish Lebanese sovereignty, such as the Palestinian fighters in Lebanon – to a pro-active role of acute political awareness and participation that would contribute to the rebirth of Lebanon; second, the re-affirmation of Lebanon's identity as a sovereign state and the securing of Arab and international support for an independent and prosperous Lebanon; and third, his personal relations with heads of state and leaders of major developmental and financial institutions all over the world, even including privileged relations with the Vatican which dedicated special efforts to devise a future path for Lebanese youth in harmony with each other, and irrespective of religious differences.

The Sunnis traditionally carried the banner of Arab nationalism. In Lebanon they represented a significant force supporting Nasserite policies until 1967, and later they advocated freedom for Palestinian fighters to attack Israel from the Lebanese borders. The first breakaway movement in the Lebanese army to favour the Palestinian resistance movement, irrespective of repercussions on Lebanon's status, was led by a Sunni officer, Ahmad al-Khatib.

In essence, by the time Palestinian fighters were evicted from Beirut to Tunis in September 1982, the two Lebanese factions that were considered pro-Palestinian were the Sunnis and the Druze. Saeb Salam, the leading Sunni politician in Lebanon, who was far more influential than the prime minister at the time, had withdrawn his support for Arafat and the PLO well before their forced departure.

Hariri had started working in Lebanon to restore infrastructure and achieve political rapprochement before 1982. It was an uphill struggle to restore Sunni credibility, but he had perseverance, as well as substantial resources provided by the Saudis to bolster up Lebanon. By 1989, when the Taef Conference was held and voted a new constitution for Lebanon, Hariri had gained sufficient recognition for the Sunni role that Lebanese parliamentarians voted constitutional changes, which transferred many of the previous powers of the Maronite president both to the council of ministers and, to a lesser degree, to the prime minister. Traditionally, until Taef, the ranking of the top political leaders was considered in the following order: president (Maronite) – first order and singular powers; president of the chamber of deputies (Shiite) – second order of political ranking; prime minister (Sunni) – third order of political ranking.

This tradition was inherited from Lebanon's Constitution, drafted in 1926. At that time, Article 95 of the Constitution stipulated that most senior political and administrative positions would be equitably apportioned. There was no specificity about the religious identity for each position. In fact, there had been a Greek Orthodox Lebanese president (Charles Debbas), and a president of the chamber of deputies who was a Sunni Muslim religious figure (Sheikh Muhammad al-Jisr).

Distribution of responsibilities by religious denominations became the practice after Lebanese independence in 1943. Christians agreed to turn away from France as the trustee of their cultural, political and economic aspirations, and Muslims implicitly agreed to abstain from calling for the integration of Lebanon into a larger Arab entity, possibly Syria, or a Greater Syria that would extend to Jordan, Iraq and Palestine.

This balance in religious political designations was maintained, although it came under critical pressure in 1958. At that time, sectarian tensions were diffused by moving to an electoral system that would give Christians and Muslims equal seats in parliament and in senior administrative positions, as opposed to a 6:5 ratio in favour of Christians that had prevailed before.

The civil war of 1975 nearly shattered all implicit agreements between religious sects. After Israel withdrew from Beirut in late summer 1982, and Bachir Gemayel was elected president, only to be assassinated three weeks later, his brother Amine Gemayel took the helm of the presidency.

In the first year of his rule, Gemayel seemed to have gathered the reins of presidential direction, but by autumn 1983 the country was divided, and in February 1984 the army was split and government was dispersed. It was certainly true that, as of that date, any major decision had to pass the test of three significant religious groups (Maronites, Sunnis and Shiites) and to secure as well Druze blessing by Walid Jumblatt. Lebanon became a collection of religious fiefdoms devoted to the exercise of political power and securing economic benefits. The country was no longer a state, and the crowning of divergences came about after Michel Aoun, as the designated prime minister by Gemayel in September 1988, waged his war first against the Syrians, and later the Lebanese forces, to cement his control politically and emotionally over what is termed Christian Lebanon.

Before the Taef Conference in 1989, Hariri had reintegrated the Sunni community within the greater Lebanese society. He exerted tremendous efforts, supported and sponsored by the Saudis, to bring about reconciliation between the Lebanese, including two conferences in Switzerland and the Tripartite Agreement in Damascus in 1985. All these efforts came to nothing. Taef was a last-ditch attempt sanctioned by the King of Saudi Arabia, King Muhammad V of Morocco and President Chadli Benjedid of Algeria.

The success of Taef in stopping the fighting and paving the way for peace confirmed the pivotal role the Sunnis would play in reconciliation, and in any future constitutional changes in running the affairs of state in Lebanon. All this was to the credit of Hariri. Ambassador Johnny Abdo, former head of army intelligence from 1976 to 1982 and a close advisor to Hariri, confirmed that Hariri wrote the text of the Taef Accord himself. It is well known that Hariri benefitted from the advice of the late Nasri Maalouf, a distinguished lawyer, jurist and linguist. Also, Hussein Husseini, speaker of the House, and George Saade, at the time head of the Phalange Christian party, contributed to the text.

Hariri had supported Makassed, the oldest and most venerable of Sunni charitable educational societies. Moreover, Hariri's team had cleared the rubble from Beirut after 1982, where a significant proportion of all Lebanese Sunnis live, and from Sidon, his home town, which is predominantly Sunni. Once he became prime minister on his birthday on 1 November 1992, Hariri had the powers and will to strengthen his sect and its role in governing Lebanon.

Formation of the first Hariri government in November 1992 was subject to strong sectarian demands. Some of these went beyond Hariri's tolerance, as he was certainly religious, but not a fanatic. Still, he designated the ministry of finance to a Sunni, as well as the ministry of justice and the ministry of telecommunications. He wanted to achieve progress on reconstruction of schools, government buildings, roads, waterworks, electricity, telecommunications, etc. He was the first Sunni nominated as prime minister to come from a humble background. All his predecessors had come from established families with a religious or political heritage. In Hariri, Lebanon had its first prime minister selected because of his contributions to peace and welfare. He enjoyed success and had drive, an open spirit and great optimism. It was his belief, until his assassination, that the Lebanese are gifted, strong and, given half a chance, loyal and nationalistic.

To abbreviate debate, Hariri expanded the role of the Board of Reconstruction and Development (BRD) and entrusted it with both planning and execution. He gave the position of head of the BRD to one of his trusted associates, an engineer with literary ambitions, Fadel Chalak, who had worked with him for a number of years in Saudi Arabia. By 1993, the Sunnis – thanks to Hariri – were involved in the affairs of state to a large degree and had acquired anew a stake in the success of Lebanon. Their role was now better defined and more important as per the new constitution.

The Sunnis in Lebanon were drawn more firmly together by Hariri and were given very serious responsibility in regaining for Lebanon its previous role and recognition. Together with this formation of the ranks, Lebanese Sunnis were sponsored and supported by the Saudi regime, which to the Sunnis represented the political core of their religion. Hajj duties were facilitated and organized under Hariri's watchful eye. For a number of years, during Ramadan (the Muslim holy month of fasting), Hariri gave *iftars* (the meals that Muslims take after prayer and sunset). These *iftars*, a Muslim habit of generosity, were never held only for Muslims. In fact, in the holy months when Hariri held these *iftars*, no less than 30,000 Lebanese would partake of food together and they were of all creeds and factions. Hariri saw Lebanon in this perspective, a country of nationals that live together in harmony and respect.

Perhaps Hariri's most overt move to fly the Sunni flag was demonstrated in the rehabilitation and enlargement of the Grand Serail, which was supposed to accommodate the offices of the prime minister and his residence.

At Taef, the accord stated that the three political leaders would have state-financed residences and offices that would be under the tutelage of each new leader. The Grand Serail has a unique position on a hill overlooking Beirut's city centre, where lie the parliament building, the ministry of finance, the ministry of telegraph and telecommunications, and the crux of the banking community in Lebanon.

Hariri added a third floor to the two that already existed, and which were built in sandstone by the ruling Ottomans around the turn of the nineteenth century. Reconstruction and rehabilitation works took five years, and the prime minister's offices are the most imposing and best quality quarters in the Lebanese Republic. These quarters are an important symbol to Sunni Muslims and were intended to be so. Today, 500 metres to the east of the Grand Serail is the new splendid mosque of Muhammad al-Amine, which was built at Hariri's expense and which now shades his grave at its northern corner.

As fate would have it, when Hariri completed the Grand Serail in summer 1998, he had etched above its entrance the religious saying: 'Had it been perpetuated to another, it would not have been in your trust.' Ironically he had to hand over his power and position by November of that year and he stayed an outcast for two years.

Hariri's network of Arab and international relations was meticulously woven. He had two constraints, which he always took into consideration on his forays beyond Lebanon. Saudi Arabia, the country from which he drew his main support, distrusted Saddam Hussein, and so did Syria. Hariri kept his distance from Saddam irrespective of attractive offers that were made by envoys of Saddam in respect of oil deliveries. They pointed out that Jordan and Syria were both benefiting from discounted prices on large deliveries. They also offered to spend 25 percent of the income from the sale of oil to Lebanon, on Lebanese goods. These offers fell on deaf ears: Hariri believed that keeping away from Saddam would save him a lot of trouble.

Contrary to his position *vis-à-vis* Saddam Hussein, Hariri made it his business to maintain strong and open relations with Hafez al-Assad, the

Syrian president, and King Fahd of Saudi Arabia. He forged a close relation with President Mubarak of Egypt; with the Ruler of Kuwait; as well as with each and every ruler of any Arab sheikhdom or state in the Gulf. In Dubai, which was developing as the centre for tax-free activities and advanced technology representation, he developed a partnership with Sheikh Muhammad bin Rashed for launching a youth-oriented television channel, and although this venture in itself did not succeed, Sheikh Muhammad sensed the great opportunity for making Dubai the multimedia centre for the Middle East. This objective is clearly being achieved in the early twenty-first century.

Hariri's international outlook was developed on the basis of a strong friendship with President Chirac of France, meaningful representation, activity and investments in the United States, close relations with the World Bank's president, and a network of personal ties with leaders as diverse as the Brazilian president, the president of Malaysia, the president of Iran and the Turkish prime minister. All these relations and ties served Hariri and Lebanon well, particularly following the tragedy of Qana in 1996, in which 109 people were killed by Israeli forces (see page 79).

The events of April 1996 have been narrated in full in Chapter Three, which deals with Hariri's first stretch as prime minister from 1992 until late 1998. Lebanon signed an agreement with the UN, the US, France, Israel and Syria, and an international supervisory commission was established to review the application of this agreement. Although Israel and Syria both signed the agreement, they were not really happy with it. Israel could no longer castigate and attack at will, and Syria was no longer the single arbiter of Lebanese affairs. Somehow, the Lebanese identity was no longer submerged.

Hariri, from the date he first became prime minister of Lebanon in November 1992, felt the need to reach out to the Christians. There had been widespread criticism of the electoral law by the majority of the Christians, particularly the Maronites.

The reasons for Christian alienation were numerous. On the one hand, the Taef Accord transferred significant political powers and duties from the president (a Maronite) to the council of ministers, which was and still is headed by a Sunni prime minister. In October 1990, General Michel Aoun, who held stubbornly to the position of prime minister in a cabinet of three, all Christian officers (including himself), was ousted from Baabda by a military operation conducted by the Lebanese army with support from the Syrians. Irrespective of the legitimacy of Aoun's claims or lack thereof, he enjoyed a surprising degree of support amongst Christians. The forced departure of Aoun was a second grievance sustained by the Christians. Taef, Aoun's removal, and a bad electoral law were sufficient reasons for the majority of Christians to boycott the elections of 1992. Later, many prominent Christian politicians declared their regret over the boycott decision.

Hariri, the Sunni Muslim who came to power with popular enthusiasm, was very close to the Saudis, who represent the religious and moral leadership for Sunni Muslims. While Lebanese Christians welcomed Hariri's nomination, they remained wary and stood on the sidelines watching the political and developmental turmoil.

In February 1994, fifteen months after Hariri came to power, Samir Geagea, leader of the Christian Lebanese forces, was held prisoner because of suspicion that he organized the blowing up of a church in Zouk, a northern suburb of Beirut. To many Christians, the accusation seemed fabricated, and eventually Geagea was tried for a different crime. He had been asked to join Hariri's cabinet but declined, although that portfolio would have given him immunity from prosecution. Geagea remained in prison for eleven years, he was held in a cell underground and secluded from visitors except his wife and a Maronite prelate.

Taken together, all these factors caused a great deal of disenchantment for the Christians, and largely because of feeling aggrieved, many Christians started protesting that public projects were concentrated in Muslim areas. A wall of resentment was building up in Hariri's face, and the man himself, although religious, was not fanatic, and realized that Lebanon could only grow if its Christians and Muslims worked together.

Patriarch Sfeir, the head of the Maronite Church, enjoyed close relations with Pope John Paul II. He was, moreover, on friendly terms with Hariri and appreciated his aid to education. Patriarch Sfeir himself devotes a lot of his time to reading and learning via the Internet. He reads and speaks six languages and enjoys open-air walks and discussions. The Patriarch, moreover, is considered by the Maronites as the authority of last resort, and the arbiter between political leaders.

Hariri sought the assistance of Patriarch Sfeir to traverse the spiritual divide with the Christians. Patriarch Sfeir advised Hariri to seek a close relation with Pope John Paul II. The Vatican had started a Synodos (study circle) for Lebanon in 1991. Catholic priests, including a select list from Lebanon, were involved in the task, which took years. The Synodos was finally held in November and December 1995 and came out with a 'Papal Instruction' that called for cooperation and love between all religious sects in Lebanon, which was described as a Holy Land.

Before that date, in 1993, and with the help of Patriarch Sfeir and the Papal envoy in Lebanon, Cardinal Pablo Puente, Prime Minister Hariri visited the Vatican to meet the Pope and ask for his support in bringing about closer relations between Christians and Muslims in Lebanon and the Middle East. It appears that Pope John Paul II listened closely to Hariri's request, for Hariri visited the Pope on numerous further occasions, both on his own and with his wife.

On 10 May 1997 Pope John Paul II visited Lebanon. On 11 May, he held an open-air mass in the centre of Beirut that was being rebuilt. The cleared area was a stretch of land near the port of Beirut, and Lebanese of all religious denominations attended this mass. In the history of Lebanon, until that date there had never been a turnout as huge and as orderly. This visit came about as a consequence of repeated requests from Hariri for the Pope to play a role in getting Christians and Muslims closer together, not only in Lebanon but in the Middle East as well, including Syria. The address of Pope John Paul II included the following words, which summarize the spirit of his papal instruction for Lebanon:

Let us pray today that God's blessing touches all those suffering in

Lebanon. Let us pray to be the source of spiritual power to you all. To the Church and the nation so that Lebanon fulfills its role in the Middle East amongst its neighbours and the world at large.

Please God put your light and love in the hearts so that reconciliation between individuals and within families matures, and between neighbours and in villages and cities and within institutions of the civil society.

Please God let your force unite all the people of this country so that they walk together with determination and courage towards peace and a life defined by mutual respect for the dignity of individuals, their liberty and prosperity for the good of this country and all its people.

This address by Pope John Paul II was given great political significance as it was really calling for Lebanese independence and peaceful recognition of Lebanon's regained status among the community of nations. Pope John Paul II had been credited with a significant contribution to the crumbling of communist regimes, and was viewed internationally as the most potent figure in the rebirth of religion in communist countries with all the consequences of that awakening. As a Pole himself, the Pope had supported Solidarity and its thrust in Poland in 1989. Because of his role in battering communist ideology he was considered, in Arab circles, as a close ally of the United States. This evaluation was mistaken but nevertheless widespread in the Arab Middle East. Here was a pro-West Pope calling literally for Lebanese independence and peaceful and neighbourly relations in the region. The Pope as well showed friendship and love for Rafiq Hariri, a Sunni Muslim who had reached out to the Pope to contribute towards closer ties between Lebanese of all creeds.

The significance of this relation was not lost on leaders in neighbouring countries. By April 1996, when Hariri had met with President Chirac, Prime Minister John Major, Chancellor Kohl and President Yelstin, as well as President Clinton indirectly, and the Pope, his stature had become awesome. Whether the bitter taste of his success was felt more in Israel or

Syria, one cannot predict, but resentment of Hariri, although undeclared, ran deep in Damascus and Tel Aviv. Hariri was taking away Lebanon from the hegemony of Syria, and to Israel he seemed to be restoring the country's credibility in important international circles.

Although Hariri had achieved a measure of Sunni solidarity, and regained for Lebanon Arab and international recognition as well as special support from the Pope, these successes in themselves would not have brought about his assassination. Each of the objectives outlined at the beginning of this chapter, and discussed above, is positive and, as such, does not represent a direct threat to powers in the region or international political targets. On the contrary, to attract an assassination plot Hariri must have elicited political fears and hatred.

It has been claimed that Hariri was behind Security Council Resolution 1559 of 2 September 2004, which calls for the disarmament of all militias in Lebanon and the withdrawal of foreign forces. There were even accusations that Marwan Hamade and Dr Ghassan Salame worked on the draft of the resolution. An attempt was made on Hamade's life on 1 October 2004, and Salame declined a ministerial nomination after Hariri's assassination because of fears for his safety in Lebanon.

President Chirac, a close friend of Hariri, was a sponsor of the resolution. Many countries' interests were impacted adversely by this resolution, and any one of these countries or political groupings touched by its ramifications could have borne a grudge against Hariri to the point of wishing to eliminate him. This type of thinking and action has been manifested in East and West in years past, as well as in more recent years in the Middle East. The motivation seems to have existed and the Mehlis report summarized in the following chapter provides a more thorough and focused picture.

NINE

The Siniora Cabinet
and the Shadow of Detlev Mehlis

The United Nations Security Council established by Resolution 1595 an Independent International Investigation Commission (UNIIIC) for exploring all evidence related to Hariri's assassination, which was classified as a terrorist act of regional and international impact. Detlev Mehlis, a German prosecutor with experience in this field, was chosen to head the UNIIIC. The official start of the commission's work was 25 June 2005, for an initial period of three months and possibly renewable for a similar period. Team investigators numbered thirty, from seventeen different countries, whereas the total number of investigators, experts, recorders, security specialists, etc reached 120.

At about the time of formation of the UNIIIC, the results of the Lebanese parliamentary elections were clear. These elections were held on time in the second half of May and the first half of June 2005. The Mikatti government composed of members who did not run for election did a good job in organizing elections that proceeded without major security incidents or overt distortion of results. International UN observers and a team from the European Union followed the elections and issued a report which gave the government a clear bill in this respect. International observers, however, noted what most Lebanese recognized: the electoral law is distorted by the administrative classifications. These, for instance, give Shiite Muslims overwhelming power to determine the success of Christian nominees in districts lying south and east of Beirut. By contrast, Sunni Muslims have this power in Beirut and northern districts.

Due to the importance of leading parties in the Shiite community, their nominees were sure to be elected. Saad Hariri, who had taken on the mantle of his father, was the undisputed Sunni leader. He chose to cooperate with Walid Jumblatt, leader of the Progressive Socialist party (PSP) and the strongest Druze chieftain, and the Qornet Shahwan grouping, a Christian group of opposition parliament members supplemented by a number of intellectuals and Christian political party chiefs, as well as partisans of the Lebanese forces.

Hizbullah and Amal swept the elections in the south and the Beqaa, whereas Hariri and Jumblatt prevailed in Beirut, Chouf, Baabda and Aley. This happened in the first two days of elections, which were to be followed by elections in Metn, Kesrouan and Byblos, and later Batroun, Koura, Zgarta, Tripoli and Accar in the north.

Previous contacts with General Michel Aoun, who had left Lebanon in October 1990 and had remained a political exile in France, paved the way for his return to Lebanon on the eve of the elections. He came back to an enthusiastic welcome and soon assumed the position of decision-maker in respect of nominees for elections in Metn, Kesrouan and Byblos. Due to the sweeping success of Hizbullah and Amal in the south and the Beqaa, and Hariri's and Jumblatt's success in Beirut, Chouf, Baabda and Aley, Aoun benefited from the sectarian voting instincts of the Christian electorate, bringing to parliament 21 candidates. He turned to the elections of the northern administrative district and there he faced failure because Sunnis responded to Saad Hariri, first and foremost, and because the Lebanese have, in elections, a self-corrective tendency that operates to limit the powers of any one group. This can only be expected in a political society that endorses elections on sectarian bases, and where political representation is often linked to favouritism.

Irrespective of disproportional importance for particular sects in certain districts, and better representation that could have been achieved with a better law, the new parliament had a number of distinctive characteristics. Parliament has 61 new members out of 128. In previous elections the change rarely touched more than 20 percent of the members, whereas in 2005 the change was in the order of 41 percent. Among the newly elected members, one can point out distinguished figures in their own professions. Moreover, youth is more important in this parliament than before. This is a change that could affect trends and policies, particularly because the largest bloc composed of seventy-two deputies is led by Saad Hariri, a thirty-five-year-old.

The strength of Hizbullah and Amal in the south and the Beqaa, and Saad Hariri and Jumblatt in Beirut and the Chouf, meant that a number of contestants for parliamentary seats were elected without contest. Uncontested winners were seventeen in number out of a total of 128 deputies. The largest proportion was in Beirut where eight nominees on Saad Hariri's list, including himself and Dr Ghazi Youssef, were uncontested. In Sidon, Bahia Hariri was not challenged, and as an expression of respect the voters endorsed her choice of Usama Saad who had been a strong critic of Rafiq Hariri and his policies. Amal and Hizbullah gained four uncontested seats in the south, whereas Jumblatt and his ally and close friend Marwan Hamade were clear winners.

Competition was stronger in other electoral districts, particularly because General Aoun chose to challenge all other Christian nominees unless chosen and designated by him. Due to this attitude, he contributed to the loss of a number of outstanding parliament members or nominees such as Nassib Lahoud, Fares Souaid and Camille Ziade.

Choice of a new prime minister follows parliamentary elections. Saad Hariri was expected by many observers to take this role, but he wisely chose to abstain as he felt he needed more experience and certainly more security. His sources and assistants warned him of murderous intentions against him, and since mid-summer 2005 he has been continuing his parliamentary duties from Paris, Jeddah and Riyadh.

Hariri's bloc proposed Fuad Siniora, the former minister of finance in successive Hariri governments, a non-parliamentarian and a leading figure in the Hariri camp. This choice was due to Siniora's intelligence, experience, hard work and patience. Most elected parliament members felt the need to honour Hariri's memory and provide a chance for serious efforts to uncover his assassins. Siniora would do his best to achieve both objectives and had sufficient experience to lead the country in difficult times.

In October 2004, before Hariri gave up on forming a government, Siniora had asked to be relieved of any ministerial duties in the incumbent government of Hariri. He was drained by the constant and meaningless friction that cripples government actions and that prevented fulfilment of the commitments made by Lebanon at the Paris II Conference in 2002. In fact, in his budget proposal for 2005, submitted in September, Siniora had proposed a far-reaching programme for administrative reform, one that would be difficult to implement in the political atmosphere prevalent at the time.

Siniora formed a well-balanced cabinet in July. He needed over three weeks to fine tune the structure and secure the president's approval for all nominees. He could have imposed his choices but he worked tirelessly to bring about a measure of understanding with the president. The cabinet that came about incorporated a member of Hizbullah, Muhammad Fneich, who was shouldered with the ministry of electricity. It is well known that a significant proportion of unpaid electricity invoices was concentrated in the southern suburbs where Hizbullah Shiite families are the predominant group of residents. Minister Muhammad Fneich was thus given two difficult tasks: to smooth operations of EDL (Electricité du Liban) with improved efficiency and clear contracts for fuel supplies and maintenance contracts, and to improve the settlement of electricity bills. On all his visits to secure negotiations, whether in Syria, Kuwait or Qatar, the minister's integrity created a good impression. Yet there is still a lot of hard work ahead of him. To further placate and involve Hizbullah in actual governing, Siniora allotted the ministry of labour to a Shiite university professor close to Hizbullah, Dr Tarad Hamade. American officials who protested against the post for Fneich, who is a member of Hizbullah, established a rapport with Hamade who visited Washington after becoming minister.

For key positions in the ministries of finance and economics, Siniora brought in clean-slated figures each of whom was well known to him. Dr Jihad Azour had worked with Siniora in the ministry of finance for four years, on loan from UN agencies. Although Azour had been brought in by George Corm, the former minister of finance and a harsh critic of Hariri, Siniora appreciated Azour's way of thinking, training and clear actions. The second choice by Siniora was that of Dr Sami Haddad who was heading the International Finance Corporation's[1] programme in Egypt. Haddad, with his knowledge of the Middle East and respected stature within the IFC, could provide a reliable and interactive link with the IFC and the World Bank.

To soothe the president, who had come under heavy criticism about the efforts of security agencies to uncover Hariri's assassins, Siniora chose to leave the president to decide on the minister of justice, who had to be a reliable figure that could coordinate efforts between the UNIIIC and the Lebanese judiciary. Choice settled on Charles Rizk, an erudite Maronite who had experience with government work as director general of the ministry of information, and as chairman of Lebanese Television up to the early 1980s when it enjoyed a monopoly. Rizk, a close friend of President Lahoud, enjoyed credibility with the Maronite Patriarch and Siniora and was, therefore, nominated minister of justice. He has worked well with Detlev Mehlis and foresaw the evolution of work of the UNIIIC.

The president's two other nominees were his son-in-law Elias Murr, as minister of defence, and the mayor of Beirut, engineer Yacoub Sarraf. Elias Murr was nearly killed on 12 July 2005 by a car bomb planted near his house in a residential area north of Beirut. During his treatment in Switzerland for wounds sustained in this attack, Murr accused the former

---

1. The International Finance Corporation is the World Bank agency for private sector participations in developing countries.

head of the Syrian intelligence services in Lebanon, Rustum Gazale, of the attempt on his life. Sarraf, who had been the mayor of Beirut since 1998, appointed by the al-Hoss government, had thwarted Hariri's attempts to develop the commercial centre of Beirut. As minister of environment, he had to resign his position as mayor, and already public advertisements have been placed for this position.

The cabinet as it was formed had representatives from all major political parties except the bloc of General Aoun, who claims repeatedly that his bloc is the only true representative of the majority of Christians. Irrespective of this omission, the cabinet received strong support at its traditional summary programme, submitted to parliament for a vote of confidence, and achieved this result with a significant majority.

Siniora's new government stressed the following objectives: the unravelling of Hariri's murder and punishment of the perpetrators, organizers and executors irrespective of their nationalities and positions (this objective also required open cooperation between Lebanese judicial and police authorities with the UNIIIC, and constant cooperation with UN authorities and friendly governments). The cabinet undertook to apply the terms of the Taef Accord, which would define relations between the three branches of government and, particularly, between the president and prime minister, which were skewed in favour of the former by Syrian hegemony as of 1991. Reduction of budgetary deficits was stressed as an objective, together with efforts to gradually reduce public debt. It is important to note that, in this respect, the government stressed administrative reforms, privatization and securitization as avenues for achieving better government administration and reducing public debt.

As to the political issues raised by UN Security Council Resolution 1559, the cabinet chose to stress that it would apply the Taef Accord. This refers clearly to these issues and will commence a process of debate and negotiations to achieve the desired results. This part of the cabinet's programme seemed couched in wishful thinking, although clearly public opinion favoured immediate disarmament of the Palestinian groups at least.

Finally, the cabinet emphasized its intention to maintain the best relations possible with all Arab countries, and particularly with Syria, for a number of obvious reasons. In addition, the cabinet pronounced its intention to maintain good relations with the international community of nations and international, regional and specialized organizations.

The statements and stated objectives seemed too broad and in certain respects unachievable, at least in the near future. Syria had faced unprecedented international pressure and it had to give in to total withdrawal from Lebanon of its army and intelligence forces. As I have already mentioned, Minister Kassar conveyed to Undersecretary Satterfield at the dinner held on 28 February 2005 that Syria would close its borders to commercial traffic and transit passage from Lebanon. This initiative came about just a few days before Siniora's cabinet received its comfortable vote of confidence. Hundreds of trucks carrying perishable and non-perishable products were stranded on the Lebanese-Syrian border. Syrian authorities claimed they were concerned about trucks that could carry explosives and explosive devices, and that they were implementing new security measures on their borders.

These trucks and their drivers were of different Arab nationalities, causing problems for Lebanese, Syrian, Jordanian, Saudi and Iraqi drivers. Transit operators faced losses, and Lebanese agricultural exports on the trucks perished, whereas other agricultural produce for export rotted on the ground in the Beqaa. This crisis continued for nearly three weeks, at which time Prime Minister Siniora visited Damascus to meet with his counterpart and request an end to the crisis. Three days after Siniora's visit, the crisis was resolved, probably due to the fact that the Americans had started delaying Syrian trucks and trade with Iraq, just as Undersecretary Satterfield had predicted.

Internally, Siniora emphasized constitutional terms by insisting on holding weekly meetings of the council of ministers, alternating the venue between the Grand Serail, the base of the prime minister's offices, and the Presidential Palace. The role of the president was no longer that of the final decision-maker – he could no longer, as he had previously with Syrian support, secure a two-thirds majority vote in the council of ministers in favour of his decisions on disputes with the prime minister. Before the end of July 2005, Siniora had established rules of engagement, something Hariri had never been able to achieve due to Syria's overt support of Lahoud.

By August 2005 Siniora started to acquire the image of not only a senior politician but of a statesman. In previous years, he had assumed the difficult and unpopular role of a thrifty and tough minister of finance. He succeeded in raising government revenues from 18 percent of GDP to 24 percent, and introduced significant improvements in customs clearance and collection procedures, recording of real estate transactions, and preparation and implementation of VAT. His capability and dedication were never in doubt but his public persona was always a matter of debate. For Siniora, responsibility and authority offered challenges that enabled him to broaden his role in securing national objectives and, in the process, secure national support.

On 25 August 2005 Detlev Mehlis submitted his first summary report to the minister of justice, who in turn forwarded it to the new attorney general in Lebanon, Said Mirza, and the investigating judge in the Hariri affair, Elias Eid. Mehlis suggested detention-on-suspicion of all four heads of the security services in Lebanon. On 30 August Jamil al-Sayyed, the former head of internal security, Raymond Azar, the former head of army intelligence, Ali al-Hajj, the former head of internal security forces, and Mustafa Hamdan, the former head of the Presidential Guard, were all picked up from their residences by Lebanese security forces, together with available evidence, and taken to prison. The impossible had finally happened. The persecutors and dominant security lords were imprisoned like ordinary citizens and their bank accounts and assets were frozen (in the case of Jamil al-Sayyed, it seems he kept petty cash at home in the order of $700,000).

By early August, when the Syrian borders had reopened to commercial traffic, Siniora turned his attention to other immediate problems. He realized that Lebanon's situation had worsened since Paris II, and that a level of aid that had seemed adequate then would no longer suffice. He had one particular immediate problem, that of electricity generation and fuel costs. An agreement signed with Syria for deliveries of natural gas by pipeline to a 450-megawatt gas oil or natural gas powered station in the north of Lebanon was suspended by the Syrians. The Lebanese had paid $34 million for construction of a pipeline from Syrian delivery points to the Lebanese power station. Calibration equipment for measuring gas quantities were installed, but the Syrians did not want to deliver the natural gas quantities that had been contracted for. Fulfilment of this contract could contribute a saving of $130 million per year for the Lebanese, in addition to environmental benefits resulting from burning low sulphur natural gas as opposed to medium sulphur gas oil.

Minister Fneich visited Syria and hoped that, due to his political affiliation with Hizbullah, which continued to support Syria, he would set the agreement into motion. He returned empty-handed, and visited Kuwait to secure deliveries of government-to-government gas oil to substitute for the natural gas that was not coming. Contracts with Kuwait brought about, on account of prices and credit terms for 270 days, savings in the order of $55 million instead of the $130 million achievable with gas deliveries.

It was clear from the first efforts of the prime minister and the minister of electricity that the whole question of energy supplies represented the main challenge for Lebanon. Total consumption is in the order of 5.3 million tons, which by 2005 prices could cost anywhere between $2.8 and $3.2 billion. Simply put, the energy issue has to find a solution, and the government is looking at different possibilities. This issue will certainly figure in the international aid conference that was called for on 19 September in New York by Secretary of State Condoleezza Rice, and which is expected to happen in the not-too-distant future.

Imprisonment of the security chiefs inevitably raised questions. There were protestations that this action was not yet justified. Many commentators without a professional background or credibility accused Mehlis of being inept, or of being an American agent or a politicized figure. The Lebanese president's position was seriously weakened, as the heads of security services were his protective shield against criticism or deteriorating relations with Syria. Still, he went on record to praise the officers detained and to ask for comfortable circumstances for their detention, and he went so far as to declare that Mustafa Hamdan, the head of the Presidential Guard, was one of the most honest officers in the Lebanese army and that he had saved Lahoud's life in 1983.

Calls for the resignation of the president increased in intensity, as Hizbullah and Syrian supporters increased their criticisms of Resolution 1559 and levelled indiscriminate criticism against Mehlis. The allegations against Mehlis became all the more vicious as he sought to interview a number of Syrian officials. He had addressed requests to this end in June, and met with stone-walling tactics, as his letters took a month to be answered. On 26 August 2005 Commissioner Mehlis finally met with a representative of the Syrian ministry of foreign affairs in Geneva.

Finally, between 20–23 September, interviews were conducted at the Monte Rozza resort in Syria, which is situated ten kilometres from the Lebanese border. All interviews were conducted in the presence of representatives of the Syrian ministry of foreign affairs, with translators and re-orders of proceedings as well as a video recording. In the end, and as the Mehlis report of 25 October to the UN states on page 10, 'It was apparent that the interviewees had given uniform answers to questions. Many of those answers were contradicted by the weight of evidence collected by the UNIIIC from a variety of other sources.' The report continued to say, 'if the investigation is to be completed, it is essential that the government of Syria fully cooperate with the investigating authorities, including allowing for interviews to be held outside Syria and for interviewees not to be accompanied by Syrian officials.'

This last sentence in the Mehlis report to the UN authorities, together with other incriminating evidence, including the bank accounts of Syrian officials who played an important role in Lebanon, like Ghazi Kanaan, Rustum Gazale and his assistant Jameh Jameh, persuaded all Security Council members to unanimously endorse Resolution 1636. The resolution was passed on 1 November 2005 (which would have been Hariri's sixty-first birthday), and asked Syria to fully cooperate with the UNIIIC or risk further retaliatory measures by the international community.

Before the date of UN Security Council Resolution 1636, a momentous event occurred in Syria. On 12 October, as President Bashar al-Assad was conducting an interview with CNN to try to prove that Syria had nothing to hide, Ghazi Kanaan – the tsar who ruled Lebanon with an iron hand for twenty years from 1982 – committed suicide in his office where he presided as Syria's minister of the interior, according to an official Syrian announcement.

Kanaan, on the morning of his alleged suicide, conducted a rare interview at his request with a well-known Lebanese talk radio personality, Warde. He stressed the constructive role of Syria in re-establishing peace in Lebanon after Taef, and admitted that Syrian officers had received benefits in Lebanon through corruption. He ended his interview by saying, 'probably this is the last interview or public announcement I will ever make.'

There is little doubt that Kanaan's apparent suicide can be related to events in Lebanon, particularly the assassination of Hariri. It is well known that Kanaan was opposed to the extension of the term of President Lahoud, which was imposed by Bashar al-Assad in spite of Resolution 1559. Moreover, Kanaan openly ridiculed the Syrian press, which is totally government-controlled. His family claimed that he was liquidated to eliminate opposition to the regime's policies. Yet no matter what, the death of Kanaan pushed the Syrian regime towards further concessions to international pressures.

Siniora kept his course in spite of these tumultuous developments. He even ventured the opinion that it was best for President Lahoud to resign, but he added that this was a constitutional issue. He succeeded in maintaining cabinet solidarity, and the official Lebanese line remains: full support for the UNIIIC and its work, which has been extended at the request of Mehlis until 15 December 2005, when six months would have elapsed since the start of its work.

In September, at the time of the opening of the United Nations sessions, Siniora attended a conference called for by Condoleezza Rice to pledge aid to Lebanon. This conference was held on 19 September when President Lahoud was at the UN, but he was not invited to attend. Siniora was charged with the task of preparing a programme for the salvation of the Lebanese economy. The US, Britain, France, Russia, China, Japan, Saudi Arabia, Egypt, the European Union and the World Bank expressed strong interest in providing aid.

Since early September Siniora has been working with a core of his ministers on developing a programme that incorporates corrective measures in respect of the National Social Security Fund, social safety nets, energy requirements, budgetary improvements, administrative reforms, privatization moves, securitization possibilities, energizing and organizing the financial market, drafting legislation for encouraging investments and various other structural steps. There is no doubt that the task is immense, and it was agreed during the visit to Lebanon by the US Deputy Assistant Secretary of State for Near Eastern Affairs, Elizabeth Dibble, on 8 and 9 November that the proposed conference would be held in early February 2006. Siniora affirmed that the programme for action and financial support would be drafted by Lebanese in Lebanon. It is to be hoped that a positive response can be solicited from the international community. It might seem to observers that Siniora's task in Lebanon, to secure endorsement of a multifaceted reform programme, might be more difficult and challenging than securing aid. This might well be true.

At the time of writing, at least two months before the international conference, it is impossible to provide a detailed outline of what will be presented. But it is not too difficult to guess what could be requested. We can start with two important statistical indicators with which to project a meaningful perspective. Total cumulative public debt at the end of 2005 will probably amount to the equivalent of $38 billion, 53 percent in foreign currencies and 47 percent in Lebanese pounds. Interest payments are likely to hover around $3.3 billion a year until the principal of the debt is reduced. In order to make any impact, progress has to be at a rate of growth of 5–6 percent a year. It is possible that the GNP will have contracted by 2 percent in 2005 due to the ramifications of Hariri's murder. The desired rate of growth is not impossible, and was achieved in 2004 to a large extent because of trailing benefits from the Paris II Conference. Assuming debt repayment is evenly spread over twenty years, settlements by Lebanon have to start in 2006 at the rate of 1.8 (principal) + 3.3 billion (interest), or $5.2 billion a year. This outcome cannot be achieved unless Lebanon secures long-term loans for low-interest rates of $10 billion and $2 billion in donations, whether in cash or kind (oil products, for example). If this should come to pass, then public debt will be reduced to $36 billion by the end of 2006 and interest payments will fall to less than $3 billion. Privatization could yield $2 billion a year in 2007 and 2008, which would reduce debt to $32 billion, and with 5 percent growth a year, the GNP might reach $26–27 billion, and the ratio of total debt to GNP would fall to around 120 percent – a tolerable level that allows growth.

The inflow of transfers and investment will either be complementary factors that facilitate success, or contribute to failure. If Lebanon achieves a volume of transfers of $5 billion a year and an inflow of direct investments of $1.5 billion a year, the desired results will materialize. It should be noted that, as has been mentioned previously, these figures were $4.5 billion and $1 billion in 2004. The required improvement is not impossible to achieve. Provided there is political harmony internally – that is, within the tolerable limits of 'normal' political bickering – and the financial market is activated properly, the desired results are within reach for Lebanon.

It is useful to provide an example of what a developed financial market can contribute to Lebanon. Investcom, a telecommunications enterprise developed by two Lebanese, Taha Mikatti and his brother Najib (who was prime minister during the period of the 2005 parliamentary elections in Lebanon), developed its services and partnerships to cover 1.8 million cellular subscribers in twenty-three countries, including Egypt, Cyprus, Syria and Algeria. After years of hard work, they wished to market 25 percent of the shares of Investcom. Tasteful advertisements on CNN briefly told the story of the company, and its value was estimated to range between $2.4 and $3 billion.

The Mikattis wanted a liquid environment with an active financial market and no taxation on foreign earnings. They chose to launch their offer out of Dubai, where Investcom was registered. The demand for 25 percent of the shares at the higher bracket of the quotation was ten times the $750 valuation. Investors with deposits in Lebanon alone pledged $5 billion for purchases.

Assuming Lebanon creates the tax and regulation requirements necessary for an active financial market, it is possible to project a listing of a number of Lebanese high-tech and trading enterprises with a market value over $20 billion. There are at least four enterprises, two high-tech and two trading with international networks, which are Lebanese owned, in which the volume of sales exceeds $500 million a year, and in one instance reaches $5 billion. With total yearly sales of $8 billion, these four enterprises account for the equivalent of 35–37 percent of Lebanon's GNP.

With wisdom, tax incentives, easy procedures and tax stability, and clear and fast legal proceedings, these companies and others could be attracted to the Lebanese scene. In this context, it is perhaps useful to recall what happened in respect of Solidere shares. A year ago, at $4.5 per share, the total shareholding of Solidere was worth $720 million. At $13.4 on 10 November 2005, Solidere shares in total had a value of $2.3 billion. In one year, the value of these shares had increased by $1.5 billion essentially because the stock was listed on highly liquid markets in Kuwait and London. By January 2006 Solidere shares were at $20.

An active, well-organized Lebanese financial market could attract Lebanese-controlled companies with a market value exceeding $30 billion. Such a market could be tied up with advanced and active markets in the Gulf, Western Europe, North America, Australia and South America. Activity generated could be in the order of $4 billion a year – and Siniora's government aims to achieve this result.

Prime Minister Siniora, Condoleezza Rice and Elizabeth Dibble repeatedly confirmed that the proposed international conference for aid to Lebanon does not attach any political preconditions, particularly the requirements of UN Security Council Resolution 1559, in respect of Palestinian armed presence in Lebanon or the military arm of Hizbullah. By contrast, the success of the conference will hinge on the programme for reform adopted by the Lebanese, and concrete measures must be decided upon in respect of the electricity sector, the National Social Security Fund and a number of private organizations that came under public control, such as Middle East Airlines, as well as budgetary deficits.

By contrast, the Lebanese government is expected to show reform initiatives in respect of certain political issues. Already, Prime Minister Siniora has started initiatives on two fronts.

International observers of parliamentary elections held last May and June in Lebanon did not observe any foul play in the process. They felt and reported that procedures and practices allowed all Lebanese of voting age to exercise their free will. Moreover, no recorded attempts at tampering with results were confirmed. Still, the observers echoed the Lebanese public's concerns about the electoral law and the distribution of electoral districts that seemed to skew the results. International observers recommended a revision of the electoral law.

One of the first decisions made by the Siniora cabinet was the formation of a committee composed of eminent jurists for reviewing all proposals and to initiate a project that serves to bring about election results that better reflect individual choices. The committee that has been given this task is headed by Fouad Boutros, a distinguished jurist, former judge and long-serving minister of foreign affairs. It is expected that in early 2006 this committee will present a draft law for elections, with full explanation for this choice. After that, it will be the responsibility of parliament to study the draft proposal, possibly introduce certain adjustments, and finally approve and vote a new law.

The second initiative taken by the Siniora government which meets international requirements was advertising in the Lebanese and international press to attract applicants for senior positions in government agencies. A committee of independent experts was formed to review applications and provide recommendations by assessing abilities and past records rather than sectarian or political affiliations. Positions were advertised for mayor of Beirut, secretary of the Higher Council for Privatization and chairmanship and board memberships of the Beirut financial market, and there remain many other functions to fill. It is not yet possible to judge the success of this initiative, and certain boards await further legislation, but progress is certainly being made. There are many sceptics who believe that serious changes are not to be expected, but the prime minister and most of his cabinet members are in favour of this process.

The third initiative is multifaceted. It includes the issue of legislation allowing the free establishment of political parties and/or social and educational societies; notification to the ministry of the interior is sufficient. This move broadens the scope of political liberty. Also, economic legislation intended to facilitate the start-up of companies and organization of the Beirut financial market was completed.

Expectations of economic and political progress could have been better if relations with Syria had proceeded on a rational and civilized basis. The Syrian leadership, however, has been very bitter at having to abandon Lebanon. This is apparent from recent events. For example, before the end of October 2005, Palestinian fighters in the Palestinian Front for the Liberation of Palestine – General Command (PFLP–GC), led by Ahmad Jibril – who was an officer in the Syrian army – started staging military manoeuvres beyond Palestinian camps. This action released many frightful ghosts from the days of Palestinian–Lebanese fighting in 1975–6.

Representatives of the Palestine Authority and the Palestine Liberation Organization, including Abu Mazen, worked hard to avert any clashes in Lebanon. Moreover, they declared that Palestinians in Lebanon must abide by Lebanese law. By contrast, Prime Minister Siniora, while refusing to accept the proliferation of armed Palestinians outside the camps, has called for improvements of social, educational and work conditions for the Palestinians and the restriction of arms within the camps. Attempts by the Lebanese government to negotiate with various Palestinian groups are not yet bearing fruit. The PFLP–GC's leaders do not wish to abide by the commitments of other Palestinian factions because they are so instructed by Syria.

That the Syrian leadership does not wish Lebanon well has been made clear from the breaking of an agreement to supply natural gas to Lebanon after all technical works were completed in Syria and Lebanon. Imposition of the blockade on commercial traffic in July and early August, until Syria faced similar treatment on the Iraqi border, was another clear example. Finally, Bashar al-Assad spelled out his bitterness against the Sunni Lebanese leadership and the Lebanese media.

According to al-Assad, the Lebanese prime minister and the leader of the largest parliamentary bloc are no more than agents of the great powers that have been developing plots for control of Syria. All Lebanese journalists were assumed to be agents of Saad Hariri. The Syrian president asserted: 'Every article has its price; every television interview has its price...' He was certainly reflecting his experience in Syria where 90 percent of the press and television is state-controlled and run by Ba'athist employees. The 10 percent that is private is essentially controlled and owned by sons of leading Syrian officers or relatives of the Syrian president.

President al-Assad has confirmed that Syria is ready to cooperate with the international community in respect of the application of UN Security Council Resolution 1636, which calls on Syria in strict terms to fully cooperate with the UNIIIC, headed by Detlev Mehlis. Al-Assad said that Syria has invited Mehlis to visit Damascus, and that he was invited to do so by a newly appointed Syrian judge to head a Syrian commission for investigating Hariri's assassination. Al-Assad is overlooking Mehlis's reservations, expressed after his earlier visit in September. Syrian interviewees were accompanied by numerous observers fulfilling apparently routine functions such as secretarial, interpretation or security duties. Mehlis rejected this method of indirect pressure on

Syrian witnesses, and has again been invited by the Syrian president to play the role of a buffoon.

Syria is not showing signs of realizing fundamental changes in the manner of cooperation between nations. Feeling threatened by further punitive international sanctions if Syria does not fulfill the requirements of Security Council Resolution 1636, the Syrian deputy prime minister for economic affairs declared that 'Syria has self-sufficiency in oil and gas and food. It can, therefore, face the consequences of economic sanctions without fear of major losses.' By contrast with this self-assurance, President al-Assad indicated that he abstained from accepting an invitation to attend a European Union meeting in Barcelona in November because the European Union, although it has initialled a cooperation agreement with Syria, has not moved to the final stage of signing a working agreement.

We might ask what the Syrian position is – an isolationist and proud singularity, or a close affinity with the international community. What appears to be clear is that Syria has not made up its mind. The leadership on both regional and international levels claims openness and readiness for cooperation. Yet for the public, brainwashed over decades, Syria's leadership is not ready to admit that these two faces are irreconcilable, and that internationalization and globalization are now overwhelming features of tomorrow's world.

TEN

Findings of the Security Council International Independent Investigation Commission (UNIIIC)

The United Nations Security Council adopted two specific resolutions relating to the assassination of Rafiq Hariri and twenty-two other persons on 14 February 2005.

The Security Council's Resolution 1595 was put into effect on 16 June 2005, and it formed the UNIIIC under the direction of Commissioner Detlev Mehlis, a fifty-seven-year-old German judge. This commission came about as a consequence of recommendations made by a fact-finding mission headed by Patrick Fitzgerald, a deputy commissioner in the Irish police force, who was dispatched to Lebanon in March 2005. After one month of searching for facts, interviewing security chiefs and reviewing the procedures followed and the reports finalized by Lebanese agencies, the Fitzgerald team concluded (as previously mentioned) that Lebanese security agencies were negligent in carrying out a thorough investigation. Moreover, according to Fitzgerald, they did not enjoy public credibility. Accordingly, the creation of an international investigation team was recommended. The Security Council endorsed this recommendation, and Mehlis was asked to lead a 120-person team of experts, and given an initial timeframe of three months, to be renewable for a similar period if necessary.

On 25 October 2005 Mehlis submitted his report. In the meantime all heads of security organizations in Lebanon had been detained because of strong indications of criminal intent, complicity and action. Mehlis indicated that he had benefitted from the work of the Fitzgerald team, and from initiatives by Lebanese authorities, who were freer and more energetic after the withdrawal of Syrian military and intelligence personnel from Lebanon on 26 April 2005. One of Mehlis's important conclusions – that the detonation charge was 1,000 kilograms of high-density TNT and that it was loaded on a small Mitsubishi truck and detonated above ground – is based on findings of a team of Swiss experts invited to help by Lebanese authorities.

Mehlis requested an extension of the term of his commission for three months near the end of August 2005, when he submitted an executive summary report to Secretary General Kofi Annan. Mehlis needed more time to interview witnesses, collect additional evidence and interview Syrian security officials, particularly a number of leading figures who exercised responsibility in Lebanon or over Lebanese affairs from Syria. The first request to interview Syrian witnesses was sent on 11 June, and an evasive answer was only received by mid-July. Another written request was forwarded on 17 July, to be answered on 25 August without a clear commitment. Finally the Syrians, feeling strong international pressure, sent Dr Riad Daoudi, a legal advisor on international law, to meet with Commissioner Mehlis on 9 September in Geneva. This meeting took place fifteen days after Mehlis had submitted his executive summary report in which he protested against Syrian tactical delays.

The dates for interviews were set for 20–23 September in Syria, and were conducted at the isolated Monte Rozza Hotel resort, which is located ten kilometres from the Lebanese border. Those interviewed included the Syrian minister of foreign affairs, Dr Farouk al-Sharaa, and the deputy minister of foreign affairs, Dr Walid Mouallem (also a former ambassador to the US and envoy to Lebanon) who was entrusted in January and early February 2005 to work on smoothing relations with Rafiq Hariri and President Lahoud in Lebanon. Other interviewees included Ghazi Kanaan, head of the Syrian security operations in Lebanon from 1982 until 2002; his assistant Rustum Gazale, who took over his responsibilities in 2002; and Jameh Jameh, assistant to Gazale.

According to Mehlis's evaluation, the Syrians interviewed seemed to have rehearsed their sessions in order to maintain a coherent image and, in certain cases, submitted written testimony that aimed to divert from the truth, as evidenced by other convergent and more independent testimony. In the case of Mouallem, his written statement contradicted a recorded interview with Hariri in early February in Beirut.

In addition to these flaws, Mehlis considered the presence of a number of Syrian government observers in witness sessions as representing undue indirect pressure on the liberty of each interviewee. Consequently, the UN commissioner stressed that Syrian witnesses had to be interviewed individually, possibly only with legal counsel, and outside Syria. As these requests went unheeded, on 1 November 2005 the UN Security Council unanimously endorsed Resolution 1636, which obliges Syria to cooperate with Commissioner Mehlis on his terms. Otherwise, the Security Council would endorse sanctions against Syria, possibly even including the use of force.

The date for submission of Mehlis's second report was set for 15 December 2005, six months from the date of start up. In case Syria proved non-cooperative, it was understood that sanctions would be adopted. Arab as well as Western and Eastern (Russian and Chinese) pressure mounted on Syria.

In typical Syrian style, and as proof that Syria, with really a one-party system, had fallen behind emerging international attitudes, President Bashar al-Assad delivered a defiant speech on 10 November 2005. It stressed Syria's readiness to challenge the major powers, and denounced the Lebanese prime minister as well as Saad Hariri, the leader of the majority parliamentary bloc in Lebanon. Al-Assad, however, did not go overboard in respect of the international community. He said at the end of his speech that Syria respects international organizations and would cooperate in unravelling Hariri's murder. As proof, he cited Syria's nomination of its own investigation committee into Hariri's murder. The judge nominated to head this commission, albeit nine months after the murder and seven months after Syrian withdrawal from Lebanon, had invited Mehlis to visit Damascus for consultations, but Mehlis declined to accept the invitation.

On 24 November 2005, at the Meridian Hotel, Mouallem and Riad Daoudi told members of the national and international press that an agreement had been reached with Mehlis, guaranteed verbally by a member of the Security Council, with veto powers to interview Syrian witnesses in Vienna. All Syrian officials would return to Damascus. It was expected that five witnesses would be interviewed shortly afterwards. However, both officials neglected to mention any undertaking to dispatch any other witnesses requested by Mehlis in the future.

The delaying tactics of the Syrian regime, which left the decision to cooperate until the last acceptable moment, as well as Syrian press accusations against Mehlis and his 25 October report, plus attacks against the Lebanese government, were best understood by Mehlis himself. Mehlis had investigated the bombing of the La Belle nightclub in Berlin, which took place in August 1986, killing a Turkish citizen and two American servicemen and wounding 230 others. Over ten years, he worked meticulously to establish the responsibility of the Libyan perpetrators of the attack, and of the Libyan regime. To achieve his results, he studied the psychology of senior officers of dictatorial regimes. When Secretary General Annan chose Mehlis to manage the UNIIIC work for clearing the murder of Rafiq Hariri and twenty-two others, he took into consideration this aspect of Mehlis's experience.

Uncovering the perpetrators and executors of the La Belle bomb attack required more than savvy about the psychology of servants of totalitarian states. Mehlis utilized the evolving technology of monitoring telephone communications to establish dialogue and commands between the Libyan embassy in East Germany and the perpetrators of the crime. Moreover, he listened to and reviewed all monitored communications between the Libyan embassy in East Germany and Tripoli, the capital of Libya. Mehlis's findings sent three conspirators, along with the German wife of one of them, to prison for lengthy terms.

It is well-known that the Syrian intelligence services were organized, trained and indoctrinated by the Stasi, the former East German intelligence agency. Methods of interrogation, infiltration, disinformation and brutal extraction of confessions were meticulously hammered into the minds of Syrian intelligence officials by senior Stasi agents. In fact, it was a matter of pride for Syrian intelligence officers to stress that they had been trained in East Germany. In this respect, Mehlis had an advantage, as on a previous assignment he had had the opportunity to study the intelligence files of the feared and effective Stasi. Accordingly, he had an understanding of Stasi methods, and it is not impossible that he knew the background of many Syrian intelligence officials and their training. For this reason, in his search to uncover the truth about Hariri's murder, he concentrated on communications, lines of authority, use of funds and methods of interrogating civilians.

Work by the UNIIIC was far more extensive than the preparatory work of the Fitzgerald team. This was only to be expected: the means made available to the UNIIIC were substantial, and the team members came from seventeen countries to provide rich and varied experience, as well as to distance themselves from any possible accusations of prejudice. Still, the most important factor of all was represented by an improved political and security atmosphere in Lebanon after the withdrawal of Syrian military and intelligence personnel on 26 April 2005.

Before the date of the withdrawal, and during a period in which imprisoned heads of intelligence services in Lebanon were still in control, tampering with evidence took place as well as negligence of proper procedures and objective reporting. Moving the vehicles of Hariri's bombed motorcade by midnight of 14 February 2005, less than twelve hours after the explosion was, to say the least, a suspect decision. Ali al-Hajj, the former head of the Internal Security Forces (ISF), supervised the transfer of the vehicles to an internal security barracks in Beirut. He was told to do so by Mustafa Hamdan, who headed the Presidential Guard troops and who had no authority over al-Hajj, except for his close contacts with the Lebanese president. Reports on the facts and findings of the crime scene were incomplete and misleading. Ashraf Rifi, who replaced al-Hajj, finalized a highly critical review of the reports and acts of senior internal security officers who supervised the crime scene.

According to the second report of the UNIIIC submitted on 12 December 2005, al-Hajj – already incarcerated – had tried to hide evidence. In paragraph 54 of the second UNIIIC report it states that investigators 'discovered several electronic media, including removable data tapes, stored in a safe. A preliminary examination of these electronic files and accompanying documentation revealed that they comprised classified intelligence reports on a wide variety of topics which were obtained by General al-Hajj from the ISF and illegally kept by him'.

In spite of tampering with evidence, distorted reporting, diversionary tactics and stonewalling by Syrian officials, Mehlis was able to build a case that provided sufficient evidence to convince the newly appointed attorney general, Said Mirza, and the investigating judge, Elias Eid, to issue warrants for the arrest of heads of Lebanese security agencies on 30 August 2005.

Lebanese, British and French divers helped retrieve shards of the blown-up truck, which had been loaded with TNT. The serial number of the truck was identified, and witnesses and satellite shots proved it was parked at a quasi-military camp outside Damascus in September 2004. The Abu Adass fable, which included a televised confession on al-Jazeera by Abu Adass, presumably an Islamist political martyr, was shown to be fabricated. Abu Adass has not been heard from since. He is presumed dead in the Mehlis report. What was proven is that on 14 February, a contact by telephone was established with the correspondent of al-Jazeera Television to tell him that the videocassette of the film could be found on a tree branch near the ESCWA building in downtown Beirut (al-Jazeera is located in an office in the block adjacent to the ESCWA building and, therefore, the cassette could be retrieved within minutes). Former senior Lebanese security officer Jamil al-Sayyed asked for the original cassette immediately after it went on the air.

Five hundred witnesses provided testimony in the investigation into Hariri's murder, probably due to the integrity and independence of newly appointed judges and senior security personnel, although some preferred to maintain anonymity. In paragraph 14 of the second UNIIC report it states that: 'Between 7 October and 10 December, fifty-two witness statements, sixty-nine investigators' notes and eight suspect statements were issued. Three searches were conducted and seven exhibits were obtained. A total of 37,000 pages of documents have been entered into the case file.' The additional witness statements included those of the five senior Syrian officers interviewed in Vienna between 5 and 7 December, according to the standards of the UNIIIC and Lebanese legal procedures for interrogations. Also, President Lahoud had been interviewed twice, once for a period of six hours.

Convergence of witness statements showed written and oral statements by Syrian officials concerning Syrian relations with Hariri to be false. Implied threats were recorded in the interview between Hariri and Mouallem, and outright threats of sabotage and street demonstrations against Hariri were echoed in recordings of Rustum Gazale, along with a number of senior Lebanese politicians and minor leaders. Only one such recording has been printed in detail in the 25 October report, but many others can be provided. The UNIIIC had photographs of the truck used in Hariri's assassination which linked it to a camp outside Damascus, and had in their possession recordings of Gazale and others wishing the elimination of Hariri, or, in the case of Mouallem, his subjugation. Surveillance cameras of the HSBC Bank established the slow progress of the truck just one minute and fifty-seven seconds ahead of Hariri's convoy. All indications suggest a well-organized and thought-out plan. The negligence of senior Lebanese security officers in conducting the investigation, their deliberate acts to tamper with the evidence and their untruthful statements were all factors in the decision to detain them. Moreover, they were all subject to Syrian direction and reported on a daily basis to their Syrian masters.

As of summer 2004 and Hariri's declared objections to the renewal of the term of President Lahoud – even for three years instead of six – Hariri was criticized, accused of malpractice and insulted by a plethora of Syrian-sponsored politicians or political aspirants. These included Asssem Kanso, head of the Syrian Ba'athist party in Lebanon; Najah Wakim, a former member of parliament who in 1998, as already mentioned, had written a libellous book against Hariri; Nasser Kandil, the parliament member imposed on Hariri; and Wi'aam Wahab, who was appointed minister of the environment in the Karame government of October 2005, and who continues to be a vocal critic of the Hariri-Jumblatt alliance.

Al-Sayyed, one of the four officers in prison, had conducted a series of interviews with *al-Hayat* newspaper after Hariri's assassination, in which he asserted his innocence and the need for a 'fair dictator' to govern Lebanon – implying himself. Since the commission's 1 October report, it had learnt that al-Sayyed had operated an illegal fund out of his office, which financed secret operations. Based on this information, paragraph 71 of the second UNIIIC report states that investigators recovered twenty-one binders of documents, records and other evidence from the Sûreté Générale and questioned several witnesses. Al-Sayyed's frozen accounts and assets showed him to have $10 million worth of real estate, including a summer house of more than 1,500 square metres and three swimming pools, in addition to bank deposits of $24 million.

Of the four officers in prison, the man who had come to his position last, Ali al-Hajj (in summer 2004), had been chief of security for Hariri. Hariri suspected that al-Hajj was passing information about his movements and opinions to Gazale. He trapped al-Hajj by uttering a mild criticism of Gazale; the following day Gazale called Hariri to express his anger at the criticism. Hariri fired al-Hajj, who was, soon afterwards, appointed head of the internal security forces.

Al-Hajj had $4 million of bank deposits, and real estate properties worth $3 million. He had given a huge party at his newly completed residence in the Beqaa in honour of Gazale. On 1 November 2004 he reduced Hariri's official security contingent from forty to eight. By contrast, his personal guards numbered in excess of twenty, and those in the service of al-Sayyed numbered seventy-two.

Corruption was not only the preserve of Lebanese security chiefs. It was also evident among Syrian senior officials who, due to their influence, could obtain rich rewards. The accounts of Kanaan, Gazale and his brothers and Jameh, which were frozen with banks in Lebanon or transferred by the same officers and their family members abroad, far exceeded the wealth of al-Sayyed. Further, both Kanaan and Gazale and/ or their family members acquired important real estate in Lebanon.

In respect to Hariri's assassination, the available evidence – of political pressure, coercion of decisions and the truck and explosives – does not identify the perpetrators of the crime. On the basis of the evidence provided, the most that could be said was noted in paragraphs 7, 8, 9 and 10 of the Executive Summary of Mehlis's report of 25 October 2005:

7. It is the Commission's view that the assassination of 14 February 2005 was carried out by a group with an extensive organization and considerable resources and capabilities. The crime had been prepared over the course of several months. For this purpose, the timing and location of Mr Rafiq Hariri's movements had been monitored and the itineraries of his convoy recorded in detail.

8. Building on the findings of the Commission and Lebanese investigations to date and on the basis of the material and documentary evidence collected, and the leads pursued until now, there is converging evidence pointing at both Lebanese and Syrian involvement in this terrorist act. It is a well-known fact that Syrian Military Intelligence had a pervasive presence in Lebanon at the least until the withdrawal of the Syrian forces pursuant to resolution 1559. The former senior security officials of Lebanon were their

appointees. Given the infiltration of Lebanese institutions and society by the Syrian and Lebanese intelligence services working in tandem, it would be difficult to envisage a scenario whereby such a complex assassination plot could have been carried out without their knowledge.

9.   It is the Commission's conclusion that the continuing investigation should be carried forward by the appropriate Lebanese judicial and security authorities, who have proved during the investigation that with international assistance and support, they can move ahead and at times take the lead in an effective and professional manner. At the same time, the Lebanese authorities should look into all the case's ramifications including bank transactions. The 14 February explosion needs to be assessed clearly against the sequence of explosions which preceded and followed it, since there could be links between some, if not all, of them.

10. The Commission is therefore of the view that a sustained effort on the part of the international community to establish an assistance and cooperation platform together with the Lebanese authorities in the field of security and justice is essential. This will considerably boost the trust of the Lebanese people in their security system, while building self-confidence in their capabilities.

UNIIIC established sufficient cause for recommending detention of the heads of security services in Lebanon. From the above quotation, it is obvious that UNIIIC would have recommended similar treatment of senior Syrian security figures who supervised the work of their Lebanese counterparts. As the crime was committed in Lebanon, detention of the criminals would be best achieved in Lebanon. By the time the report was submitted, even by the time the earlier summary report was submitted on 25 August 2005, all the Syrian security officials who served in Lebanon were assuming functions in Syria. There was need for further corroborating evidence to strengthen the case against organizers, perpetrators and actual executors of the crime. It is probable that the driver of the Mitsubishi truck loaded with explosives died in the blast. Consequently, the actual executor of the crime might not be alive to stand trial. Criminal accusations by Lebanese law equalize the guilt of the organizers and perpetrators with those who execute a crime. UNIIIC's search concentrated on identifying such organizers and perpetrators. Three successive missions by forensic experts from Germany, the Netherlands and Japan worked on this question from July to the end of September 2005. Based on their findings and the initiative by Prosecuting Judge Elias Eid to explore telephone communications and records, the following picture comes about:

144. Investigations by both the ISF and Military Intelligence have led to [the discovery of] six prepaid calling cards, which telephone records demonstrate were instrumental in the planning of the assassination. Beginning at approximately eleven o'clock on 14 February 2005, cellsite records show that cellular telephones utilizing these six calling cards were located in the area stretching from Nejmeh Square to the St George Hotel, within a few-block radius and made numerous calls with each other and only with each other. The phones were situated so that they covered every route linking the Parliament to Kuraytem Palace: that is, cellsite records demonstrate that these telephones were placed to cover any route that Hariri would have taken that day. One of the cellphones located near the Parliament made four calls with the other telephone lines at 12.53 – the time that Mr Hariri's convoy left Nejmeh Square. The calls – and all usage on the cards – terminated at 12.53 on 14 February, a few minutes before the blast. The lines have all been inactive since.

145. Further investigation has revealed that these six lines – along with two others – were put into circulation on 4 January 2005, after calling number 1456 activated them. They were all activated at the same location in northern Lebanon between Terbol and Menyeh. Since they were first purchased in early January 2005, until the time of the explosion, the lines only had calls with each other. In that time period, until the assassination, there appears to be a correlation

between their location and Hariri's movements, suggesting that they might have been used to follow Hariri's movements in that time period.

146. The Commission, in conjunction with the Lebanese authorities, continued the investigation of the origin of these telephone lines. The six prepaid cards originated, along with four others, from the Powergroup Company, Beirut, a store owned by a reportedly active member of al-Ahbash with close ties to Sheikh Ahmad al-Abdel. According to company records, the lines were delivered to the store's Tripoli branch. One of the employees of that Tripoli store reported that on 30 December 2004, he received a telephone call from Raed Fakhreddin, the owner of another cell shop in Tripoli and the nephew of Tarek Ismat Fakhreddin, a prominent businessman. Raed Fakhreddin reportedly urgently wanted to buy ten prepaid cards; the Tripoli store employee noted that the inquiry itself was unusual as Raed Fakhreddin did not customarily buy lines from the Tripoli store nor typically have commercial dealings with the Tripoli store other than mobile handset purchases. However, the ten calling cards bearing these particular lines were located, and Raed Fakhreddin sent a messenger to pick up the calling cards bearing these lines from the Tripoli store. That messenger reported to the Commission that he paid $700 in cash at the Tripoli store to purchase these ten lines and deliver them to Raed Fakhreddin. The forms legally required for purchasing cellular lines were not filled out that day, however, but rather over two weeks after the lines had been sold, on 12 January 2005. The supporting identification required for the purchase, which was provided by Raed Fakhreddin, proved to be false. On 14 September 2005 the ISF arrested Raed Fakhreddin, along with others involved in the transfer and sale of these calling cards. Raed Fakhreddin was subsequently interviewed as a suspect by the Commission. In that interview, while he admitted that he purchased the lines, he denied any knowledge of the use of six of the lines in connection with the Hariri assassination.

147. Of the ten mobile phones used in connection with these ten cellular telephone cards, five have been traced to a store in Tripoli.

Conclusion

The investigation of the prepaid telephone cards is one of the most important leads in this investigation in terms of who was actually on the ground executing the assassination. This is a line of investigation that needs to be pursued thoroughly.

Conclusion

It appears that the jamming devices in Hariri's convoy were operational and functional on 14 February at the time of the blast. Further investigation may provide information about how the IED [Inplanted Explosive Device] was activated.

Conclusion

It appears that there was interference with a telecommunications antenna in the crime scene area during the time of the crime. This is a line of enquiry that should be thoroughly pursued.'[1]

As of the end of November 2005, interviews of Syrian witnesses by the UNIIIC were scheduled to begin in Vienna. The location was agreed upon between Riad Daoudi and Detlev Mehlis. Syrian sources emphasized that instead of a detailed protocol over procedures, they had accepted a Russian guarantee that Syrian interviewees would not be detained. There was no confirmation of this Syrian allegation by the Russians. In fact, the Americans stated that there were no guarantees to the Syrians.

Rustum Gazale and Jameh Jameh were amongst the first batch of interviewees in Vienna. There is no doubt that other witnesses will be brought forward. Considering that Gazale, Jameh and their bosses in Syria were supervising security agencies in Lebanon, it is more than likely that the UNIIIC will advise that they be detained, as happened in Lebanon. At this point, this conjecture about detention and the difficulties

---

1. From the section headed 'Use of Prepaid Telephone Cards', the Mehlis report, dated 25 October 2005.

of conducting a trial of the accused by one court have surfaced. It is certain that Syrian authorities will not accept trials by a Lebanese court. Moreover, the Lebanese government will seek to avoid conflict over this issue. Different scenarios will be proposed and debated: a Lebanese court holding sessions in a different country; a Lebanese-international court with participation from the International Court of Justice; a Lebanese-Syrian court meeting in a neutral territory preferably under the Arab aegis, etc. There is no doubt that future proceedings of the trial, passing of judgment and establishing guilt beyond doubt will require months or years. What is definite is that this crime has changed the practice of political terrorism in the Middle East.

On 12 December 2005, the day that the second UNIIIC report was submitted in New York, a heinous crime was committed in Lebanon. Gebran Tueni, a prominent press figure managing *an-Nahar* – Lebanon's leading daily newspaper – and a parliament member and leading activist for Syria's withdrawal from Lebanon, was assassinated by a car bomb that killed him and two of his assistants while on their way to work. That same day the Lebanese cabinet held a meeting to discuss the crime. The prime minister and most cabinet members, other than Amal and Hizbullah representatives, were in favour of calling for the establishment of an international court. Four ministers abstained, in addition to Minister Yacoub Sarraf, who is close to President Lahoud. The vote was approved and a cabinet crisis came about as a result.

The UNIIIC report leaves Syria with an opportunity to cooperate fully with the commission's requirements and avoid international sanctions. On 11 December 2005, in a televised interview with Russian television, President al-Assad had threatened that imposition of sanctions against Syria would destabilize Syria and Lebanon and cause international reverberations. By contrast, the UNIIIC's second report emphasized the need for at least six more months of investigation work, if not more. The following three paragraphs are directly quoted from the UNIIIC's second report:

However, it is worth noting that, despite their reluctance and procrastination, the Syrian authorities did make available for questioning the five Syrian officials that the Commission had summoned. The extensive interviews took place outside Syria, according to conditions determined by the Commission.

UNIIIC investigators were also able to interview a Syrian witness in Syria without interference. As this is the beginning of a long-awaited process, it is up to the Syrian authorities to be more forthcoming in order to make headway in a process that will be most probably a long one if it is to be judged against the pace of progress to date. (Paragraph 10 of the second UNIIIC report.)

Until now, the Commission has made steady progress on the Lebanese track. It remains to be matched on the Syrian track. For that reason, it is the Commission's view that Syria should pursue its own investigation in an earnest and professional manner and respond to the Commission in a timely way, fully and unconditionally, before it is determined whether it is complying in full with the provisions of resolution 1636 (2005). (Paragraph 11 of the second UNIIIC report.)

The second report by the UNIIIC confirms the findings of the first report and calls for detention of nineteen suspects. These include the five Syrian officers already interviewed and several others not yet interviewed, or to be interviewed again. It is not possible to predict the outcome of the ongoing investigation, although it is worthwhile to point out three avenues that have not been fully investigated, and one peculiar accident. First, on the Lebanese track, disentanglement of 97 million telephone calls with 26,000 pages of conversations for the period December 2004 to March 2005 have been summarized. Second, magnetic tapes of telephone surveillance by Lebanese army intelligence personnel, although tampered with and obliterated by intention, are being reconstructed. Third, there are the files secured from Jamil al-Sayyed's office. The accident is that of

the burning of all Syrian intelligence files about Lebanon. The commission
has been told of this by two witnesses in Vienna, and by the judge heading
the Syrian Independent Investigation Commission.

The second report strengthens the conclusions and recommendations
of the first report. Lebanese-Syrian security agencies laid out the plan
for the assassination of Rafiq Hariri, and used illegal and extorted funds
to finance this effort. Ongoing investigations, which are becoming
technically more sophisticated, are further strengthening conclusions
reached based on facts observed or uncovered.

Postscript

It is unusual to write a postscript to a book of this nature. The need for this was dictated by the nature of the crime.

Lebanon has had a turbulent history since the mid-1960s. Rafiq Hariri achieved enormous political and economic results by concentrating on educational possibilities, reconstruction, regaining recognition for Lebanon and its needs amongst Arab nations and the international community. He was gentle, generous, hard-working, ambitious and always hopeful. The only period of relative long sadness was from early September 2004 – the date of a forced renewal of the term of President Emile Lahoud – until his tragic death on 14 February 2005.

The local, regional and international outrage at his murder had never been witnessed before over a political assassination in the Middle East. At no time in recent history has the United Nations considered a political crime as a terrorist act with international repercussions. Three United Nations Security Council resolutions were voted on in connection with Hariri's murder. Resolution 1595 called for the creation of an International Independent Investigation Commission with powers to unravel the reasons behind the crime, its perpetrators and actual executors. When Syrian reluctance to cooperate with Commissioner Detlev Mehlis, entrusted to conduct the investigation, threatened the progress of the investigation, Resolution 1636 was adopted on 1 November 2005 by all fifteen members of the Security Council, calling on Syria to cooperate or face sanctions that could involve military action.

Other than identifying war crimes committed by criminal individuals for whom punishment was sought, the United Nations Security Council has never adopted such strict resolutions. One cannot but wonder: why this exigence, and what are its likely results?

The steadfastness of the UN resolutions was in consequence of Hariri's international recognition and work for peace in Lebanon and the region. The crime was regarded as a barbaric act of terrorism. UN observers were incensed by the lethargy of Lebanese security agencies and Syrian security figures in Lebanon. Initially, there was no dynamism or method in the efforts executed. It seemed that this crime, like so many others – including the assassination of President René Mouawad on 22 November 1989 – would eventually be forgotten.

The international climate *vis-à-vis* terrorist acts has fundamentally changed since 11 September 2001. If acts of terrorism with broad political ramifications were allowed to take their course without retribution, the civilized world at large could be held to ransom by terrorists. Middle Eastern awareness of this change in international perception had not been acute. Hariri's murder was considered an international terrorist act *par excellence* by the UN agencies. The international reaction was further inflamed by the demonstration of over one million Lebanese on 14 March 2005, calling for justice, removal of security officers, and the elimination of Syrian military and intelligence hegemony over Lebanon. It was obvious that Syria could no longer be entrusted with shaping the future of Lebanon.

Syria had opted in 1990 to support the Allied Forces in evicting the Iraqi army from Kuwait, which Iraq had occupied since the beginning of August of that year. Although Syria's role was marginal, it gained points with George Bush Sr, who left the Syrians with a free hand to supervise peace in Lebanon. Yet Rafiq Hariri proved difficult for the Syrians. The Lebanese had signed a new accord at Taef at the end of 1989, which restored peace amongst warring groups in Lebanon, and Hariri was given a chance to work on restoring Lebanon's institutions and characteristics.

He rebuilt schools, roads, government buildings, electricity generation capacity, water supplies, security forces and, most important of all, the hope of the people. Stabilizing the currency from 1992 provided a platform for attracting investment, and improving the infrastructure, encouraging Arabs to return to Lebanon as visitors, investors and enthusiasts. Irrespective of political obstacles and Israeli incursions, which slowed progress, Hariri persisted in his efforts to give Lebanon a rebirth. Politically, he regained for Lebanon its right to determine its own future when he succeeded in bringing about the April 1996 agreement intended to protect civilians in South Lebanon and North Israel.

It was clear from all that was happening that a dichotomy had emerged, which pitted Syrian military and intelligence hegemony against Lebanese aspirations and efforts. The two forces, one military and supported by a wide security network run by a primitive political system, the other the emerging spirit of a Lebanon growing accustomed to progress and modernity, could not be reconciled. Hariri did his best to avoid clashes, and often paid dearly for his efforts, whether in terms of patience or resources.

Syria's leadership in the twenty-first century was less flexible than its previous leadership of the late 1990s. After 11 September 2001 it cooperated with the Americans to combat terrorism. However, Syria offered shelter to extremist Palestinian organizations and, after the Americans and British invaded Iraq, Syria was constantly criticized by the Americans for doing too little to stop the infiltration of Islamic fighters into Iraq. Calls were made for Syrian withdrawal from Lebanon, but the Syrian regime turned a deaf ear and settled on the notion that the Americans needed them.

In 2004 the US applied sanctions against Syria for harbouring terrorists, continuing to occupy Lebanon, helping extremist Palestinian groups and aiding Hizbullah. The US Congress voted these sanctions. By contrast, Syria maintained absolute tranquillity in the Golan Heights. These water-rich mountains, which are more developed for a successful Israeli wine industry and for skiing, are internationally recognized to be Syrian. American-sponsored negotiations in spring 2000 were about to restore the Golan Heights to Syria, had Ehud Barak maintained his enthusiasm for peace. Still, Syria does not foment trouble in the Golan, although Israeli soldiers in there can closely monitor movements in Damascus. Since 1973 there have been no incidents in the Golan Heights between Syrians and Israelis.

While stability held in the Golan Heights, the Americans sought Syrian cooperation on other matters, but with little success. Since 2004 American sanctions against Syria have included prohibition of American investments there, forbidden flights of Syrian civilian planes in American airports, no confirmation of Syrian transfers or letters of credit by American banks and no sales of civil airplanes or spare parts to Syria. These sanctions were aimed partially at encouraging Syria's withdrawal from Lebanon. The effects of these measures remained small as the sanctions could be overcome by supplies of services and products from other industrialized countries.

In late summer 2004 Security Council Resolution 1559 was passed, calling on Syria to withdraw all its military and intelligence forces from Lebanon, and for demilitarization of Palestinian factions in Lebanon supported by Syria, as well as Hizbullah. Originally, the Syrians ridiculed Resolution 1559, but after Hariri's assassination and growing accusations against Syria, President Bashar al-Assad decided to avoid the wrath of the international community and declared, on 8 March 2005, a programme for total withdrawal before the end of April. The withdrawal was achieved by 26 April.

International initiatives multiplied. A special envoy of the UN secretary general, who was entrusted with supervising the full implementation of Resolution 1559, verified Syrian withdrawal. The UN sent a fact-finding mission to collect possible evidence about Hariri's murder and to suggest a follow-up. The UNIIIC was established, and Lebanese and Syrian moves became subject to international observation and scrutiny. At no time in recent history have Lebanon and Syria attracted as much international attention and action.

Lebanon formed a non-partisan cabinet to supervise parliamentary elections held under international observation in May and June 2005. The process of the elections was correct, but the basis for them is currently under study, with a view to improving popular representation. After Hariri's death and the intensive international attention and involvement in Lebanon's affairs, Lebanon started moving towards more democratic practices, although regular political bickering continued. The question of the arms possessed by Hizbullah is certainly urgent, and needs to be resolved. This question will require time and better regional prospects. Syria, even if it wishes to meet UN calls, cannot easily bring about the taming of Hizbullah. The one force of containment of Hizbullah's actions is represented by the April 1996 Accord, and by the alliance of the majority of the Lebanese against a fallback under renewed Syrian hegemony or assumption of the role of the 'black sheep' of the Arab world.

In the post-Hariri era Syria has been forced to interact positively with the international community. The Syrian regime, while attempting to look strong and solidly backed, has made successive concessions. Syria cannot act in ways that perturb Iraq, Jordan, Turkey or even Lebanon, and Resolutions 1595 and 1636 have put its back against the wall. Times have changed. Syria is yielding to pressure and suffering the pains of having to deliver political and economic liberalization moves. Lebanon is freer to pursue the restoration of democracy, the energizing of the economy and a broader regional role. Neither country is allowed to become a real headache for the international community. Lebanon and Syria are now neighbouring countries with an implicit obligation to co-exist in peace and, if possible, prosperity. Syria's anger and lost pride for having to withdraw from Lebanon under international pressure do not have sympathy within the Arab world or the international community, and Syria's Arab and international relations are passing through a difficult period of normalization. Claims of independence, fortitude and the ability to survive international sanctions no longer convince the Arab masses. Syria is no longer the great Arab hero. It must listen to Egypt, give due weight to Saudi advice, seek Turkish cooperation and achieve harmonious relations with Jordan and Iraq. Whenever relations with the US became too tense, Syria resorted to Qatar for intervention with that country's American allies. Syria cannot escape international cooperation and the flood of media information about worldwide political developments. In the twenty-first century, Syria must get on the ladder of progress, open up opportunity for its youth and promote economic and political freedom.

Hariri's death introduced many fundamental changes. For the first time in recent history, the death of a statesman produced an international independent investigation commission, and possibly an international court in the near future. The United Nations' efforts in developing countries concentrated on social and development issues: in Lebanon, after Hariri's death, the UN became involved in speeding up the return to democracy, and upgrading legal procedures and investigation techniques. Insistence on a form of international justice has become an established practice after Hariri's murder.

By 12 December 2005, when Detlev Mehlis submitted the second report of the UNIIIC, he reconfirmed his intention to leave his UN responsibility and resume his duties in his home country. He confirmed as well that he would support the work of the UNIIIC until the alternative head was chosen. On 13 December the Security Council extended the term of the UNIIIC for another six months ending 15 June 2006, at the request of the Lebanese government. Moreover, this term could be renewed again if need be. The Security Council also emphasized in this resolution (1644), proposed by France, Syria's obligation to cooperate fully with the work of UNIIIC. This outlook gained strength from the lack of sufficient progress in respect to Hariri's assassination, and Mehlis's indication in his report to the Security Council that Syrian delaying tactics could further stall the investigation for two years. Still, he advocated incarceration on suspicion of nineteen suspects, of whom at least seven are Syrian. In the resolution, the Security Council members congratulated Mehlis on his work and on the progress he had achieved.

Finally, in respect of Lebanon's request tabled on 13 December 2005 for the formation of an international court to judge the accused in relation to other crimes committed since October 2004, or to broaden the current commission's task to include such crimes, the Security Council charged Secretary General Annan with the task of negotiating the formation of an international court with the Lebanese government. Review of other crimes committed since October 2004 was not endorsed by the UN Security Council. Instead, the UNIIIC was enabled to offer technical assistance to Lebanese judicial authorities in their investigation of these crimes.

These decisions met the most pressing Lebanese request of extension for the UNIIIC, and although it did not respond immediately to the question of an international court, it left the door open for this possibility. In Lebanon, divergence of attitudes in the cabinet threatened its continuity over this issue. It is possible that the breathing space left could enable the Lebanese prime minister to negotiate this matter with Annan, in cooperation with dissenting ministers.

On 13 February 2006, one day before the anniversary of Hariri's assassination, the Minister of Justice, Charles Rizk, announced that two senior Lebanese judges were to visit the UN headquarters in New York to discuss the establishment of an international court that would pass judgment on individuals implicated in Hariri's assassination. It would also deal with those involved in other attempted assassinations made since 1 October 2004, when Minister Marwan Hamade barely escaped a car bomb.

In January 2006 Secretary Annan had dispatched a senior member of the UN legal department, Mr. Nicholas Michel, to discuss the scope of the proposed international court with Lebanese officials (whether political figures or senior judges). In essence, the request by the Lebanese government to the UN to look into the possibility of establishing such a court was made on 12 December 2005, but the actual process is relatively long and complicated.

Before the end of January 2006 the five ministers of the Shi'ite bloc that had withdrawn from the cabinet over the demand for the formation of an international court had rejoined the cabinet, after Prime Minister Siniora declared the government's ongoing regard for the resistance movement, i.e. Hizbullah.

At the end of 2005 television interviews with Abdul Halim Khaddam, the former deputy president of Syria – who in June resigned from his position with the government and the Syrian Ba'ath party – provided strong credibility to allegations in the UNIIIC report of 12 December 2005. Khaddam was the minister of foreign affairs in Syria from 1970 to 1984, before taking the mantle of Vice President for Foreign Affairs. He was the arbitrator of Lebanese political differences from 1982 until 1998. As already mentioned, since the early 1980s Hariri had developed a strong bond of friendship with Khaddam. During the period of condolences following Hariri's death, Khaddam was the only senior Syrian figure to come to Lebanon to extend his sympathies to Hariri's family.

In Khaddam's television appearance on al-Arabiya on 30 and 31 December, filmed at his Paris home, he strengthened certain conclusions and allegations made by the Mehlis commission, and provided information that confirms the extent of corruption by Syrian security officials, or by relatives and friends of President al-Assad. The opinions and facts given by Khaddam during these interviews increase Lebanese suspicions and, in principle, serve to push Lebanese factions to overcome their differences and work on preserving and developing Lebanese independence.

For some time Khaddam had been experiencing a conscientious change in his political perceptions. At the end of 2003 he wrote a book in Arabic, *The Current Arab System: Absorbing Reality and Exploring the Future*, published by the Arab Cultural Centre. In this book, Khaddam asserts that Arab underdevelopment was due to lack of respect for the principle of separation of powers, and absence of democracy, free political parties, thinking and the press. He was the second important Arab leader from an autocratic socialist regime to express such thoughts. In March 2002 the Algerian president, Abdulaziz Boutaflika, expressed similar ideas in his address at the Arab Summit held in Beirut, asserting that without democracy and economic freedoms, the Arab world had no future. As the president of Algeria – in his second five-year term as of 2004 – Boutaflika introduced political and economic reforms. Most importantly, he succeeded in stemming the continuous bloodbath that for years had terrorized ordinary citizens in Algeria. Khaddam, by contrast, could not implement improvements in Syria. He could only press on with recommendations. His last serious attempt was made at the Ba'ath party conference held in June 2005, but his suggestions were ignored.

Khaddam's efforts at reform would only be fully exposed by globalized media coverage, which he used. His revelations, therefore, would be viewed as an effort to stimulate an Arab reawakening. The most significant of these were the following:

- The Syrian regime resented Hariri's consolidation of the Sunnis and his suspected implicit support of the Security Council's Resolution 1559 of September 2005, which called for Syrian withdrawal from Lebanon.
- Syrian officials (including Bashar al-Assad) threatened Hariri and Lebanon with destructive acts well before 26 August 2005. These threats were levelled many times, often by security figures with limited authority.

    Until 18 August, al-Assad claimed he was not working to renew Emile Lahoud's term. This he conveyed in person to Khaddam.

- In 1998 both Khaddam and Ghazi Kanaan were against Syria's choice of Emile Lahoud as president, as they felt a military man could not govern Lebanon without destroying its plural system.
- During Lahoud's presidency, the Lebanese president and Jamil al-Sayyed kept up a barrage of disinformation against Hariri, which was forwarded to al-Assad.
- Rustum Gazale, the head of the Syrian intelligence services in Lebanon after 2002, insulted and threatened Hariri, Walid Jumblatt and Nabih Berri. Upon reviewing this matter with al-Assad, Khaddam was told that Gazale had done the same with Najib Mikatti (a close personal friend of al-Assad and Lebanese prime minister from April until the end of June 2005), and Suleiman Franjieh (a close friend of al-Assad

and the former minister of the interior).

• In addition to all these misdeeds, Gazale had extorted $35 million from al-Madina Bank. (Photocopies of cheques drawn for millions of dollars from al-Madina Bank in his and his brother's names have been reproduced in the Lebanese political weekly *al-Shiraa*.) According to Khaddam, al-Assad called Gazale a criminal and a thief. Yet no measures were taken against him. Mehlis asked for his detention after two interviews with the commission experts, in Syria in September and in Vienna last December. Moreover, the $35 million taken by Gazale does not include at least three apartments bought for him and his brother by Ibrahim Abou Ayash's personal assistant Rana Koleilat, and no fewer than ten luxury cars.

• Two relatives or close associates of al-Assad amassed fortunes in billions of dollars. The interest on this illegal wealth, according to Khaddam, could yield $600 million a year. Such wealth could not come about without the exploitation of political power, smuggling and enforced monopolies, whether in Syria or Lebanon.

Beyond these allegations and many others, Khaddam – who is a trained lawyer – confirms his belief in the professionalism of the work of the UNIIIC. He ridicules claims that the findings have been politicized, and calls on the Syrian regime to accept international scrutiny.

Syria has strongly denied most of the accusations leveled by Khaddam. Criticism of Khaddam has appeared in the government press in Syria and in the pro-Syrian press in Lebanon. Criticism has also been vociferous from members of parliament in Syria, who on 31 December 2005 voted unanimously a resolution to try Khaddam as a traitor. This example of herd mentality once again diminishes Syria's credibility as a modern state. Khaddam has been labelled as a traitor simply because he has confirmed public knowledge and the testimony of worthy figures.

After Khaddam's statements it will be very difficult to doubt the UNIIIC reports. Also, verification of corruption will necessitate review and revelation of the wealth of Syrian and Lebanese security officers and figures close to al-Assad. The ball is now in the Syrian court, and explanations are required. Security Council Resolution 1644 demands the truth, and Syrian officials must decide whether or not they can survive without implementing the resolution.

In response to the UNIIIC recommended assessment of al-Madina Bank records to uncover bribery payments to Syrian officials and potential culprits in respect of Hariri's assassination, the following facts emerge:

The Special Investigation Commission (SIC) of the Lebanese Central Bank uncovered the existence of accounts held by the Gazale family (the brothers of Rustum and his son) in a number of banks. These accounts were being fed through cheques drawn mainly on Rana Koleilat's accounts at al-Madina Bank and its affiliate, United Credit Bank. Money withdrawn from the accounts of the Gazale family amounted to $10,396,696 from one bank and $16,656,918 from the other. Remaining balances totalled $750,076.

In addition to these sums, Mr. Ibrahim Abou Ayash used his own account to cover withdrawals from al-Madina Bank and United Credit Bank made with credit cards owned by Muhamad Burkan and Nazem Abdo Gazale, totalling $12,935, 947.

On top of these sums withdrawn, spent or placed in various banks, a married female friend of Rustum Gazale was credited with LL1,752,588,478 (nearly $1.17 million) as well as $921,978.

In other words, Mr. Rustum Gazale, the senior Syrian intelligence officer in Lebanon for less than thirty months, and his family members cashed over $40 million. From these figures it is obvious that Khaddam was not exaggerating. If anything, he underestimated Gazale's acquisitions. There is, of course, the $2 million that went to his female friend and, as mentioned before, Gazale and his family acquired at least three apartments worth $2 million each and ten cars worth over $1 million, in addition to gifts of jewellery and diamonds.

There is proof of massive corruption by Gazale but no proof of a direct line between these riches and Hariri's assassination. It is clear, of course, particularly with cash withdrawals of nearly $13 million by credit cards, that Gazale had the cash to organize the crime. The question remains whether he did so or not.

The generosity of Miss Rana Koleilat and Ibrahim Abou Ayash remains unexplained. In fact, much of the money was not even their own. The whole debacle of al-Madina Bank casts a shadow over the practices of Adnan Abou Ayash, his brother Ibrahim, and Miss Rana Koleilat who was given an open guarantee by Adnan Abou Ayash, authenticated by a notary in February 2003.

None of the three characters is available for questioning by the courts. Adnan Abou Ayash is living in Saudi Arabia, working hard and keeping a low profile. Rana Koleilat travelled out of Lebanon on a false passport and her whereabouts are unknown,[1] and finally, Ibrahim Abou Ayash is constantly unavailable, presumed to be in Canada for medical treatment.

Other than the predictable official Syrian reactions to Khaddam's interview, one cannot help speculating about Khaddam's motives for confirming:

- Threats by the Syrian regime to Hariri.
- False testimony by Minister Charaa and Deputy Minister Mouallem.
- Immature decisions and reactions by the Syrian leadership.
- Syria's latent desire to hold on to Lebanon with American tolerance.
- Widespread corruption of Syrian officials and/or relatives of the president with enthusiastic participation by Lebanese parties.
- Impossibility of Syrian security involvement in Hariri's assassination without awareness at the top. This notion has also been repeatedly stressed by the UNIIIC reports.

At age seventy-seven, Khaddam has put his life in harm's way by expressing his opinions. For an intelligent, healthy and far-sighted senior statesman, such an initiative cannot but emanate from a feeling of historical

---

1. As is mentioned on page 134, Rana Koleilat was uncovered and detained on 12 March 2006 in Brazil. Her extradition awaits further procedures.

responsibility, the elements of which can also be felt in Khaddam's book, mentioned earlier, which appeared at the end of 2003. The experience of writing about and interpreting upheavals in the Arab Middle East since the early 1960s has possibly urged Khaddam to expose facts and evaluations that could contribute to a change of regime in Syria.

Some observers have gone so far as to assume that Khaddam contributed to an inevitable change in the Syrian regime in the hope of becoming president himself. These same observers claim that Ghazi Kanaan was working for a regime change and was liquidated because of it. In the case of Khaddam, it is possible to surmise that aspiring to the Syrian presidency does not excite his political appetite. He is now an elder statesman and is only afraid that his generation failed to advance the Arab nation. He is disappointed by Arab underdevelopment, and has reached the conviction that progress is the child of pluralism, political liberty and a truly independent and enlightened judiciary.

Mr Serge Brammertz, a Belgian senior judge appointed on 9 September 2003 as Deputy Prosecutor at the International Criminal Court, was nominated to head the UNIIIC's investigation into the assassination of Prime Minister Rafiq Hariri. Mr. Brammertz assumed his responsibilities as of mid-January 2006. Since taking on this responsibility he has decreased the size of the team that assisted Detlev Mehlis, his predecessor. This was presumably because most of the investigation work, other than with Syrian witnesses, had already been done. Brammertz reestablished contact with Syrian officials. During a visit to Syria he met with Dr. Walid Mouallem, Minister of Foreign Affairs, who had formerly been interviewed by Mehlis's team. The Belgian head of the UNIIIC agreed with his Syrian contacts on further interviews and procedures.

At the time he was chosen to head the UNIIIC by Secretary General Annan, Mr. Brammertz was Deputy Prosecutor of the International Criminal Court and was in charge of the Investigations Division of the Office of the Prosecutor. Before his election he was Federal Prosecutor of the Kingdom of Belgium. Mr. Brammertz also assisted the Council of Europe in 'setting up a mechanism for evaluating and applying international undertakings concerning the fight against organized crime'. He also served on the Justice and Internal Affairs Committee of the European Commission and as an adviser for the International Organization for Migration, leading major research studies on cases of cross-border corruption and human trafficking in Central Europe and the Balkans. From 1996 to 1997, he served as Deputy Prosecutor, then Chief Deputy Prosecutor at the Court of First Instance in Eupen (Belgium), before becoming Deputy to the Prosecutor-General at the Liege Court of Appeal. While a National Prosecutor of the Kingdom of Belgium from 1997 to 2002, Mr. Brammertz was also Professor of Law at the University of Liege. An author on global terrorism, organized crime and corruption, he has published extensively in European and international academic journals.

Serge Brammertz was born on 17 February 1962 in Eupen and he speaks English, French and German. He is temperamentally cautious and avoids public exposure. This was greeted positively by the Syrians who have been under international observation since February 2005.

On 14 March 2006, one year after the demonstration at Martyr's Square, Serge Brammertz submitted the third report of the Commission to the UN Secretary General. This report alleged to be closer to establishing the perpetrator of the crime. Moreover, the report encourages Syria's improved cooperation with the Commission. Proof of this cooperation is awaited in April and May of 2006.

Before analyzing salient features of the Brammertz Report, it is interesting to note the evaluation of the new head of the Commission by a Lebanese judge who has been in constant contact with Mehlis and later Brammertz: Brammertz is, according to him, a highly disciplined judge rather than investigator. His conclusions are based on what he considers reliable evidence. Moreover, he will not venture speculative opinions before reaching a verdict. It must be stressed that Brammertz does not challenge the findings of the two previous reports, although two or three witness testimonies have been discredited, and he introduces a more subtle evaluation of the layers of criminal involvement between those who conceived of, instigated and executed the crime. In his opinion, the job was very professional and must have involved someone with experience in terrorist activities.

Brammertz confirms meeting with Syrian officials twice and reaching an understanding that they will abide by the requirements of all relevant UN Security Council resolutions (1559, 1636 and 1644). He was promised an audience with the Syrian president, which was confirmed by Syrian official sources on 16 March 2006. The audience with President Assad will be in the nature of a discussion. All questions are to be answered provided it is understood to be a dialogue rather than an investigation.

The Brammertz report stipulates that one of the unidentified bodies at the scene of the crime could be that of the perpetrator. Moreover, Brammertz emphasizes the need to learn why Ali al-Hajj, one of the Lebanese officers currently under detention, reduced Hariri's security team from forty men to eight. Also, he wants to know who ordered Hariri to be under surveillance. It has been established that al-Hajj received orders from Mustafa Hamdan, head of the Presidential Guard, to move the cars of Hariri's convoy from the scene of the crime less than twelve hours after the explosion. The possibility remains that Hamdan could have ordered the reduction of Hariri's official security team.

Brammertz also indicates that Lebanese army intelligence recordings provides serious evidence pointing to Raymend Azar's involvement. Movements of a slush fund operated by Jamil al-Sayyed have to be scrutinized. It is well known that he extorted money from business and financial institutions. Moreover, as has been noted before, his own personal and family funds with banks amounted to $24 million, as well as a further $700,000 in cash at his home.

Further study of the accounts of al-Madina Bank are considered imperative. As has been indicated, the Central Bank report to the attorney general show payments of $43 million to Rustum Gazale, his family and his female friend. $13 million were cash withdrawals, which could have financed the assassination, although Brammertz does not go so far as to suggest this.

The detained officers as well as other suspects whose mobile phone use was concentrated along Hariri's route on the day of the crime are all to be investigated further, along with al-Ahbash, a fundamentalist Sunnite group. One of the members of this group was in touch with the presidential palace immediately after the explosion and he remains in custody.

According to technical evaluations, the Brammertz report indicates that the explosion could have been underground as well as above ground. This requires further evaluation of works underground nearby one day before the explosion.

One new area of assertion relates to the UNIIIC cooperation with Lebanese authorities, not only relating to Hariri's assassination, but also the fourteen terrorist explosions which preceded (including the attempt on Marwan Hamade in October) and followed the crime of 14 February 2005. These incidents total fourteen in number, and the Commission suggests there are indications that these acts were linked with the assassination of Hariri.

It is probably true to say that the Brammertz report confirms most of the findings of the earlier two reports but goes further towards identifying the criminals. Moreover, the report indicates that an international court will be formed to pass judgment. It subtly points to the possibility of involvement at the planning and execution levels of a party not yet named, which would suggest greater involvement by fundamentalists than has been hitherto mentioned.

The time for full disclosure and revelations has not arrived yet, asserts the report. Two expected developments, however, indicate significant conclusions and must be mentioned briefly.

On 29 March 2006, Detlev Mehlis will be decorated with the highest order of merit the German government confers. He also becomes the highest Federal Prosecutor in Germany. Both initiatives by the German government indicate that the work of Detlev Mehlis on uncovering the evidence related to Hariri's assassination has received worldwide recognition.

Serge Brammertz, for professional reasons, has to leave his UNIIIC post by the end of June 2006, so the formation of the international court and selection of the judges and Prosecutor General has to be completed before then. If this outcome is delayed it will become much more difficult to continue investigations into Hariri's assassination and the fourteen other crimes assumed to be linked to that terrorist act.

The Lebanese government, the Security Council, Secretary General Annan and the UNIIIC must cooperate very closely to establish the proposed court, which was requested by the Lebanese government on 13 December 2006.

The UN's scope of responsibility is no longer confined to distant persuasion. Few states, other than the superpowers, can ignore UN directives. The UN grew in authority as Lebanon and Syria were subjected to close scrutiny intended to assess democratic and legal practices in both countries.

Bibliography

Asfour, Hana, *INTRA Bank: Crisis and Lessons* (Beirut, 1969).

Bustani, Emile, *March Arabesque*, (Robert Hale Limited: London, 1963).

Chalak, Fadel, *Experience with Hariri* (Arab Scientific Publishers: Beirut, 2006).

Clinton, Bill, *My Life* (Alfred A. Knopf: New York, 2004).

Eisenhower, Dwight, *The Eisenhower Diaries* (W.W. Norton & Co.: New York, 1981).

Fisk, Robert, *The Great War for Civilization, the Conquest of the Middle East* (Fourth Estate: London, 2005).

Ghali, Boutos Boutros, *Unvanquished: A UN-US Saga* (al-Ahram: Cairo, 1999).

Halak, Aline, *Cellular Phones, The Rip Off of the Century* (All Print: Beirut, 1999).

Haddad, Gregory, *The Pope and Lebanon: The Synod and the Papal Message* (St Paul's Press: Rabwa-Lebanon, 1998).

Hariri, Rafiq, *Statesmanship in Government* (Infopress: Beirut, 2000).

Hoss, Salim, *For Truth and History: Governing between 1998 and 2000* (All Print: Beirut, 2002).

Hrawi, Elias, *Return of the Republic*, Manassa Camille, (Dar an-Nahar: Beirut, 2002).

Iskandar, Marwan, *The Lost Role, Lebanon and the Challenges of the 21ˢᵗ Century* (Riad al-Rayess Publications: Beirut, 2000).

—— (ed.), *Yearly Economic Reviews of the Lebanese Economy* (M. I. Associates: Beirut, 1993–2004).

Kaddam, Abdul Halim, *The Current Arab System: Absorbing Reality and Exploring the Future* (Arab Cultural Center: Beirut and Casablanca, 2003).

Khazen, Farid, *The Breakdown of the State in Lebanon 1967–1976* (I.B. Tauris: London, 2000).

Kissinger, Henry, *Diplomacy* (Simon and Schuster: New York, 1994).

Leverett, Flynt, *Inheriting Syria. Bashar's Trial by Fire* (Saban Center at the Brookings Institution Book: Washington DC, 2006).

Nahas, Charbel, *Chances of Avoiding Crisis and Conditions for Success* (Dar An-Nahar: Beirut, 2003).

Saade, George, *My Experience with Taef: Facts and Documents, Misunderstandings, Poor Execution and Deception* (n.p.: Beirut, 1998).

Sadat, Anwar, *Search for Identity: My Life* (Modern Egyptian Bureau: Cairo, 1979).

Wakim, Najah, *Black Hands* (The Company for Distribution and Publications: 1998).

UN Delegations or Committees Reports

- UN International Investigation Commission Report by Serge Brammertz (March 2006).
- UN International Independent Investigation Committee Reports by Detlev Mehlis (October 2005 and December 2005).
- Fact Finding Missions Report by Fitzgerald, Patrick, (April 2005).
- Lebanese Government Report to the Paris II Conference on Economic, Financial and Administrative Reform Program (November 2002).

Lebanese Central Bank Report

- Confidential Report on Suspect al-Madina Bank Accounts to the Attorney-General of the Lebanese Republic (December 2005).

Index